a Gift for:

_____

From:

_____

A MOTHER'S JOURNEY
of Love, Loss and Life Beyond
by Jennifer L. Scalise

ISBN: 978-1-936691-00-5   Hard Cover
         978-1-936691-01-2   Soft Cover

For information, contact:

Lakeland Press, LLC
St. Charles, MO 63304
www.LakelandPress.com

ISBN: 978-1-936691-00-5, Hard Cover
         978-1-936691-01-2 Soft Cover
Library of Congress Control Number: 2010932575

Publisher's Cataloging-in-Publication Data:

Scalise, Jennifer.
A mother's journey of love, loss and life beyond : a true story / by Jennifer Scalise. – St. Charles, MO : Lakeland Press, c2011.
    p. ; cm.
    ISBN: 978-1-936691-00-5 (hardbound) ; 978-1-936691-01-2 (pbk.)
        1. Daughters —Death—Religious aspects—Christianity.
2. Children—Death—Religious aspects—Christianity. 3. All terrain vehicles—Accidents—Costa Rica. 4. Loss (Psychology)
5. Bereavement—Religious aspects—Christianity. I. Title.

BF575.G7 S33 2011   2010932575
155.9/37—dc23   1111

A MOTHER'S JOURNEY

of Love, Loss and Life Beyond

a true story by
JENNIFER L. SCALISE

LAKELAND PRESS | St. Charles, MO | USA

Within this book, we have embedded links to digital content that will enhance your experience of the author's journey. You will see "Quick Response" (QR) codes tucked away throughout the chapters. You can scan these codes with a smartphone tag reader to link to videos. If you don't have a smartphone, you can access the videos by visiting the author's YouTube channel at www.youtube.com/jenniferscalise

Acknowledgements

My deepest gratitude to those who have offered tremendous support throughout this project:

To Sue Sylvia, whose passionate guidance has taught me along the way. Her expertise and broad range of talents helped to make the words of my journey something I can proudly share. Her willingness to accept Brooke into her heart and allow for her input made working together incredibly special.

To Robyn Obermoeller, I'm blessed to have been united with a friend so true. Her unsurpassed creativity and endless hours of dedication have made this memoir of Brooke simply amazing. The unavoidable pull she feels towards our cause and the connection that exists between our families proves—somehow, someway our souls are connected.

To Rhonda Hollingsworth, my dear friend who has been there for me during both good times and bad. Thank you for caring about my well-being and believing in this project so passionately that you have dedicated your professional career to be by my side. Together we can make a difference in the lives of many—something you had coincidentally dreamed of years ago.

To Briana Miesner, for always being there for me, often anticipating what I need before I can ask. I appreciate the many years of endless support and endearing friendship. Your loyalty and dedication mean more to me than you can imagine.

To Roseanne Catalano, for being my editor of choice and helping fine tune my work. Our writing style and late night work habit made us most compatible; the fact that your daughter shares the same birthday as Brooke made us destined. I enjoyed working together and feel honored that this experience has changed your life.

To Brian Kennebeck; his spiritual guidance and graceful prayers have blessed this project along the way.

To Debborah Shankelton whose heartfelt concern was obvious from the first emotional message. Thank you for your patience, flexibility, and professionalism. The loss you later endured personally, along with the discovery that your blonde, blue eyed, tall, "all legs" daughter is also named Brooke assured me you were part of the plan.

To Sandi Sewing, for her endless late night hours converting the manuscript and organizing photos. Thank you for all you have done to help our family. You were a perfect fit that fell into place unexpectedly.

I am grateful for all of you and touched by the spiritual draw or connection we share. I feel honored that Brooke's legacy will live within you always.

To my children, family and friends, thank you for not giving up on me. This journey was essential for my healing and growth. I apologize for the time it has taken me away from you. I have emerged a better person and look forward to slowing down, enjoying life, and creating new memories together. You are what matters most in my life.

To Brooke, for your constant guidance and endless love. Your faith has inspired many. I long for the day we are together again. You are my sunshine.

To God—for the gift of Your Peace and the Light of Your Presence.

For Blake, Brooke, and Paige

You give meaning to my life and inspiration for my strength.
I love you immensely and am proud to be your mother.

Author's Note

It is inevitable we will all suffer loss in our life. Regardless of whether it is the loss of a relationship, a job, a pet, or a loved one—most find it upsetting and painful. We all deal with the hurting—or grief—differently. I am not ashamed to share my journey, or fight for survival after the tragic death of my daughter. I do wish to offer hope and encouragement so others will see that they, too, can survive life's most difficult challenges.

Enduring this terrible loss has led me to look at my life more closely and helped me understand its true meaning and purpose. We have to believe and we must have faith, knowing with confidence that our lives are eternal, and our loved ones truly never leave us. We are stronger than we realize or ever deemed possible. I have found that it is in the midst of the hardest times that I turn to God to find peace. It is unlikely that if everything were perfect, we would feel the need to seek God in our lives. It is through these difficult times that we grow spiritually, furthering us on the path of our life journey.

Please don't let sadness keep you from reading my journey. I assure you I find peace and have emerged a better person.

"Heaven is both present and future.

As you walk along your life-path holding My hand,
you are already in touch with the essence of Heaven:
nearness to Me.

You can also find many hints of Heaven along your pathway,
 because the earth is radiantly alive with My Presence.

Shimmering sunshine awakens your heart,
gently reminding you of My brilliant Light.
Birds and flowers, trees and skies evoke praises to My holy Name.

Keep your eyes and ears fully open as you journey with Me.
At the end of your life-path is an entrance to Heaven.

Only I know when you will reach that destination, but I am
preparing you for it each step of the way. The absolute certainty
of your Heavenly home gives you Peace and Joy, to help you along
your journey.

You know that you will reach your home in My perfect timing: not
one moment too soon or too late. Let the hope of Heaven encourage
you, as you walk along the path of Life with Me."

I Corinthians 15:20-23; Hebrews 6:19

~ Sarah Young
Jesus Calling (Devotions for Every Day of the Year)

~ *Introduction* ~

*"The angel of the Lord encamps around those who
honor Him…and He delivers them."*
~ Psalm 34:7

A Message From Above

Nobody expected it. Nobody prepared for it. Nobody imagined facing something so tragic, ever. And nobody anticipated the impact I would have on others, even after my time on Earth had ended.

I know that to most, twelve sounds too young to die. On the other hand, many now think of me as an old soul, wise beyond my years. My mom always said I was mature for my age. My parents often had to remind me, "We are the parents!" I lived a full life and in a short time, I did so much. Maybe I experienced life differently than most children my age.

Maybe age is not determined by how we think. I believe there is more to it than just the number of years you have been physically alive on Earth. I think your physical age must be considered as well as the number of years in your planned lifetime. For instance, a twenty-year-old who will live to be ninety is still very young at twenty, but a twelve-year-old who will only live to be twelve has lived a full life.

Sometimes people, especially children, have difficulty expressing what they feel inside. I found writing; it was my outlet and a way to communicate my deepest thoughts. My family didn't see most of what I wrote until after I passed. I am thankful my letters and journals were there to give them needed strength during this difficult time. I think of my writing as a precious gift to my loved ones, and I am honored to share it in these pages.

I always had great passion for life, and I can honestly say I made the most of it. I tried to be the best I could at whatever I did and I worked hard to abide by the Golden Rule. I had fun in life, laughing and loving as often as possible. I was a Straight-A student. I tried to be a good role model for other children. I was not hung up on insecurities or vulnerable to peer pressure. In fact, I really didn't concern myself with what anyone thought about me or how silly I looked. I was all about loving life!

From a very young age, I felt a deep connection with God. I did not go to church often and my family was not very religious, but God's presence guided my life and I had amazing faith. My leaving this world came as a complete shock to many, but not to God. He knows the end from the beginning. Deep down, my soul knew, too. As hard as it is for those who love me to accept, I was prepared for my journey home.

While I miss my loved ones very much, I am so thankful for our almost thirteen beautiful years together on Earth. Even though I am no longer by their sides physically, I am forever with those I love.

I continue to send reassurances to my family and friends, giving them the peace of mind of knowing that there is no death, only life.

I am at peace now and have returned home. I understand eternal life and while to most it seems like it will be forever before we are together again, relative to eternity it will be soon, I promise. I know my parents and grandparents want to return home to be with me, but they must understand that there is a plan and a purpose for each of our lives. We all need to be open to God's plan for us. Soon enough, though, we will be reunited, and they will be homesick no more.

The saddest part of my story is that my death resulted from complete negligence and a careless lack of regard for human safety. Changes must be made to prevent this type of tragedy from occurring again. I thank the many people who have helped my family start making those changes. I thank them for all they are doing to help us protect other innocent tourists from an experience like ours. Countless others have helped my suffering family. It makes me proud to see such support offered during their time of need.

What was it like to die? As I headed up the dangerous road, I had no idea what lay ahead of me. There were no warning signs, no guard rails, and no cautioning signals from the guide as he raced ahead so fast that none of us could keep up. The sharp turn came up so suddenly, so quickly, that I had no way to stop. The dangerous spot was a tragedy waiting to happen. I didn't see the turn at all and I didn't know what was happening until I started the 260-foot fall.

I felt no pain. God immediately opened His arms and caught me. He lifted my soul home to the eternal shores of Heaven as my physical body rested on the shores below.

Deep down, I believe my soul always knew my time here would be short. Although it has been a tough road of discovery, my family now understands the purpose of my life. There are no such things as coincidences in life. Many things happened before and after my death as part of the plan to help me spread Heaven's eternal message.

In my short life here, I had a great impact, and my legacy will continue. Through my death, I can inspire so many others and bring a sense of purpose to their lives. Those who love me must understand that there is nothing I want more. With so much to be done to complete my plan, I trust that those I love will welcome the opportunity to help others as I would wish.

I am in a wonderful place here in Heaven. Someday we will all be reunited and, together, we will celebrate the many lives we have touched on our journeys. I want my family to know that I am with them in spirit, and eventually will welcome them home. Forever, hand in hand, we will share the never ending journey of love and life.

The font used in this Introduction was created from Brooke's handwriting.

"My life is my message."
~ *Gandhi*

~ Chapter One ~

"I am here on earth for just a little while."
~ Psalm 119:19

*U*p until that horrifying moment, I would have described the day as nothing short of perfect. Then, in a matter of seconds, my life changed forever. What started as a day of fun and adventure on our dream vacation in Costa Rica ended in the tragic death of my twelve-year-old daughter, Brooke Lauren Scalise.

We left for Costa Rica on July 5, 2009, to vacation with close friends—friends we had known since before the kids were born. Over the years, our families had enjoyed several vacations together. Our party included me, my boyfriend George, his son Little George (6), and my three children—Blake (14), Brooke (12), and Paige (6), along with our friends Fred and Kelly Bietsch and their children—Emma (13), Brian (12), and Sarah (7). For weeks we had all—especially Brooke—looked forward to the trip and the many adventures that awaited us.

Initially, we planned to vacation in Cabo San Lucas with only our immediate family. We had always talked about going to Costa Rica with the Bietschs, but had never planned a trip. In mid-spring, they invited us to stay with them at Kelly's family's four-bedroom condo in Reserva Conchal, located at the five-star Paradisus Playa Conchal Resort, in the Guanacaste Region of Costa Rica. The only week they could go was the week we had already planned to take our trip to Cabo.

After discussing Costa Rica with Kelly, I went to Brooke and told her we would have to choose between the two vacations.

She rushed up to her computer to research Costa Rica. Within an hour, she begged me to change our plans. We had gone to Cabo a few years before and she wanted to experience something new. She told me about the activities she had found online, starting a list of "must do" excursions. Brooke was excited about everything Costa Rica offered, and looked forward to spending another vacation with the Bietschs.

Amazingly, I was able to rebook our travel for Costa Rica without incurring any change fees, still using frequent flier miles for all six of us. We arranged to meet the Bietschs directly in Costa Rica since our flights required an overnight layover in Miami and theirs did not.

Sunday, July 5, 2009

After arriving in Miami late, we headed straight to our hotel. We ordered pizza, then went swimming. Before bed, I called the airline to see how early we needed to check in for our international flight from Miami. I was surprised when they told me we needed to check in only thirty minutes prior to departure; I knew international travel usually required an earlier arrival. Just to be safe, we allowed for plenty of time the next morning. We stood in line at the curbside check-in for quite awhile; by the time our turn finally came, it was exactly fifty-nine minutes before our flight. We had been misinformed—Miami International requires passengers to check in an hour before international travel. The computer would not allow the attendant to check us in.

The millions of miles I have flown over the years have earned me platinum airline status for life; therefore, I am accustomed to some special privileges when I travel. This, along with my firm belief that if there is a will, there is a way, led me to confidently escalate our situation to a manager for assistance. I had to talk to a few different managers, but eventually we were escorted to our flight and assured they would handle the luggage. As we finally sat down on the plane, I let out a loud sigh of relief, thinking what a disaster it would have been to have missed our flight. Yet the real nightmare lingered in the days to come.

Monday, July 6, 2009

When we landed at the small airport in Liberia, we quickly made our way through customs to the baggage claim. Our excitement doubled; we would be at the resort soon. We waited and waited until the last piece of luggage arrived—not surprisingly, our bags had not made it. We stood in line to file our claim, then walked outside.

Unexpectedly, the Bietschs had driven back to the airport, almost an hour away from the resort, to meet us. Each family had rented the largest SUV available, only to find they weren't large at all. In order to use the last row of passenger seats, we had to unfold them, taking up all the cargo space. The Bietschs figured our family of six would never fit in the vehicle along with our luggage, so they came to help. Excited to see each other, the kids divided up: the girls in one car and the boys in the other. Despite the fact that it was raining like mad, we all rushed happily off to start our extended vacation.

We stopped at a local grocery store, and were shocked to see a guard with a large gun standing watch out front. Local papers on display in the store advertised prostitutes for hire, which we later learned is legal in Costa Rica. The experience reinforced how different third world countries are from America. We hurried through the store, stocking up on what we needed. Regardless of the minor challenges we encountered, we were determined to have the time of our lives.

Instantly, we relaxed when we reached the resort. We took in the spectacular views of ocean and forest, meandering walkways, bubbling fountains, shimmering lakes and lush tropical gardens. The beauty extended inside the condo. It was the perfect getaway—large, spacious, and beautifully decorated. The main living area opened onto a large patio with inviting furniture. From the patio, we could step onto a fairway on the Reserva Conchal Robert Trent Golf Course, which overlooked the ocean. I couldn't wait to hurry up and start unwinding.

We unpacked the groceries and the few personal items we had with us. Without our luggage, we pieced together some swimsuits and set off to have a day of fun. It was pretty funny to see Brooke in a frilly pink

swimsuit that belonged to seven-year-old Sarah. I borrowed Emma's suit, Blake wore some of Fred's trunks and the others all swam in their clothes. It didn't matter; we were on vacation. We spent that afternoon enjoying the resort's enormous lagoon-style pool as well as the beach. The water felt great. The exquisite white sand beach, lined with palms and surrounded by lush

green mountains, made a tropical paradise. The big kids played in the waves for hours, while Paige, Little George (LG) and Sarah picked up seashells. The beach, Playa Conchal, is made up of tiny crushed shells, with an abundance of large, beautiful shells that entertained the little ones for hours, as they competed to see who could collect the most. Together we took in our first beautiful sunset.

Tuesday, July 7, 2009

The next day, Kelly, an experienced rider, took Brooke, Emma and Sarah on a guided horseback riding tour at the resort. Both Emma and Sarah share her passion for horses; Brooke, on the other hand, loved

any adventure, and found the experience just as exhilarating. Since I am a little intimidated by horses, I opted to live vicariously through them. When they all came back, they took turns sharing the details of their ride through the wooded hills, along the beach and even out into the water.

Our luggage still had not arrived. No biggie—this time I rigged up one of Sarah's suits with ponytail holders so it would fit Paige, and once again, we made the most of it. We had purchased toiletries when we went to the grocery store the first day, and since we were able to borrow some things from our friends, it really didn't matter. Besides, we were on vacation. Who really needed makeup or nice clothes? A swimsuit, toothbrush and deodorant literally covered our needs.

Wednesday, July 8, 2009

Together, we all headed to Flamingo Beach, about ten minutes from the resort. The beautiful beach had dark, soft sand that felt amazing on our feet. The older kids had a blast frolicking in the crashing surf, surrendering as the waves tossed them ashore time and time again. Paige, Little George, and Sarah wandered the beach in search of treasures to add to their seashell collection and merrily chased and captured little hermit crabs, which they insisted on bringing back to the condo as pets. Meanwhile, in Costa Rica's extreme heat, the adults appreciated sitting in the shade of the trees growing right on Flamingo Beach.

It was nearing rainy season in Costa Rica, so most days it started to rain around three or four. As we sat on the beach that day, the afternoon rain felt so good, like a natural shower that rinsed the ocean salt water from our skin, leaving us feeling refreshed. I look back on the fun that day in Flamingo, and cannot believe the irony. Within a matter of days, on the other side of Flamingo Beach, Brooke would leave behind her physical being here on earth.

A few minutes after we got back to the condo, a huge storm hit with the most intense lightning I have ever seen. We all sat on the patio and watched the show. The little ones played with their collection of pet crabs and argued over who had collected the most. The lightning went on for over an hour. It was incredible. We thought the storm was typical for the area, but, when we asked someone later, they said it was an unusually large storm.

We spent the evening on the patio, which had quickly become a favorite spot for all of us. It was wonderful to sit outside and talk or read, while taking in the sounds of nature. You couldn't help but relax, feeling a million miles away as you listened to the tropical birds sing and the wild monkeys call out from the trees.

The airline called to tell us our bags had arrived; they were sending them to the resort. Relieved, we went to the resort office to claim them. In the end, all the bags made it except mine. Brooke and Blake thought it was hilarious. We had looked for somewhere that I could buy some clothes, but, outside of outrageously priced resort attire, there was nothing in the area. I bought a lime green dress from a tent vendor beside the road a few miles from the resort on the way to Flamingo, then alternated between that and a few things I borrowed from Emma.

Thursday, July 1, 2009

On Thursday, our fourth day in Costa Rica, completely out of nowhere, I woke up extremely ill, with a high fever and could barely get out of bed. The adults went to get me antibiotics.

After they returned with medicine, the group packed up and left for the day; while I stayed in bed and mostly slept. I did try to read a little of a book that my mom had been encouraging me to read for months. I hadn't gotten to it, so I took it with me on vacation. It wasn't like my mom to buy a book as she wasn't much of a reader. I was surprised, that of all books, this was one she had not only purchased but also vehemently suggested I read. The book, *Holding Fast: The Untold Story of the Mount Hood Tragedy* by Karen James, told the story of the climbing trip her husband took that turned tragic.

After several hours, the crew returned. Brooke immediately rushed into my room, excited to share the details of the day. They had gone on an ATV tour, and had a CD of over two hundred pictures taken during the excursion that she couldn't wait to show me.

Brooke and Paige jumped in bed and snuggled with me, making me feel better instantly. Brooke asked if I was enjoying the book that lay open on the bed. I explained to her that it was a little dark and I wasn't quite sure why Ma (what the kids call my mom) recommended I read it.

Brooke wanted me to watch the slideshow, but I felt too ill. She understood, and went on to tell me about the most beautiful beach where they stopped to take photos. She described the small island situated right offshore and

the huge cliff located on the far side that made the beach so spectacular. What she didn't realize then, was that on the other side of the cliff, sat the secluded beach which, oddly enough, would soon become the very spot where her physical body would come to rest.

That evening, William Huyling Fonseca, the owner of a different tour company, came to the condo to meet with us to plan other excursions. I still felt too sick to get out of bed, so I was not able to participate.

William was recommended for the Rainforest/River Tour, by friends and family who had visited Costa Rica. During the meeting, Kelly shared with William how much fun they had on the ATVs that day. He went on to explain that he had just purchased ATVs and that he could offer a similar tour, combining the ATV and the Zip Line Adventure. They scheduled the Rainforest/River Tour for Saturday, figuring that would be less strenuous in case I was still not feeling one hundred percent. They booked the more adventurous ATV/Zip Line Tour toward the end of our trip to give me time to recover. The cost of the tours surprised me; in total, we would be spending sixteen hundred dollars for the two tours. However, this was new to me and both of these excursions had been highly recommended.

Friday, July 10, 2009

Since I had been too sick to get out of bed the day before, I was shocked but relieved when I woke up feeling better. I thought our run of bad luck had finally ended, but things would only get worse.

That morning, while enjoying the patio as usual, we had a few encounters with mice. Several local cats would always sun themselves on the patio and enjoy the nice furniture. This time, a cat walked up with a mouse in its mouth. We assumed the mouse was dead, but it wasn't. The mouse took off and fell through a grate into a drain. The cat pawed at the grate, attempting to get to his lost prey for some time. I didn't have the stomach to see something like that, so I stayed away from the patio. The kids, however, found it amusing to watch the cat.

The next thing I knew, Little George was crying; he had been bitten by a mouse. They had seen another mouse on the patio and, as Little George went to touch it, Brooke quickly scolded him and told him not to. Well, he did anyhow. Although the bite was not that bad, it did break the skin and, of course, raised the fear of rabies. After several phone calls to family and doctors, we concluded he needed the rabies vaccine. The resort doctor didn't have the vaccine. The medic at the resort helped track down a source for the vaccine and scheduled to have it delivered the following day for him to administer.

By midday, we finally headed out to Tamarindo Beach. When we pulled into the beach area, a man in the parking lot asked for money to watch our car and keep it safe. We feared he may rob us if we didn't pay, so we paid our money and headed to the beach. Although the beach wasn't as remote as I prefer, we still had fun. We collected hundreds of corkscrew-shaped seashells and stuffed them inside our empty soda bottles as souvenirs.

The highlight of the day for me was finding a shop in Tamarindo owned by a man from Florida. I was finally able to buy some clothes to wear. Brooke acted as my personal shopper, grabbing things and handing them to me to try on. We enjoyed one of our favorite mother-daughter pastimes—shopping. I left with a new wardrobe of dresses, cover-ups and swimsuits, and Paige and Brooke both bought a few things as well.

Blake had spotted a Pizza Hut when we arrived in Tamarindo. The kids missed their usual American comfort food, and who could blame them? So as the day came to an end, Kelly and Fred decided to take the girls to dinner, while George and I took the boys to Pizza Hut and then returned to the resort.

Kelly and Fred enjoyed their dinner on the beach with the girls. On the way home, Kelly wanted to see the beach in Avellos. Even though it was getting late, she led the group on an adventure down challenging roads that appeared to be going nowhere. Eventually, they ended up at what they described as the most beautiful beach ever, Angel Beach, just in time to see the sunset.

Overall, we enjoyed radiantly sunny days, unforgettable sunsets and memorable nights swimming late at the pool, being rowdy and loving life. The kids all got along so well. Brooke and Emma helped with the little ones. Every night Paige would ask to sleep between Brooke and Emma and they let her, rather than running her off like most big sisters would do. The older kids stayed up late playing Apples to Apples (boys vs. girls), competing to avoid the crazy dares the losing team had to do. They made up games, racing each other on the fairway, balancing cups of water, declaring the winner as whoever had the most water in their cup at the finish line.

Late at night, the older kids and an adult or two would head out to the small pool just a few doors from the condo. Fortunately, after a few days of this, Brooke convinced me I had to come be a part of the fun. We swam till the wee hours of the morning, all laughing and having the time of our lives. I will always cherish my memories of that last star-filled night we enjoyed together.

Saturday, July 11, 2009

Bright and early, William (the tour company owner) picked us up in a bus to ride out to the river in the jungle. What an amazing experience to see the wild animals there in the river and feed the monkeys. We all laughed as the monkeys came up out of nowhere and jumped on the top of the boat, one thud at a time. They would lean over the side of the roof and reach in as we fed them bananas right from our hands.

After our day on the river, William took us to a small restaurant that really appeared to be more of a residence, complete with multiple chickens walking around the dirt yard. They had prepared a plated

chicken dish for us for lunch, which most of the kids did not eat. Paige, always known to amuse us, fed her chicken lunch to the chickens in the yard. We tried to explain why she shouldn't do this but she struggled to understand why a chicken shouldn't be fed chicken.

When we got back to the resort, we took Little George to the medic to get his shot. The poor little guy was anxious about the ordeal. We were concerned as well; just thinking about the dangers of rabies made us fear something could happen to Little George. We later learned that they gave him the wrong vaccine after all the efforts we made to get it. Thankfully, Little George did not get sick, but he did have to go through the series of rabies shots once we were back in the United States—not a pleasant experience for anyone, let alone a six-year-old.

We enjoyed the afternoon together at the resort and then, that evening, we made plans for the adults to go out to dinner together. We covered all the rules with the kids and made sure they knew how to reach us in the event of an emergency. As Brooke walked us to the door, she asked,

"Now, what do we do if you are not back by one o'clock? Do we call the police?" So typical of Brooke! I just hugged her and laughed and told her we wouldn't be gone long at all; we were just going to dinner.

We had a nice dinner at a restaurant nearby and made it back in a little over an hour. Since we were getting back sooner than expected, we all joked that we were going to catch them by surprise. We stood by the door and listened, thinking we would at least catch the kids being rowdy. We unlocked the door and quickly pushed it open, saying, "Busted!"

We found Brooke on her hands and knees, scrubbing the kitchen floor. Both Paige and Little George were asleep on the couch in the immaculate condo. Brooke and Emma had made a long to-do list and spent the entire time cleaning and working to surprise us. That's Brooke. My heart swelled with love.

Sunday, July 12, 2009

Sunday we stayed at the resort and relaxed by the pool all day. The adults enjoyed piña coladas while basking in sun; the kids frequented the swim-up bar, ordering their fair share of frozen concoctions as well. We ate poolside for lunch, laughing as Blake, Brian and LG fed their french fries to a huge iguana. His appetite seemed endless until Little George fed him an entire hotdog that he shoved in all at once!

Always full of adventure, Brooke signed up for scuba lessons. Both she and Emma spent a good portion of the day in lessons. I watched, admiring her determination. She begged me to let her scuba with Kelly and Fred the following Tuesday. I had a terrible feeling about it and just couldn't get comfortable with the idea. Kelly reassured me they would only go down about 20 feet, and I spoke with the instructor who would be with them. I told Brooke I would have to think about it. I couldn't shake the nagging feeling I had, and I never did agree for certain.

That evening we joined in the resort's entertainment at the dance club. Despite the swanky, clubby atmosphere, it was a family event

where the kids were welcome. Together we enjoyed the music, dancing and variety of acts. After the show, we returned to the condo, knowing we had to get up early the next morning.

As we settled in, Brooke came into my room, upset because she had left her jacket down at the dance club. She and I went back to look for it. I think back now, thankful I had those extra few minutes alone with her. We talked and laughed for a little while by ourselves. She was happy when I found the jacket, which was a gift from her dad that was special to her. I didn't know then that she would never have a chance to wear the jacket again.

Monday, July 13, 2009

On the day of the accident, we left at eight in the morning for our ATV/Zip Lining Tour. Before we left, I walked into Brooke's bathroom as she was getting ready. I grabbed her and hugged her and kissed her twice, telling her how much I loved her and how proud I was to be her mother. Brooke was happy and excited about the day we had planned.

William met us at the condo and we followed him in our cars to a house where the ATVs were lined up in front. There were eight ATVs in total; the three youngest children rode along with adults. The guides rushed us from the start. I felt somewhat anxious, as they didn't even demonstrate how to use the controls on the manual ATV. I didn't know how to start mine and the front guide was leaving. Brian rushed off his

ATV and ran over to show me. The other drivers were more familiar than I was, since they had just ridden ATVs a few days before.

I was surprised that William didn't go with us, but two other young men did. We all wore helmets, but there weren't enough goggles for everyone at first. William went to get more, while George and I did part of the tour with just sunglasses. I thought William would join us after getting the additional goggles, but he did not. For an hour and a half, we drove along beautiful beaches and deep into the rainforest. I was last in the group for most of the tour. I preferred to be able to see what was going on with everyone in front of me, and I was the most inexperienced of all the drivers.

When we arrived at the zip lines, we were filthy. Covered in dirt and dust, we all laughed at how awful we looked. Brooke smiled as she proudly displayed her dirt-filled braces.

For the next part of the tour, we took 11 zip lines across the jungle. When I saw them, I immediately asked how safe the tour was and if anyone had been injured on the zip lines. The guides informed me that no one had. Actually, the tour was extremely safe, with multiple guides

at each platform. We were always connected to the line by the cables and harnesses at each stop. They used extreme caution, but it was still a bit frightening to me, especially being up so high.

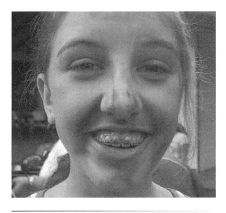

The platforms between the zip lines were made out of dark mesh steel that we could see through. When I was on a platform, looking down was not an option. As I stood in line, waiting my turn, I kept my eyes focused anywhere but down and tried to calm myself by remembering I was attached by a cable and harness. Brooke and Blake, on the other hand, loved the tremendous thrill. They both rushed ahead of me, enjoying the sensation of freedom as they swung through the trees. Brooke had so much fun that day as she soared from zip line to zip line, laughing and smiling as she enjoyed the last few hours of her life.

Personally, I felt relieved when I finally finished the last line. I think Paige was, too, though she would never admit it. She pretended to be having the time of her life because that is what she saw her siblings doing, but for someone that small, I imagine the experience was a little scary.

Before getting back on the ATVs, we ran through the gift shop and bought a few items. Brooke helped me pick out a big wooden bowl that now holds the sea shells she collected in Costa Rica. We bought a few other souvenirs that never made it back with us after the accident. In all honesty, I am not even sure how the bowl did.

We continued on the same path we had come on, but then stopped at a beach restaurant in Flamingo for lunch. I took a video of the group

and Brooke danced for the camera, happier than ever, clearly having one of the most memorable days of her life. We joked that we couldn't believe we were eating out, as dirty as we were. The camera recorded what would be the last captured images of Brooke alive.

We ordered cheeseburgers, quesadillas and nachos, and discussed what we wanted to do for the rest of the day. I am not sure what prompted me to do it, but while we were enjoying lunch, I encouraged Brooke to call her dad, Sean. We had been gone nine days at that point, and the

kids had not spoken with him since we left. Busy enjoying her cheese quesadilla, Brooke told me she would call him when we got back to the resort. Paige overhead us and excitedly said, "I want to talk to Daddy!" so I went ahead and called him then instead of waiting until we got back. Blake, Brooke and Paige all spoke with him and told him how much they loved him and missed him. Within a few miles of the end of the tour, we left the restaurant to head back to the resort.

Use your mobile tag reader
to see a video of
our Costa Rica vacation.

"Nothing is worth more than this day. "
~ Goethe

~ Chapter Two ~

"Happiness is a choice that requires effort at times."
~ Anonymous

When I think of my childhood, I think of many wonderful memories and a family full of love. People might assume otherwise when they hear my story, but there really were great times. Some of my bad memories, however, are extremely painful.

My childhood wasn't easy. I faced many challenges early on; my alcoholic father was both physically and verbally abusive. Like many other men his age, he suffered great mental anguish from the years he spent in Vietnam. He struggled to overcome the vivid memories of the nightmare he had lived through. In addition, he had scars from many years of abuse by his father. I believe he was a good man, but he suffered mentally from the hell he personally had experienced. Instead of getting the help he needed, he turned to alcohol. Drinking triggered his depression. After drinking too many beers, he would snap and become a different person.

Strangely, his anger was never directed at me, only my mom. He loved me more than anything. After living through Vietnam and his childhood, I believe he vowed never to hurt a child. I don't think he understood how terrifying his actions were to me, regardless of whether or not I was the target. All the way back to my earliest childhood memories, his violent and abusive behavior left me scared, confused and worried about my mom. Almost weekly, for years, we ran from him and hid overnight, afraid of what he was capable of doing.

My mom did not know how to escape. She worried about my well-being and tried to distance me from the violence by sending me to visit with other family as much as possible. I stayed with my grandparents a lot, and spent most of my summers living in Arkansas with my Aunt Cheryl and my cousins Beth and Jeff.

In 1980, when I was ten, my dad seemed to be slipping into a deeper depression and the situation at home grew more serious. Sensing the imminent danger, my mom knew she had to keep me away, so she sent me to live with my grandparents. I changed schools, and while it was upsetting to leave my good friends behind, I settled in quickly and made lots of new friends. I loved living with my grandparents. They spoiled me rotten, and even though they had six kids, they treated me like their princess. My grandma would bring me McDonald's to school for lunch; I felt so lucky!

An only child at that point, I longed for a brother or sister. When I lived with my grandparents, I got to be with their three youngest children, Lori, Nancy and Mark. I shared more of a sibling relationship with them, and still do to this day. After staying there for a semester, I returned to my home and my original school. That summer, I went to stay with my Aunt Cheryl in Arkansas, which I always begged to do, as I loved to be with my cousins.

One extremely hot July day, I remember being out in the steel pool in the backyard with my cousins, Beth and Jeff. The three of us were running in circles to create a whirlpool, then trying to swim against the current. We were surprised when my aunt came home from work early; immediately we noticed she was acting strange. She told me she wanted to take me somewhere. I got dressed and then we left alone, just the two of us. We pulled into their church. I was really confused and not sure what to think at this point. We went into the empty church and sat down in a pew. Then she broke the news to me.

She asked me if I understood how sick my dad was. I did; I knew he was trying to get help and had enrolled in a program at a local hospital to quit drinking. In the end, he wasn't strong enough to handle it and had fled the hospital. She explained to me that he had taken his own life.

He had quit rehab one other time, and on that day was threatening to run again. The hospital called my mom and asked her to come as soon as possible. They told her that he wanted to leave and that she needed to be firm with him and make sure he understood if he left the hospital, she would leave him for good. She rushed to the hospital and did what she could to stop him. As directed, she held firm and made it clear, this was his last chance. He grabbed her purse, dumped it out on the table, took her keys and left.

My mom knew from his actions the outcome was going to be tragic, she could sense the danger. Her inner voice warned her not to go home; that he would kill her. Terrified, she called her aunt to come get her and stayed with her in hiding overnight.

After fleeing the hospital, my dad went to his mother and step-father's house and stole a gun. When he got home, he waved the gun in the face of our next door neighbor, telling him that the minute my mom walked through the door—POW, as he gestured the shooting motion. It was clear he had snapped, but the neighbor had no way to reach my mom and warn her—this was still years before cell phones. My dad tried to find my mom, but for her protection no one told him her whereabouts. Later that evening, he called his sister, Nancy. In the midst of their phone conversation, unable to overcome his depression, he shot himself.

Accepting the death of a parent is hard on any young child, especially a suicide. I felt sad, but my dad had been a very sick man, with no faith whatsoever to give him the strength he needed to over-come his weaknesses. He had fought to find peace for many years. I loved my mom so much and was happy I would never again have to see her hurt. I mourned the loss of my father and worked to digest the shock of it all, but I recognized that his death had given us the opportunity to turn our lives around and find the happiness we deserved.

It didn't take long. On December 27, 1981, not even six months later, my mom went to a holiday party at the home of my father's sister, my Aunt Nancy. A mutual friend introduced her to Jim Albrecht, a wonderful man, whom we would both quickly grow to love and respect. At the time of the party, I was out of town at my Aunt Cheryl's house in Arkansas. My mom called me, excited to tell me she had met someone and she couldn't wait for me to meet him.

I remember how tickled I was the night we first met. They took me and my best friend Kim to the movies to see a Goldie Hawn film. I was overjoyed; they got along great and it felt so good to see my mom truly happy.

My parents were married the following August. My mom's three sisters, Cheryl, Lori and Nancy, were the bridesmaids and I was the junior bridesmaid. We all wore different color pastel dresses. My beautiful pale yellow dress made a perfect contrast to my dark hair. I was so excited the day of the wedding that I felt guilty and conflicted, but I knew we deserved this happiness.

Jim adopted me shortly after they were married, and he has been there for me ever since. He is as much of a father to me as any father is to their child, regardless of the fact that our relationship didn't start until I was ten. On occasion, someone will refer to him as my stepdad, and I always correct them, "No, he is my dad."

From that point on, life for my mom and me got much better.

"Let your hopes, not your hurts, shape your future."
~ Robert H. Schuller

March 22, 1983

Dear Jennifer —

In a couple weeks you will not be my
little girl anymore; you'll be my teenage daughter.
My, how the past 13 years have flown by. I
remember how proud I was the day you were
born and how excited I was when I learned
I had a beautiful daughter.

You have given me many, many reasons
to be very proud of you over the past years.
You've done so well in school. Dad and I
hope you will keep up the good work!

We have certainly been through alot together, haven't we? Just the two of us.
There's been happiness and sadness.
You have only multiplied my happiness.
I'm so thankful I had you during the
more difficult times. I don't know what
I would have done without you. Our
lives have certainly changed for the better
thanks to one very special person. As
you told me not so very long ago,
"It's so nice to be so happy." I couldn't
agree with you more.

I'll never forget how you used to
bug me for a baby brother or sister.
Remember what Dad told you? "All things
come to those who wait." It did, didn't
it? You were so impatient (you've always
been that way), but Dad was right, wasn't
he?

(10)

What will be next? With you, it's very difficult to predict.

I love you very, very much and consider myself so fortunate to have such a special person in my life. Every mother should be so lucky.

With Love,
Mother

Dear Jennifer:

No father could be more proud or happier of his daughter than I am of you.

You are blessed with many gifts that someday will bring you great happiness, I hope for this with all my heart, you are a very fine young lady.

I know that sometimes I do things that you may think are unfair or unjust. These are decisions I make as a father for the good of his daughter, someday you'll understand.

Your my daughter, I love you and always will.

Love, Dad.

~ Chapter Three ~

"You don't choose your family.
They are God's gift to you, as you are to them."
~ *Bishop Desmond Tutu*

I still longed for a sibling. I despised being an only child, especially through all the hard times. As soon as my parents got married, it was all I could think about and I literally drove them crazy as I would cry for them to have a baby.

My best friend at the time, Kim Fronabarger, lived two doors down from us. She had a new baby sister and I loved to go there and play. I couldn't help envying Kim. We had been only children together and I had wanted a sibling so badly. Now she had one and I didn't. She was so lucky to have a little sister. All I wanted to do when I was with Kim was play with the baby.

In November of 1982, on Thanksgiving Day, my prayers were answered and my baby sister Meghan Leah was born. At that time, her birth marked the high point of my life. When Meghan was little, she slept with me every night. I got a job at the daycare Meghan attended and rode my bike miles to work by her. Every time I saw her, as her class walked by or out on the playground, my love for her filled me. She would run to me and hug me.

Once in a while I would get lucky enough to work in her class. I was completely biased and convinced she was the cutest thing ever; I gave 99% percent of my attention to her, so unless there was no alternative, they did not assign me to her class. That same summer, I worked as a lifeguard in addition to working at the daycare. I loved bringing

Meghan to the pool with me and showing her off to everyone. Over time, I got busy with my teenage social life—friends, boyfriends and cheerleading—but Meghan always meant the world to me and I loved her unconditionally. I was so thankful to have her in my life.

"What greater thing is there for human souls
than to feel that they are joined for life—
to be with each other in silent unspeakable memories."
~ George Eliot

~ *Chapter Four* ~

"Making the decision to have a child is momentous.
It is to decide forever to have your heart
go walking around outside your body."
~ Elizabeth Stone

*W*hen I think of my successes, without a doubt, I consider my greatest accomplishment being a mother to my children. Just thinking of them brings a smile to my face, and sends a warm feeling of peace and happiness throughout my body. They are most definitely the jewel of my life. I cannot imagine a life without children. Don't get me wrong—they wear me out and keep me on my toes, but they are my pride and joy; the source of so much of my happiness.

While my children have clearly been the greatest pleasure of my life, as a mother I have faced challenges with each of them. To say it hasn't been easy for me would be an understatement. Regardless, I would go through any amount of pain or suffering over and over again, for one moment of the amazing love they give.

I met my high school sweetheart, Sean Scalise, during my freshman year, when I was fourteen and he was seventeen. After college I spent a year in outside sales with Mirex and then, in 1992, I started my career with a company named TeleCredit (the same company I am with today, currently known as FIS). After nine years together, Sean and I married on September 11, 1993. Initially, Sean and I agreed we would wait five years to have kids. It didn't take long for us both to feel differently. Within six short months of marriage, we felt the itch to start a family.

In June of 1994, I suspected I was pregnant. Father's Day weekend was coming up and I thought it would be the perfect time to surprise Sean. Even though I felt certain, the tests continued to show negative. Sean left to spend the weekend with his dad and his brother on a guys' trip to Chicago for Father's Day. As I drove him to the airport, a car cut in front of me; the next thing I knew, I was crying. That confirmed it for me—my hormones were clearly out of whack. I was so happy when the test finally showed positive, and I couldn't wait to surprise Sean with the news when I picked him up at the airport.

Being pregnant for the first time was such a magical experience. I sat in the baby's room for hours, rocking in the rocking chair as I sang to the baby. I had never been happier.

I traveled extensively throughout my pregnancy, and when I periodically had some issues that concerned me, I would refer to my copy of *What to Expect When You're Expecting* and self-diagnose. Each time, I determined it was normal. Little did I realize I had been having contractions for several weeks and was leaking amniotic fluid.

I woke up one morning with terrible cramps and concluded I had better see the doctor. Sean was at work and I didn't want to falsely alarm him, so I called my girlfriend Tracy and asked her what I should do. She drove me to St. John's Hospital. To my surprise, I found out that I was in labor. At the time I was only 31 weeks pregnant and the doctors didn't want me to deliver the baby. Fortunately, they were able to stop the labor and stabilize my condition.

The doctor explained to me that I would be given a series of steroid shots over the next several days to develop the baby's lungs, and that I needed to remain on complete bed rest. It was likely that I would be in the hospital for weeks.

We saw no point in Sean being there all day and wasting his time off before the baby was even born, so he continued to work. I had a new employee starting that week at work. I really wanted to train her before I went out on leave. Since I knew her well and had personally recruited her, I figured, what else did I have to do as I lay in the hospital bed? So

I had Sean empty out my file cabinet at home and bring me everything I needed to set up an office there in my hospital room. I think the nurses thought I was crazy.

Each day, Kristy came to the hospital to meet with me. She sat next to my bed in the rocking chair as we spent long hours reviewing what she needed to know in her new position, stopping occasionally for routine ultrasounds and monitoring sessions. On the morning of January 5, 1995, after almost a week in the hospital, a nurse came in to take me to be monitored.

By that time I was frustrated. No one gave me any indication of what was going on, and my regular doctor had been on vacation all week. While Kristy was there with me, I asked the nurse what she thought might happen. The nurse insisted that I needed to remain on bed rest, but told me not to worry—she thought I would get to go home soon.

Whew, I felt better! The nurse wheeled me down to the room to be monitored, and Kristy and I picked up where we had left off. After about an hour, the same nurse came up, put her hand on my shoulder and said to me, "Honey, I am sorry. It looks like I was mistaken; your white blood cell count has gone up and we are going to need to start inducing labor."

Since this was my first child, I didn't quite know what to think; I was pretty overwhelmed. Kristy and I looked at each other, tears welling up in our eyes. I looked back to the nurse and asked if Kristy could at least stay with me. I called Sean to tell him he needed to come to the hospital.

At that point, I was 32 weeks and my body truly was not ready. The labor was long and painful, but after over 20 hours, I gave birth to our beautiful son, Blake Alan Scalise. Blake weighed only 3 pounds and 2 ounces; he could not breathe on his own. A team of doctors immediately started working on him; he was quickly put on a respirator and whisked off to the NICU (Neonatal Intensive Care Unit).

I needed to remain in recovery, so I could not go with Blake. I felt sad and depressed on top of being petrified worrying what was happening with Blake. I couldn't believe I had just had a baby, and I couldn't see him or hold him. I was given a heavy dose of medication. Finally, exhausted, I went to sleep for some time.

The next day, several family members and friends came to visit us. I felt overwhelmed at one point, when the number of people in my hospital room made it look like a party. The nurse finally came in and asked everyone to leave so I could rest.

I was scheduled to go home 24 hours after delivery, but I couldn't bring myself to do it. I was so upset. How could I leave the hospital without my son, especially since I had not even gotten to hold him yet? It seemed like a bad dream. I begged the doctor to let me stay; I couldn't leave my son. Finally, he conceded, and I had one more day to at least sleep under the same roof as Blake. Unfortunately, I had only delayed the inevitable. I did have to leave before I ever got to hold him.

Each morning, bright and early, Blake's doctor called and gave me an update on Blake's status. I'd get up after he called and head to the hospital to spend the day in the NICU. I knew I should have been

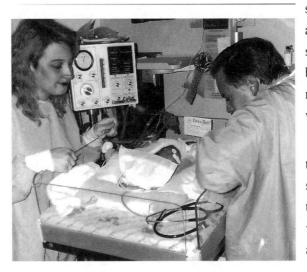

staying in bed and allowing my body some time to heal, but I couldn't—I needed to be there with Blake.

Sean returned to work, but would still manage to get to the hospital for a visit during the day and then back again for the evening. Finally, when Blake was five days old, we got to hold him. It was the most amazing experience and we both sobbed. Unfortunately, we couldn't hold him long and we had to keep oxygen with him, but he was getting better.

This routine continued on for over three weeks, during which time we took advantage of the opportunity to learn as much as possible from the NICU staff. Caring for a premature child is altogether different than caring for a full-term newborn, and we weren't experienced with either. At first it was overwhelming, but we caught on quickly and soon made sure one of us was always there to attend to Blake's needs. Because of our involvement, the staff felt comfortable allowing Blake to go home earlier than expected. To help us prepare and prove we were capable of doing it on our own, they required us to stay at the hospital overnight and care for Blake, alone in our own room.

Boy, were we in for a surprise! There were two of us in the hospital overnight and we still couldn't keep up; we were exhausted. Blake took hours to drink just a few CCs from the tiniest bottle imaginable. He did not have the strength in his tongue to suck properly, so we had to feed him a certain way, applying pressure and movement under his chin. Preemies tend to have reflux, so, typically, after he finished eating,

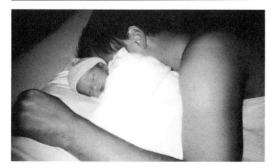

he would projectile vomit everything we had just fed him and we would have to start all over.

Finally, after what seemed like an eternity, we brought our baby home.

He was still so small, weighing only three pounds, five ounces. We told our family and friends we did not want any visitors on the first day, and asked that we be given some privacy to enjoy our son to ourselves. He came home with a heart monitor that we had to use when he slept. Still, Sean and I hovered over him together, making sure that he was breathing. We were scared, knowing that premature children are prone to sleep apnea and often have to be patted on the back to take the next breath.

Though we had a lot to take in as new young parents, we only cared that Blake was with us. I couldn't believe what I felt inside and how much I loved this child. Never had I felt a love like this, or even known something so wonderful existed. I was certain this was the greatest love of my life.

Blake was so cute—so tiny that Sean could actually slide his wedding ring on his wrist. At one point we took a picture of him next to

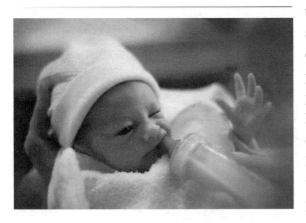

the cordless phone and he was truly only the size of the phone. He still had problems eating and keeping his food down, so it seemed like feeding Blake was a never-ending process. He didn't have the strength or skill to nurse directly from me, but his health made it essential that he have nothing other than breast milk. This required double the work for me, because I had to pump continuously and then feed him.

Blake had his days and nights mixed up, so literally, I got no sleep. Regardless of how tired I was, I would hold him on my chest and lie with him for hours. I thought about how blessed I was to have this beautiful baby and what a miracle it was that he was there with us. I felt a connection with him unlike anything I had ever experienced.

Over time, Blake grew up to be no different than any other child. He quickly filled out, becoming the most adorable toddler ever. I look at him now, amazed that he weighed only three pounds when born. At 15, he towers over me at 5'10', 170 pounds and a size 11 shoe. To this day, I keep in my room the first outfit he ever wore. I hold it often to remind me of the miracle that he is.

Like most mothers, I am extremely proud of my child. He does incredibly well in school, with close to a 3.8 grade point average. Instead of taking the easy route, he challenges himself by taking the maximum number of honors classes. Like me, he has a passion for writing and is an incredibly deep thinker. He has amazing faith, carrying on his relationship with his sister Brooke, his very best friend in life, spiritually. He talks me through my toughest days and is still the love of my life. He proudly wears his cross necklace with Brooke's name on it, always on the outside of his shirt, to keep her close to him at all times.

*"I never knew how much love my heart could hold
until someone called me Mommy."*
~ Unknown

~ Chapter Five ~

"While we try to teach our children all about life,
our children teach us what life is all about."
~ Angela Schwindt

Both Sean and I enjoyed having a child so much; Blake was the light of our life. Sean is very close in age to his brother Jeff; they are only 18 months apart. When I was young, I wanted a brother or sister more than anything. So we decided to have another child right away. By the time Blake turned one, I was pregnant.

My pregnancy was considered high risk because of what happened with Blake. I had to have a lot more tests and precautionary procedures. Again, I traveled extensively throughout my pregnancy, but by the time I reached the third trimester, I needed to be on bed rest. I did suffer from preterm labor and spent many nights at the hospital having the contractions stopped. Thankfully, all the precautions helped. In the end, everything was fine and I carried the baby full term.

I felt certain the baby was a boy. I had multiple ultrasounds due to my condition and always told the doctors I didn't want to know the sex of the child. Still, in one of the images, I was pretty sure I saw the infamous "turtle" as they call it, which told me it was a boy. My longtime best friend Tammy took me to one of my ultrasounds, and they asked if she wanted to know the sex. I told her it would be fine if she found out, but not to spoil it for me.

While I felt excited about this pregnancy, on occasion I found myself worried and guilty, certain I could never love another child as much as I loved Blake. I stressed over this often and felt terrible, thinking I would always be biased.

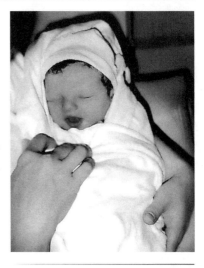

Giving birth this time was a completely different experience since I was full term. We could enjoy celebrating the occasion instead of being worried about the wellbeing of our child. On August 4, 1996, I gave birth to Brooke Lauren Scalise. A beautiful little girl; I couldn't believe it. Sean and I both sobbed.

Sean was completely shaken by Brooke's birth. I assumed then that he was overjoyed from the experience of having a daughter. Now, I often wonder if there was more to it. His love for her was apparent and we felt truly blessed that she was a healthy baby. This time, they handed us our baby to hold right away.

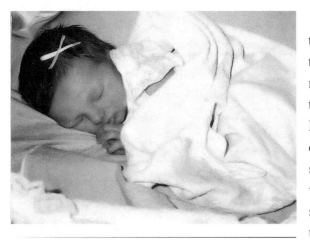

Sean went out to the waiting room to tell our parents the news and invite them to come to the room. It was such a blissful day. Everyone was shocked that the baby was a girl. I proudly showed her off. Sean took Brooke from me and handed her to my mom, who cried tears of happiness as she looked into Brooke's eyes for the first time. My mom handed Brooke to Mary Sue, Sean's mom, and we watched her marvel at holding their family's first baby girl. Finally, after two boys and a grandson, she had a little princess to love. Everyone was elated to hold Brooke, a wonderful experience we appreciated more than usual, since we were not able to do so with Blake.

I had been so confident that I was having a boy that I did not purchase a single girl's outfit. I had washed all of Blake's baby clothes and arranged them all in the drawers by sizes. Fortunately, Tammy knew I was having a girl, and like a true best friend, she showed up at the hospital with an entire wardrobe for Brooke.

Little Blake, the love of my life, seemed so confused when he came in to see Brooke. He proudly wore his Big Brother shirt and Big Brother pin (which are still on display in his room today). He didn't like seeing me in the hospital bed, so instantly he started to cry and put his arms out to come to me. He was so cute, only 18 months then.

As an experienced mother this time, I asked for a private corner room, and told my family and friends I wanted to be alone to rest and bond with the baby. I kept Brooke with me the entire time I was at the hospital. It was obvious right away how special Brooke was. I held her and cried as I realized that a mother can love each of her children as much as the other. Mothers are blessed with a love I had not understood until I had a second child. Each child is unique, their own person. Loving one is not like loving the other, and a mother's love doesn't have to compete. You love each of them more than anything for the unique child they are. I was so happy and overwhelmed with pride.

That night, I asked the nurses to disrupt us as little as possible and reassured them I would take care of all of Brooke's needs. She was a perfect baby, a complete angel. She slept nine hours that first night at the hospital, and from that point forward, she slept through the night every night. I figured I was being blessed this time because I missed so much sleep caring for Blake when he first came home.

The same day I had Brooke, my good friend Nicci Scanlan gave birth to her daughter, Maddison, in Columbus, Ohio. Nicci worked for me, so it was a bit inconvenient for our sales team when their manager and their manager's manager both went out on leave at the same time.

She and I joked that it was just a sign of our teamwork. The announcement they sent out at work talked about the double delivery. This time I begged the hospital to release me early and was discharged in less than 24

hours. I could not wait to go home to be with Blake; I missed him so much.

Blake and Brooke's bond started immediately. We never said one name without the other. Today, it is so hard to just say Blake. It was always Blake and Brooke, or if you were in a rush, Brake and Blooke. He felt so proud of his baby sister and was determined to help. He loved to climb into her car seat, bassinet, and swing—he thought they were all for him. He was still tiny then, not yet caught up from having been premature. He loved to

help with the baby, constantly rubbing her head and sticking her pacifier in her mouth. More than once he caused me to panic when I returned to the room to find him in her bassinet with her while she slept.

Even though they weren't twins, they were as close as any two siblings could ever be.

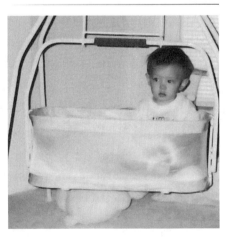

They shared a tight bond and a tremendous love from the very beginning. As children, they always remained close and rarely ever fought. I have many wonderful memories of the two of them together, memories that make me both laugh and cry. It breaks my heart at times to think how hard this is on Blake, but he is doing well and still feels the connection to Brooke even though she is no longer here in the physical world.

"Our real lessons often appear to us in the shape of pains, losses, and disappointments; let us have patience, and we shall soon see them in the proper figures."
~ Joseph Addison

~ Chapter Six ~

"Other things may change us,
but we start and end with family."
~ Anthony Brandt

As a family, we enjoyed many wonderful vacations together. We took the kids to Disney World more times than I can count—and more times than I had wished.

By the time Brooke turned three, her favorite ride was the Tower of Terror. They would put her in a seat on its own in the top middle row because it was the safest spot for the smaller kids. She was tall, but thin. One day, both she and Blake insisted that we do the ride time and time again. I am not necessarily a fan of the Tower of Terror; each time, as the elevator plummeted, leaving my stomach behind, I prayed this was the last time. After four times in a row, I finally told her I couldn't ride it again or I was going to be sick.

We took several cruises over the years, a favorite for all of us. Although Brooke wouldn't leave my side to go to the kids' camp and scheduled activities, she still

had fun. Blake, on the other hand, wanted to do nothing but go to the camp. They both enjoyed going to the formal dinner every night and eating pizza and ice cream any time they wanted. We made it a tradition to have pizza and cookies at midnight. The entertainment was always a highlight of the trip. As a family, we marveled at the fantastic performances the cruise ships put on.

I had always dreamed of going to Hawaii. Since I travel often, I wanted to be considerate of my fellow travelers. I had decided years ago that I would wait until I knew the kids were old enough to behave well for seven hours on a plane. I worked toward saving enough frequent flier miles for the four of us to fly first class and enjoy a two-week vacation.

Since we planned to use frequent flier miles, and there are only a certain number of award seats available on each flight, I booked the trip far in advance. At the end of the summer of 2002, I made the reservations for the following March. The kids helped me plan the vacation; they were ecstatic and couldn't wait.

Sean and I were both always on the go and our life seemed to be getting more and more hectic. Raising two young children and the constant stress associated with our careers made for a tough combination. Although we had considered having another child, we really weren't certain our fragile marriage could handle much more.

I can't say for certain if my soul knew what my future held, or if it was a type of motherly paranoia, but I had a strange worry that something might happen to one of my children. I remembered how I felt growing up alone, and knew I wouldn't want that for my child. My rationale was that by having a third, it was less likely one of our kids would ever be an only child.

Sean and I went to Florida in September for a quick getaway to try to revive our struggling marriage. We needed time to focus on each other for a change. When we got to the hotel, I called my grandmother for some reason. I probably wanted to check on my grandpa, who was pretty sick with cancer. Grandma seemed very excited. She said, "Guess what? I am going to be a grandma again!"

For the life of me, I couldn't figure who could be expecting. None of her six kids were really in a position where you would expect them to have a baby. Dumbfounded, I asked her who was pregnant. She told me it was Lori, one of the three youngest, who is more like a sister to me than an aunt.

Lori and Randal had four boys already; her youngest, my godson Brandon, was twelve. Lori would turn forty that year. She had her first child, Tommy, when she was only eighteen years old. Starting over again meant they would spend over forty continuous years raising children under the age of eighteen. Surprisingly, over the years they still managed to keep a very active social life, thanks to wonderful grandparents, but starting over at their age seemed like a shock.

I called Lori as soon as I hung up with my grandma. I am so close with her that I didn't hold back. I started laughing hysterically, so hard that I cried. Sean saw the humor in it, too, and together we laughed until our stomachs hurt.

Sean and I ended up having a nice trip, but we were glad to settle back in at home. We had missed the kids and were happy to be with them again. A few weeks later, I noticed I wasn't feeling well. It didn't take me more than a minute to figure out that I had jinxed myself!

I called Lori, and this time she and Randal laughed hysterically. We were excited and figured it was God's plan—even though we were much older than in our previous pregnancies. I would be 33 when I had Paige and Lori would be 40 when she had Dylan.

Brooke was absolutely ecstatic—happier than ever. Of course, Blake and Sean were excited, too. Our only dilemma was what to do about Hawaii. We had waited years for the kids to be old enough to be well behaved on a flight that long; it would be another five years before the baby would be old enough to go. Should we cancel or go now?

If we took the trip as scheduled, I would be between 32 and 33 weeks. Blake had been born at 32 weeks, so I knew the baby would be fine at that point, which was comforting if I was going to go that far from home. Since this pregnancy went better than the others and I felt great, we decided to go ahead with our trip as scheduled instead of delaying it another five or six years so the new baby would be old enough to handle it.

All through my pregnancy, Brooke acted like a little mom. Involved in every aspect, she couldn't wait to find out the sex of the baby. Even though we didn't know with the other two we decided to ask this time since the kids wanted to. Blake, of course, wanted a boy and Brooke, of course, wanted a girl. We had said that Blake could name the baby if he was a boy, and Brooke could name the baby if she was a girl. On the day of the ultrasound, we let the kids stay home from school to go with us. Brooke grinned from ear to ear when she found out she was having a baby sister.

I had so much fun being pregnant when the kids were older. They really got into it; we experienced everything together as we prepared for our baby. Brooke loved looking at the little girl clothes. For her, it was a dream come true, since all she ever wanted to do anyhow was play with her baby dolls.

We left for Hawaii in mid-March. Even though I was seven months pregnant, we had a wonderful vacation. It was the most beautiful place I had ever been. The kids loved exploring the tropical beaches, all so different from one another. We spent part of the trip in Oahu and then part of it on the Big Island of Hawaii. On the Big Island, we stayed at the Hilton Waikoloa Village, a resort that the kids had picked out. A great family hotel, it came complete with tons of waterslides, lagoons, golf course, putt-putt—just tons for them to do. We relaxed and took

in the spectacular views from the many hammocks that hung throughout the property. Every night we would go out to watch the sun set; it was simply too beautiful to miss. The gorgeous grounds of the hotel included an adorable little chapel overlook-

ing the sparkling turquoise waters. Weddings were held there. Brooke visited the chapel often and made me watch a few weddings from afar—I even took videos of them for her, and then later the inside of the chapel as well. She told me that she wanted to get married there. I believed her, and up until the accident, had always imagined someday I would see her standing there as the bride.

After two fantastic weeks that included a submarine excursion, a visit to Pearl Harbor, a whale-watching trip, hikes at Hawai'i Volcanoes National Park, and visits to multiple beaches throughout the islands, we were all finally ready to come home. We had never been away two weeks in a row, and although we were all together, we felt homesick.

The only flight available for our return had been a red-eye flight, and we were all dreading it. We flew back to Honolulu and then departed for St. Louis from there. We were in first class and fortunately our seats reclined almost completely. Sean and the kids slept, along with almost everyone else in the plane, but I was so uncomfortable I couldn't relax. As I lay there with my back killing me, my contractions started. I thought to myself, "I can't believe this. Why now? Why here?" I had

not had any preterm labor during this pregnancy. My doctor had agreed I was doing great and had cleared me for the trip.

I couldn't understand why this was happening now. I told myself not to panic; this wasn't completely unusual for me. I worked to calm myself down and focused on relaxing. I figured I could get the contractions to stop in no time. After they continued for a while, I decided I needed to get another pillow and wedge it in the crease of the seat. If I could get pressure on my side, I was sure I could stop it. I thought about waking Sean, but he and the kids were sleeping so peacefully. I decided to wait and see if I could get the contractions to subside. I walked up to the flight attendant and asked for another pillow. She asked me why I needed it; I think she could tell by the look on my face that something was wrong. I casually told her that I was having some contractions and I want to put some pressure on my side. She reacted quickly, obviously concerned for my wellbeing.

The attendant made me a bed in the galley and insisted I lie down. She timed my contractions, panicking a little herself. I kept reassuring her I would be fine, I had experienced preterm labor before and this was not uncommon for me. I think that only sent her further into panic mode. She told me that the airline had to follow procedures in a situation like this and as much as I tried to convince her to wait, they feared for my safety, and I had no say. An announcement came over the intercom, "If there is an obstetrician on board, can you please ring your call button."

At that point, Sean came up to us and I told him I was fine. Another announcement, "If there is a doctor on board, can you please ring your call button." By then, my contractions were getting stronger and I was in a lot of pain. I was glad they were finding someone on the plane to help. Then another announcement, "Ummm, if there is an RN on board, will you please ring your call button." Sean left to talk with the flight attendant and I lay in the galley by myself, not quite sure what to think. All of the sudden, the captain came on the PA, "This is your captain speaking. I am sorry to disturb you, as so many of you are sleeping, but I need to let you know we are going to make an emergency medical landing in Salt Lake City, Utah. Flight attendants, please prepare the cabin for landing."

In denial, I thought, "This can't be happening, Surely this isn't real." The flight attendant who had been with me the entire time kept reassuring me this was best. Several medics on the plane, the captain and the airline personnel they have to contact during emergencies had decided unanimously—land the plane as soon as possible, do not wait to get to St. Louis. So the huge wide-body plane, completely full, headed for Salt Lake City. I was so embarrassed, but what could I do?

They landed the plane and I was immediately carried off on a stretcher. At two in the morning, the airport was deserted except for the multiple emergency vehicles that were standing by. In the middle of a sea of red flashing lights, I still couldn't believe this was really happening. The flight attendant helped carry some of our belongings as she escorted Sean, Blake and Brooke off the plane with me. They looked confused and tired. Brooke got in the ambulance with me, while Sean and Blake went in another emergency vehicle. They took me to LDS Hospital in Salt Lake City.

Since we had just left Hawaii, we all had shorts on and we landed in Salt Lake in a blizzard. We had the bags that we carried on, holding our cameras, my purse, and the kids' games and toys. We did not have any clothes or toiletries, and we were in a strange city where the only person I knew was my local sales rep. Fortunately, everyone at the hospital was so nice. They understood our predicament and worked to accommodate us. The nurses gave Sean and the kids a room next to me so they could try to get some rest. I knew the drill, so it was pointless to ask; there was no way they could tell me what would happen until they monitored me for a while and saw how I responded to the medicine being used to stop the labor. We had to wait, so I rested.

The kids were complete angels; Sean and I couldn't believe how good they were. They wanted to help me in any way they could. From my hospital bed, I could see splendid, huge, snow-capped mountains out the window—such a contrast to the lush green mountains and ocean

views of Hawaii. We took pictures of the view and joked about how we were going to explain these pictures at the end of our Hawaii Vacation Photo Album.

Eventually they were able to stop my labor and determine why my contractions had started. I had spent so much time in the ocean in Hawaii while pregnant that I got an infection. The body's natural reaction to an infection is to protect itself by forcing labor in an effort to remove the baby. They gave me the antibiotics I needed and continued to monitor me. The following day, thankfully, we were

released to go home.

American Airlines was amazing. Representatives called throughout the morning and the next day to check on me. In addition, the flight attendant called to talk with us several times. Once we found out I would be released, they told us what we needed to do. They booked us on a return flight in first class, just as our previous flight had been.

The entire ordeal had taken place so quickly. It was surreal and almost felt like it really hadn't happened at all. We snapped pictures on the plane as we departed Salt Lake, the only evidence of the odd finish to our Hawaiian vacation.

"Every hour of every day is an unspeakably prefect miracle."
~ Walt Whitman

~ *Chapter Seven* ~

*"What you leave behind is not
what is engraved in stone monuments,
but what is woven into the lives of others."*
~ Pericles

We had a lot happen in our family during the spring of 2003. Ironically, the other aunt I am close with, Nancy, unexpectedly ended up pregnant, too. Her sister, Lori, gave birth to Dylan on April 30. Then, two days later, my grandpa passed away.

This was the first tragic death we had really had in our large, close family since my dad, Dale. This loss was extremely hard on all of us. Grandpa had been sick with cancer for five years. He fought it hard and had been in remission on and off over the years. Recently, we had learned that the cancer had spread to his lungs; he had just started radiation treatment.

My mom and dad had gone to my grandparents' house on May 2, 2003 to watch the Kentucky Derby with my grandpa. They had a nice visit and Grandpa was in good spirits. My parents left to go grocery shopping, then home. After they left, my grandma made dinner. Shockingly, while my grandpa ate his dinner, he choked on a piece of steak, possibly caused by swelling in his esophagus due to the radiation. My grandma called for help and the paramedics came to work on him, but it was too late. There wasn't anything they could do.

For five years, our tightly knit family had feared the death of the man we all loved and looked up to. In the end, it happened so fast. It was hard to accept that his death was real. We tried to find peace in knowing that he did not suffer a long, painful death as he most likely would have with lung cancer.

The services were tough and our family spent days together. Brooke took it really hard. My Grandma Albrecht had died when Brooke was too

young to remember, so this was the first death she had to deal with. She and my grandpa had been extremely close. He adored Brooke and always called her his Brookie Cookie.

Grandpa was a retired city fireman, and his fellow firefighters showed up to give him a proper goodbye. As they stood proudly by his casket and spoke at his service, we were all touched by the respect he was so deservedly given. Fire trucks led the funeral procession. When we pulled into the cemetery, I was awestruck—two fire trucks were at the front, ladders fully extended, forming an arch for the procession to drive through. He deserved that; he was always so proud of being a fireman.

We were happy Grandpa had gotten to see Lori's new baby, Dylan, before he passed. Throughout the funeral, we fought over who got to hold the baby. We held him tightly, welcoming the feeling of this new love at the time of such great loss. It was a difficult year, but thankfully God gave our family three unexpected babies to help us survive.

On June 9, 2003, I woke up early, having intense contractions. We got the kids up and we all headed to the hospital. Brooke was so excited. Unlike my other labors, this one went fast. I was already dilated

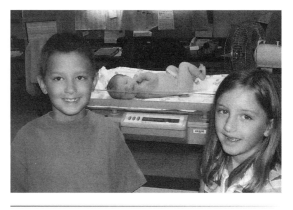

to seven centimeters by the time we arrived. They were concerned I wouldn't be able to wait long enough for the doctor to arrive. He made it just in time to catch the baby. Brooke held the baby proudly in her arms and named her Paige Elizabeth Scalise. We all cried; it was an incred-

ibly joyous day. Sharing this experience with the older children made it all that much more wonderful.

Brooke didn't want to leave; she wanted to stay there with me and Paige, but it was against hospital policy. She spent the day next to me in my bed and we bonded with Paige—our first girls' day together. Once again, my heart melted as a new, most amazing love began. I marveled at my ability to love each child so much the same, yet so differently, individually, for who they were.

Paige was a really good baby. At first I joked that we should consider having one more. Of course, it was wonderful to have the extra help from Brooke, who did everything with her, and from Blake, too. Brooke was my

little helper, right there to assist me in every way she could. Her maturity astonished me.

As I went back to work, it became difficult to balance it all. I loved my job and had always been extremely committed to it. We had a new executive running the organization at the time and we were going through major changes. I had assumed additional responsibility and was in charge of a

massive rebuilding effort out west, which required a fair amount of travel to California.

I struggled each time I left, reminding myself that I worked hard to provide a good life for the kids. Fortunately, we had a much better support system than most. That gave me peace of mind while I traveled. Sean was more involved than the typical dad and extremely dedicated to raising our children, which helped tremendously. Both my parents and Sean's were always willing to assist.

In addition, my sister Meghan, the ideal aunt, stayed with us constantly over the years to help with the kids. When Blake was little, he nicknamed her Me Me (may-may) and the kids have called her Me Me ever since. For several years straight, you wouldn't see Aunt Me Me without one of them in her arms. She loved to be with our

children, and when I traveled, she would often stay with Sean to help out. Meghan has been extremely close with Blake, Brooke, and Paige, but she and Brooke shared a special connection. Coincidentally, Brooke and Meghan were 13 years apart, just like Meghan and me. They were every bit as close as Meghan and I are as sisters.

Our babysitter, Teresa, was part of our family from the beginning. She is almost a second mom to the children. I interviewed and hired her when I was pregnant with Blake. She met all three of our babies when they were newly born, and anticipated the day she would have them to love full-time, once I returned to work. Teresa played a major role in raising our kids and deserves so much credit for the beautiful individuals they are today.

Nothing shy of a saint, a true angel sent from Heaven, Teresa is the most loving, patient woman you could ever meet. She has always watched several other children in addition to ours, and I often wonder how in the world she does it.

The stress of my job continued to escalate and things at home got worse. Paige grew past the baby stage; she was pretty high energy already and very active. She required a lot of attention to make sure she didn't get hurt. If I turned my head for a minute, unlike Blake and Brooke, Paige would find something to stick in her mouth or a way to climb up the cabinets. Even Teresa joked about it. She told us that at nine months old, Paige had officially had more time outs than Blake and Brooke combined over all the years that she had cared for them.

Life was crazy at that point. Blake was busy with hockey and Brooke was busy with soccer, in addition to their normal school activities. My job, Sean's business, doctor appointments, dentist appointments, orthodontist appointments, and everything else left very little time for Sean and I to do anything as a couple.

One thing we always had in common was our love for the kids. From the beginning, we wanted them by us all the time, and being a little soft, we quickly fell into the habit of having the kids sleep with us. Since I traveled and had to be away from them often, I absolutely loved having them next to me when I slept. By the time Paige was born, we were so set in our ways that Paige never once slept in her crib. With the kids' rooms upstairs and the master bedroom on the main level, I of course rationalized my actions by thinking she would just be too far away. So she always slept in our room, even for her naps.

Over time, Sean and I had grown apart. We could not seem to come to agreement on anything. We were both very unhappy and the kids were suffering from our deteriorating relationship.

While I knew I would always love him and care for him as the father of our children, I didn't want to have an unhappy life together or raise our kids in that type of environment. In 2005, we filed for divorce.

"Life's challenges are not supposed to paralyze you,
they're supposed to help you discover who you are."
~ Bernice Johnson Reagon

~ *Chapter Eight* ~

"Children are the hands by which we take hold of Heaven."
~ Henry Ward Beecher

I have always been in awe of the vast differences between my three kids. It bewilders me that two parents can mix the same set of genes and come out with completely different results, so night and day diffreent from one another in some ways, yet so much alike in others. It also amazes me how soon a child's personality becomes apparent. Before they are even a year old, they already possess the many traits that will always make them who they are.

Even before he was a toddler, Blake has always been reserved and laid-back, like his father. Extremely smart with a hunger to learn, he has demonstrated intense passions, to the point of obsession sometimes! Today it is paintball; his childhood fixations ranged from Star Wars to NASCAR to hockey to Yu-gi-oh and Pokemon Cards. He has always been into something "to the extreme."

Surprisingly, I think he is the most sentimental of all the kids. His attachments were obvious early on. When he was in the hospital when he was a baby, they used white rags in the NICU instead of burp cloths. Blake grew attached to "his rag" instead of a blanket like most children.

Just like me, he insists on keeping everything that has a memory tied to it, ranging from his first stuffed animals

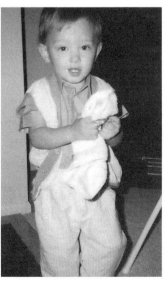

(many of which are still proudly displayed on the shelves in his room) to his favorite toy collections. Over the years, getting him to clean his room has been a real task. He never wants to get rid of anything. Years ago I made the mistake of gathering a bunch of his possessions and putting them in a bag to donate. When he realized what I had done, he threw a fit. We compromised by putting them in a basket in the corner of his room, where they still rest today.

One of the things I love most about Blake is his laugh. Just thinking about it makes me smile. He has always laughed a lot, especially at his sisters! He has a great sense of humor and does like to cut up and be silly at times. I like this balance and love to see him have fun and laugh often.

Blake appreciates the simple things, and doesn't like a lot of change in his life. Any time I redecorate something or change anything in the house, he insists he doesn't like it and would prefer it the other way. In his room, he has an outdated corded phone that lights up when it rings.

He got the phone when he was young and he refuses to let me replace it. He won't let me change his bedspread or his bedroom furniture; he tells me he likes it just as it is.

Blake is a leader, not a follower. He speaks out about what he believes in and is very direct, like me. He doesn't worry about what people think of him, and he never pretends to be someone he is not. He isn't afraid

to show affection; even as he got older, he did not get embarrassed at all, or ask me to stop, when I'd kiss him good-bye or tell him how much I love him, at school in front of other kids. He has a thirst for knowledge, and from a young age has always asked countless random questions such as: Why is the sky blue? How do planes fly? What makes magnets

attract? Why is cereal named cereal? How do batteries work? Where does fog come from? Most of the time I replied, "Good question, but I have no idea." Blake still teases me that unless it relates to the business world, he isn't asking me because I won't know the answer. It is not surprising that on the rare occasion when Blake watches TV, he watches the Discovery Channel or the History Channel.

He has a good head on his shoulders, understands right from wrong, and is determined to not let peer pressure influence him. He is very open and honest with me. He confides in me often and openly; we discuss the dilemmas teenagers his age face in their daily lives.

As he has grown, Blake has become more motivated. He is determined to be the best that he can be. He has come a long way from the age of six, when I asked him what he wanted to be when he grew up, and he proudly blurted out, as if it were the most sought-after job in the world, that he wanted to be the guy at the roller coaster who presses the button.

Blake is extremely loyal and has known his best friends since they were little. Matt and Blake became friends as toddlers together at Teresa's; Blake and Andy were in class together in first grade. He has also known his other close friend, Johnny, since he was young. Blake has been an exceptionally good kid and I am blessed to have a child like him. He keeps me grounded.

For the most part, Paige is the spitting image of me. She can be somewhat mischievous and a jokester on occasion. That gene definitely comes from her dad, but otherwise, it is kind of scary how she not only looks like me, but acts like me. By far the most colorful of the three kids, Paige is adorable and knows how to work it. A little bitty thing, she still wears sizes four and five now, and she is about to turn seven. She epitomizes "small but mighty." The most independent child you will ever meet, Paige could easily be Kevin in the movie *Home Alone* and spend a week on her own. Her first words were, "No, me do!" She refuses to ask for help with anything.

A very creative child, Paige has an imagination that is out of this world. When she was little and we went shopping, any time she saw a mirror she would talk to her imaginary friend "Jaynet"—her own reflection in the mirror. When she was three, I walked into the room to find the blinds hanging sideways and a cord cut from one. She threw her hand over her mouth, acting shocked. She looked me in the eye and said, "Momma, look what Elmo doed."

Like her mother, Paige is a bundle of energy and has two speeds, on and off. I swear she is talking and telling me what she wants for breakfast before she even opens her eyes in the morning.

Paige is a natural leader with tremendous confidence in herself. She believes that she can do anything, and she is not intimidated by anyone. By the age of three, she would boss the big kids around and issue orders, certain she was in charge. She has several older friends and she hangs with them quite well. As a matter of fact, she ends up being the one that leads.

A few months ago, Little George came running up from the basement, crying and extremely upset. Big George ran to see what was wrong and he told his dad that Paige had thrown something hard at his head. Big George took him to put ice on it, and I saw Paige go running upstairs to Brooke's room. I found her standing in the corner, in time-out. I knew it must be bad. So I asked what she had done and told her she needed to go apologize. She quickly turned around, her arms crossed in anger, and said, "He didn't apologize to me." I asked again what had happened.

She shouted, "Little George said I can't aim, and that he can because he played baseball. So I said, 'Oh yeah? Think I can't aim?' and I picked up a battery and threw it at him and hit him smack middle of his forehead!" She served her timeout, I checked on Little George, who was fine, and then couldn't help laughing at what a little stinker she is.

She can be both stubborn as a mule and sweet as can be. I have struggled with finding effective discipline for her. She does not respond to anything except positive reinforcement. We have never spanked Blake or Brooke. With Paige, by the time she was three, I spanked her

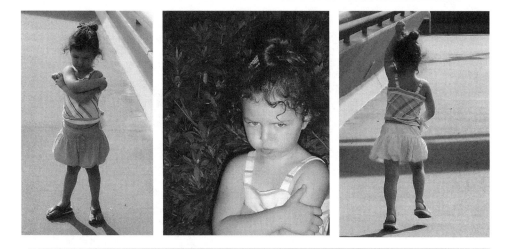

good. She had a big red handprint on her butt and my hand throbbed, but she looked me directly in the eye and said, "That didn't hurt." But when she is sweet she makes you melt. She often wakes up in the middle of the night and throws her arms around me, and says, "Momma, I love you so much." When she leaves me messages telling me she misses me so much she can't stand it, all I can think about is when I get to snuggle her again. But then, when I rush to call her back, she says, "What do you want?"

There have been many unforgettable moments, like the time she got angry because someone finished a box of cookies she had set aside for Santa, and when I made her eat soap for saying damn, and she told me she was going to tell Jesus on me. When Paige was three, she and Brooke were sliding down the steps in a sleeping bag. I asked them to stop. Brooke did and told Paige they couldn't do it anymore. Paige looked at Brooke and said, "It's okay, we will just do it when she is gone!" Not surprisingly, before Paige started school she told everyone how when school started she was going to spend a lot of time in the "princess' office" (principal's office).

When Paige was a toddler she hated to wear clothes. It didn't matter if it was summer or winter, she preferred to be in the nude. Trying to keep clothes on her when we were at home became an endless battle. I will never forget the bitter cold winter day when Sean left to go somewhere and Paige didn't get to tell him good-bye; she ran out the door after him without a stitch of clothing on. By the time I got to her she was in the snow-covered driveway with her arms thrown around Sean completely oblivious to the freezing cold or the fact she shouldn't be out in it, naked!

Just like her mother and her grandmother, she is a complete sappy mess when it comes to sad movies. We discovered this early, when she was only three and we watched *Flicka*, a movie where a horse was injured. She couldn't understand why she was crying. She looked at me with this pitiful look on her face and said, "Momma, why am I twying (crying)? My eyes are all wet!"

A responsible girl, Paige could run the household if I let her. She has a motherly, nurturing side and loves to take care of both the dog and the hamster. She treats them like they are her babies and she is the momma. As young as she is, she works hard to be strong and control her emotions. She is positive and happy despite any circumstance.

Somehow I knew, as did others, that something about Brooke was special. My mom knew it, Meghan knew it, Teresa knew it, and George knew it. We couldn't explain it, but she was wise beyond her years. Something let us know she was unique.

Always incredibly mature for her age, Brooke often shocked others with the level of conversation she could carry on. Sometimes, even I couldn't believe what she understood and the advice she gave. One night before we went on vacation, Brooke and George stayed up talking after the rest of us went to bed. I woke up when George finally came

to bed. It was after two in the morning. I remember how he shook his head in amusement. He explained, "I just can't believe Brooke is only twelve. If I didn't know better, I would swear I was talking to you or another adult, not a child."

Quite intense at times, Brooke focused deeply on whatever activity she was doing. She was extremely determined like I am, but particularly organized like her father. Brooke had to make a detailed to-do list for everything, even listing mundane activities such as "put on deodorant" and then "wait two minutes" before listing the next to-do, "put on shirt."

She loved to have fun and had more passion for life than most people. Whether dancing in Halloween costumes on the deck in the snow, or dancing on the mailbox and waving as the cars drove by, she always created some kind of fun just by being crazy and loving life with her friends. You never saw Brooke without a smile on her face and a sparkle in her eye. She found a way to appreciate just about anything or anyone.

On the other hand, Brooke was insanely responsible, reminding both Sean and I constantly of things we needed to do. She acted like a mother to Paige and took her under her wing from the day she was born. After the divorce, she looked after Sean and always reminded him of everything, from locking the doors to tying up the boat properly. When the kids were with him, she always helped take care of Paige.

Boy-crazy even in her preschool years, Brooke gave Matt (Blake's best friend from Teresa's) a plastic "engagement ring" when she was three, and asked him to marry her. He still has the ring today. On her first day of kindergarten, when I went to be with her in her class, Brooke asked, as serious as could be, "Now what do I do if I love a boy? Do I write a note, or do I just tell him?" She loved to hang out with her brother's sports teams, hockey or baseball, and had a boy on the team she was in love with each season.

Brooke was a worrier and did, on occasion, stress herself out over little things. Like Sean, she was a perfectionist and would spend hours making sure her clothes were folded exactly right in the drawer. She loved to make us proud. She was hard on herself and insisted on being

the best she could. She was a Straight-A student because of the effort she put forth; teacher after teacher told us what an incredible role model and positive influence on the other children she was.

Brooke liked everyone. It didn't matter if you were tall, short, rich, poor, older, younger, foreign, native, black, white, purple or green—Brooke had no prejudices. She could find the good in anyone, always. She knew to love people for what mattered most—their character. She had many friends over the years that she was proud to be friends with because of who they really were as a person, regardless of anything else.

I remember when Brooke was only two, we went shopping and let her pick out a baby doll—any doll she wanted, we told her. She decided quickly; she knew exactly which one she wanted. Brooke selected an African American baby. Sean tried to show her a few others, to see if she wanted one that looked more like her, but she refused. She was adamant that she wanted that doll.

For years, Brooke took her favorite doll with her everywhere, usually without clothes on. You would only see the dark brown fabric that made up the body. Since Brooke named every one of her dolls Sally, she had to find a way to differentiate between them. She called this one Tan Sally. Of course, we still have Tan Sally. Skin color, hair color and eye color meant nothing to Brooke. She didn't feel the need to have her baby look just like her. I was proud of her ability to see us all as one. Regardless of anything else, I was proud she was able to see we are all God's children. I believe Brooke always understood this. Early on, Brooke expressed a desire to learn about God. We were not a religious family and rarely went to church. This was true for my parents as well as Sean's. Brooke had very little religious influence from us, yet she always talked about God and had a special relationship with Christ. Brooke wrote me letters asking for us to go to church more. At five years old, she drew pictures of Jesus and wrote how much she loved her parents and would pray for them. She drew random drawings of angels when she was only 5 years old.

Brooke knew Teresa (her babysitter) was a devout Christian with a close relationship with God. She asked Teresa to read her the Bible and help her learn about Jesus. Brooke's interest was so great that she got the other kids excited to learn more, too. She had favorite videos of Jesus that she would ask to watch when she was at Teresa's. She could never get enough and always asked to learn more.

Sean and I took the kids to Meramec Caverns back when Brooke had just turned four. As we were entering the cave, the tour guide explained to us how outlaw Jesse James had hidden in the cave. He went on to say that Jesse James had been a bad man: a bank robber and a murderer. During his story, Brooke spoke up loudly, telling the whole group that it was okay, that God would forgive Jesse James. Sean and I were both quite startled by her comment, since we didn't go to church. The guide just looked at us and asked how old she was, while the other visitors all chuckled at her wisdom.

Brooke believed in herself and knew that as long as she was doing the best she could and having fun, nothing else mattered. She was silly and random, genuinely happy for others' good fortune and without a jealous bone in her body. She loved to spend quality time with me, and no matter what, she put this time before anything. Always happy, her laughter was contagious to those around her. She loved hugs and affection and liked to be close to me. She slept in my room with Paige

and me until she was twelve, when I regretfully made her start sleeping in her own room. Yet Brooke was not overly sensitive and emotional. When we watched a sad movie and I bawled at the end, she couldn't understand why I cried. She knew it was just a movie and could separate herself from it. On the other hand, she always called me Mommy.

Brooke lived by the golden rule, treating others as she would like to be treated. She had a deep compassion for other people, especially the less fortunate. When she and I took trips together, she loved to feed the homeless people. She got such a rush from helping those in need. She tried not to judge or criticize others, but looked for the good in everyone. It took her some time to understand that not all friends her age were capable of viewing things as maturely as she did. At first she let it bother her and her feelings were badly hurt, but she later learned not to take it personally, and to forgive others if they were judgmental. She faced two situations that really upset her, but she made them opportunities to learn and grow, to be a bigger person.

Brooke was a beautiful child, but she needed extensive orthodontic work. She had a very narrow bite, plus some issues with the structure of her mouth, which required major jaw surgery to correct. The surgeon did not want to do surgery until after she had reached a certain stage in her growth. He also did not want her to get braces too soon before the surgery. Brooke looked forward to getting her teeth corrected, but she wasn't going to let crooked teeth keep her from smiling.

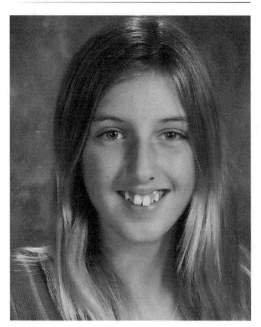

Brooke came home one day, though, extremely upset. It had gotten back to her that one of her close friends had said Brooke would be pretty if it weren't for her teeth. She took it really hard; she didn't understand how one of her friends could say something like that. In the end, she let her friend know it hurt her feelings and why, but forgave the girl for it.

The other situation was similar, only this time

Brooke overheard someone making fun of her. Brooke loved to dance, but she had absolutely no rhythm. In kindergarten, her music teacher struggled to teach her, and told her to hit plastic bottles on the floor for homework to try to learn rhythm. She just didn't have it. As she got older, dancing was one of her favorite things to do, but she danced to the beat of her own drum, so to speak, and did not care. She always danced with her best friend Lauren, an extremely talented competitive dancer, not caring that their skills were like night and day. She and Lauren had fun and that was all that mattered.

Eventually, Brooke and her best friend Gina decided to join a hip-hop class at a dance studio nearby. They enjoyed the class, as well as seeing some other friends there. One evening, when I picked Brooke and Gina up after class, Brooke was bawling. When class ended, she had walked up to her instructor (the owner's daughter) and one of her own friends, only to hear them making fun of her. I could look at her and see how hurt she was; it crushed me. Gina too, was shocked by what had happened.

When we got home, I called the studio owner and told her Brooke would not be attending anymore. I would not support having an instructor who behaved so inappropriately. I encouraged her to have a talk with her daughter; they wouldn't be in business very long if that was how they made little girls feel. Brooke's friend who had made fun of her apologized and Brooke forgave her. They remained friends. Brooke never stopped dancing, nor did she care what anyone thought. The dance studio soon went out of business.

By her actions, I knew Brooke loved God. She wore the cross necklace that Teresa gave her all the time. In her room, she posted sticky notes that said "I love God" and "I love Jesus." I also knew that on her MySpace page she had listed the Bible as her favorite book and written of her love for God. Even though I knew this, I still wasn't prepared for the overwhelming love Brooke had for God, and the deep personal relationship she had with Him.

*"It takes courage to grow up
and turn out to be who you really are."*
~ Anonymous

Mommy-

I just wanted to let you know that you mean the world to me and I love spending ~~quality~~ time with you (which I wish we had more of) and I have a blast when I am with you. But, I wish we could go to church a little more

♡ Brook

2 God

*Use your mobile tag reader
to see two videos of
Brooke just "being Brookie."*

~ Chapter Nine ~

"There is no such thing in anyone's life as an unimportant day."
~ Alexander Woollcott

*E*ven before our vacation, it had been a busy summer for Brooke. She and her best friend, Lauren, would be turning 13 in August. They had a tradition of celebrating their birthdays together. Since 13 was a milestone, I told Brooke they could choose: I would throw a big party, or take them both on a trip to San Francisco. They decided they definitely wanted to go to San Francisco. I worked with Becky, Lauren's mom, to choose a date.

The girls had church camp at the end of June, they had soccer tryouts, we had our Costa Rica trip, and Lauren had commitments at dance. In the end, we could only take the trip when they first got out of school at the beginning of June. So we made reservations, deciding to celebrate their birthdays early, something I am now so thankful for.

Going to San Francisco had become an annual tradition for Brooke and me. It is my favorite city and she quickly grew to love it, as well. Brooke and I had taken two trips together to San Francisco prior to our trip with Lauren. The day before the first trip, our very first mother-daughter trip together, she broke her ankle in a soccer game. She was crushed to think we would have to cancel it, so I took her in a wheelchair. It was tough pushing her up the hills on Powell Street, all the way to California Street, but we made it. We even managed to ride on a cable car, which is not easy in a wheelchair.

Brooke, Lauren, and I had a blast together on the trip. As usual, they were extremely silly and we laughed nonstop. The trip was special then, but even more so now. I will treasure those memories forever.

My best friend Bridget lives in San Francisco, in the Marina District. She and I have been extremely close since the third grade, but she moved to California when we were the same age as Lauren and Brooke. Bridget spent a lot of time with us when we were there, which made the trip that much more special. When Bridget and I watched Brooke and Lauren, it felt like we were watching ourselves and the crazy things we did together when we were twelve.

Bridget had been there for me during my toughest childhood years. Not long after she moved to California, her mom passed away from breast cancer. Back then we didn't have Facebook, email, or cell phones, but we managed to stay in touch through cards and letters. Bridget and I didn't get to see each other again until we were adults, but to this day, we consider each other the very best of friends.

Over the years, I have visited San Francisco many times for both business and pleasure. I love going there because I get to see Bridget, but also I like how the city opens my eyes to the world around me. When I am there, I ride the bus and take the time to notice the lives that other people live. I stop to appreciate how truly blessed I am. On one occasion a few years ago, I rode the bus around the entire city on a Saturday night, just to take in what I saw. Bridget's house in the Marina is the very last stop, as she is only a block and a half from the Golden

Gate Bridge. She was out of town then, and I was staying there by myself, enjoying a relaxing weekend. I was upset over something that I now consider trivial in the grand scheme of my life. I decided I needed a reality check so I would stop feeling sorry for myself. The bus ride worked, believe me.

As a parent I wanted to share that lesson. I believe most children would benefit from witnessing firsthand that other people are so hungry that they thank you, with genuine gratitude, for your leftovers as you leave a restaurant. What we waste half the time, a homeless person could live from. When I explained this to Brooke on our first trip there, she was so touched. I think sharing our food really became the highlight of our trips to San Francisco.

On our trip with Lauren, we had given food to one particular man every day. Both girls couldn't believe how much their kindness meant to him. They felt good knowing they were helping him. On the last day we went to take him food before we left, but couldn't find him. We needed to get back to the hotel because we had a ride scheduled to the airport, so I told them we could give our food to some other people in need; unfortunately, there were plenty. So we did and as we headed back to the hotel, they saw the man and felt awful. They asked if we could give him money, which I typically don't like to do—I prefer food, but I gave in when I saw how much they cared. They ran over to him and gave him the money. He looked as happy as if he had won the lottery. His reaction clearly moved them and their good deed left them both smiling.

Helping this man touched Brooke so much that when I returned to San Francisco for Bridget's wedding after Brooke passed, I looked for the man. I wanted to give him more, as I know Brooke would have wanted, but he wasn't there.

During our girls' trip, Brooke and Lauren wanted to do a Segway tour, but we were not able to. For safety reasons, only people who weigh 100 pounds or more can do the tour. Brooke weighed only 90 pounds. She was upset, but joked that she would eat tons of food to gain ten pounds. I had never been on a Segway and did not know why the policy was in place, so I asked for my own edification. They told me that a rider needed to weigh a certain amount in order to be able to stop the Segway and control it safely on turns. This is a perfect example of the difference between traveling in the United States and traveling abroad. In the United States, this tour agency would not compromise our safety for their profit. Outside of this country, I have learned the hard way that profit seems to matter far more than safety.

At the end of June, Brooke went to church camp with her best friends. Brooke had many friends, but she had three best friends. They called themselves the Fantastic Four—the greatest group of girls you could imagine. Brooke, Gina, Kristen, and Lauren had all been best friends since they were five and six years old. The girls went to summer camp with several of their other close friends; they were all so excited about it. Brooke found church camp to be such an inspiration. This was her second year attending; she loved being there and worshipping God.

The girls had to leave camp early that year to try out for the Tony Glavin Select Team. They had all played soccer together for years and hoped to move to this team. Two of Brooke's other good friends, Maddi and Morgan, already played for the Glavin Team. If the Fantastic Four (Brooke, Gina, Lauren, and Kristen) made it, it would be a dream team for Brooke with her closest friends all together on one team.

Brooke was excited about tryouts, but a little nervous, too. The team the girls had played for previously was breaking up. At least half the players would be trying out for the Glavin Select Team, so there would be a fair amount of competition. Brooke worked hard to prepare for the tryout. It was a scorching hot weekend with temperatures well over a hundred degrees, but she practiced in the yard constantly. She even focused on behavioral attributes that she believed were important for her to demonstrate, like commitment, dedication, drive and leadership.

After Brooke passed away, I found a document with a list of to-dos she had made for the tryout—it wasn't something you would expect a twelve-year-old to write.

- bring ball that is the correct size
- eat a nutritious snack 2 hours before tryout
- drink a lot of water before tryout starts
- bring LOTS of water
- be early to the tryout – it shows commitment.
- no jewelry
- hair up in pony tail
- have stuff on before tryout begins
- be warmed up
- introduce yourself to the coach
- never interrupt
- call them coach...
- use sir when answering a direct question from the coach
- dont mess around w/ soccer ball when the coach is speaking. hold the ball or put it between your feet.
- make eye contact with the coach
- dont let other players distract you
- you are there for soccer, so don't goof off
- don't be afraid to go first on drills if you know what you are doing
- don't be first all the time......try to do it faster and better than the kids in front of you
- be the first one back from the water break
- do not play around during water breaks
- tuck your shirt in
- wear your shorts with the waistband at the waist
- keep cord of shorts tucked in
- don't complain or whine
- try not to say that it is really hot
- don't tattle on other players
- never say I can't do it
- after the tryout, pay attention to what happens next
- tell the coach bye and thank you
- gather up everything you brought to the field
- don't ask the coach if you made the team
- the best way to handle the stress is to get outside and continue to work on dribbling, juggling, and shooting skills
- don't be upset if you are not put on the team
- try out for a different team later on

Brooke knew she could do it and gave it her all. She did a fantastic job and had no problem making the team.

"*I wished to live deliberately,*
to front only the essential facts of life,
and see if I could not learn what it had to teach,
and not, when I came to die,
discover that I had not lived."
~ Henry David Thoreau

"Shattered dreams are never random.
They are always a piece in a larger puzzle.
A chapter in a larger story.

The Holy Spirit uses the pain of shattered dreams
to help us discover our desire for God,
to help us begin dreaming the Highest Dream.

They are ordained opportunities for the spirit to awaken,
then to satisfy our Highest Dream."

~ Dr. Larry Crabb
  Christian Psychologist and Author

~ Chapter Ten ~

"Let me prepare you for the day that stretches out before you.
I know exactly what this day will contain,
whereas you have only vague ideas about it.
You would like to see a map,
showing all the twists and turns of your journey.
You'd feel more prepared if you could somehow
visualize what is on the road ahead.
However, there is a better way to be prepared
for whatever you will encounter today:
Spend quality time with Me."

~ Exodus 33:14
from the book "Jesus is Calling" by Sarah Young

As we left the restaurant after lunch, we were surprised when the guide took a different route. Since the tour was over, we thought we would head back to our cars. For whatever reason, the guide led us in a completely different direction, on a paved road in Flamingo. Brooke was in front of me and George had Paige with him, bringing up the rear. The guide who was supposed to be at the end of the line was gone. He had left our group, something he did often throughout the tour. As we neared the bottom of a steep hill, Brooke stopped. Initially, I thought something was wrong with her ATV, but she said it was fine, and then accelerated ahead of me. We all climbed the steep road.

We could not see the guide in front, so we rushed to catch up. Trailing farther and farther behind him, we sped along the road with no warning signs to alert us of danger, or guardrails to protect us from what lurked below. We had no idea that the narrow road ran less than a few feet from the edge of a sheer cliff. Unaware, we drove on beside the 260-foot drop.

When I came to an extremely sharp turn in the road—at least a ninety-degree turn—Emma was off her ATV, standing in the road, screaming hysterically at the top of her lungs, a piercing shrill scream that echoed through my ears. It took a minute to register. Brooke had been just far enough ahead of me that I did not see her go around the bend.

Confused, I tried to comprehend what had happened as Emma sobbed that Brooke had missed the turn and had driven off the cliff. I thought to myself, there is no way this could be happening, this isn't real. I didn't know what to do. I began to scream at the top of my lungs, "HELP! HELP! AYUDA ME! HELP!" George pulled up to find me screaming and in complete panic. He immediately secured his ATV and took off to find a way down the cliff.

I don't know how to explain it, but in that tragic instant, I felt in my heart that Brooke was gone. Something inside me instantly felt different.

We all screamed for help as loudly as we could. I was terrified to look over the edge of the cliff for fear of what I was going to see, but when I peered over, I could only see the ocean sparkling far below.

I was out of control; I was losing it. People were there; I have no idea where they came from, but they heard our screams and came to help. Most did not speak English, but they tried to calm me. Paige was crying; she was so scared watching this play out. I remember a woman trying to hand her to me, but I couldn't stop my frenzied breakdown.

Instinct took over, and without even thinking, I called Sean. While neither of us can remember much of the conversation, I know he was confused. He had just talked to Brooke, not even a half hour ago, and now I was telling him she was gone. I do remember Sean kept asking, "How do you know for sure? Maybe she is just injured." But I knew and I told him, "I can feel it, Sean. George is trying to get to her, but there is no way she survived. I don't think there is anything he can do." Sean sobbed—his heart was breaking—he wanted to do something but he felt helpless, thousands of miles away. With the phone still to my ear, I fell to the ground and rolled in the middle of the road in pain, a part of me dying.

When I was on the phone with Sean, desperate, I looked at Kelly and irrationally begged her, "Please do something, please." Not knowing what else to do other than to try to save Brooke, Kelly started climbing down the cliff near the spot Brooke had gone off. She stopped when she felt nothing under her feet. Some locals quickly ran to help her and pulled her to safety. The attempt left her badly cut up and bleeding. The same men got a rope and tried to figure out a way to get down to Brooke.

At some point, Blake and the rest of our group came back. Later, Blake told me he noticed we were not behind him, so he stopped and ended up having to scream for the guide. He said the guide didn't speak English, so Blake finally had to yell at him in Spanish to get him to stop.

As I saw the tour guide come closer, I became crazed. I was so angry. I wanted to throttle him. I just kept yelling at him, "WHY? WHY? WHY would you lead us up this dangerous road?!!" The young guide was so upset he was vomiting. In the police report it came out that he was underage and inexperienced with ATVs and should not have been leading a tour. He was just a kid on a joy ride, hired by the tour operator, and we followed him.

Blake kept saying that maybe she just broke some bones. Trying to be optimistic, he said maybe she was fine. I told him no; we held each other and cried as I told him she was gone, I was sure.

Suddenly, I saw George making his way back up to us. He looked completely deflated; it was obvious that she was gone. His head hung down. It took everything he had to look me in the eye, and that said it all, he didn't have to say the words. I lost it entirely and went into complete shock. I have no idea how the phone call ended, but at some point I disconnected Sean.

I told George he had to take me to her. I am not sure how we made it, but somehow we got down the cliff. I remember I just started sliding at one point until George grabbed me and told me we could not go that way. When we finally made it down near Brooke, the police were there. (I later learned that they had come by boat. A family from Florida, walking up the road, had seen Brooke drive off the cliff and had run to a police station only 200 feet up the road to get help.) The area was marked off and the police stood guard, protecting the site.

All I wanted to do was hold my baby one last time.

I screamed at them, begging to go to her. They ignored me and did not say a thing, but made it very clear they would not permit me near her. I was capsized. *How could they keep me away from my child? Why weren't they trying to help her? Why was there no medical support?* George begged them, pleading for them to try to help her. We asked if they could try to shock her, or do something to try to bring her back. They continued to ignore us.

Although I was an emotional wreck, I was coherent enough to know this was wrong—extremely wrong. Knowing this, and powered by strength from the love of my daughter, I begged George to go back up to the top and get help. I told him to get the camcorder and video the road. Somehow I knew we needed to document that the police would not help us. He was unsure of my request and reluctant to leave my side. He kept asking me if I was sure I wanted him to do this, and I said yes, too much time had gone by. I kept thinking, *What if my baby is alive and they are keeping me from her?*

When George left to go back up the cliff, I again cried out for help, and again, my sobs were ignored. I felt helpless and desperate. Somehow I had managed to hold onto my cell phone. I thought maybe I could get a helicopter to come rescue her. There had to be someone willing to help us. I called 911 for help, and I remember pleading for a helicopter, but I am not certain if I actually ever spoke with someone or what their response was. It wouldn't have mattered either way; I later learned Costa Rica does not have emergency medical services like helicopters; very little can be done to save someone in an urgent situation there.

George did as I asked and made it up the cliff a third time. His muscles barely worked; he had to stop to get water and help from some construction workers. When he got to the top, he took a video of the road and the spot Brooke drove off. Somehow I knew I would not return there.

George went to Blake and told him what was happening. He discovered that there were two ambulances at the top. He was confused because they were not trying to get to Brooke and he actually asked if she was in one. Doing everything he could, he led the EMS workers down to us.

In the meantime, Kelly begged the police to help her get the kids out of there and safely back to the resort. That portion of the road was too dangerous to even have the kids standing there, in the road or anywhere near the cliff. There was only the narrow road with hardly any room before the sheer drop-off.

Kelly and Fred moved the kids up the road to a concrete wall on the other side, away from the cliff. Angry that the police would not help her,

Kelly continued to holler at them. She did not want the kids to have to witness any more of this nightmare; they needed to know they were safe.

After George and the medics made it down to the beach, he begged them to help; to do something for Brooke. Very matter of factly, the medic told us Brooke was gone and there was nothing he could do. He was not nice or sympathetic about it. Coldly he said, "She died probably more than a half hour ago. You can tell by the color of her skin." I will forever hear that sentence over and over again in my head.

George and I fell to the ground, crying over the loss of Brooke. We could not believe this nightmare was happening to us. We couldn't understand why it took so long to get help and why there was no sense of urgency through any of this.

With my voice hoarse from all the screaming, I cried, "I want to hold my baby. I NEED to hold my baby!"

George cried, "She can hold her can't she?" They continued to ignore us, said nothing and refused to let us near Brooke. The pain was unbearable. I rolled in the rocks and sand in agony, begging, "Just hose me off and knock me out." I was filthy, my entire body covered in dirt and sand. *I wanted to cleanse away the filth that covered my body and escape this nightmare that was engulfing my life.* Accustomed to how things are done in the United States, I mistakenly thought they might care how I felt and about my wellbeing during this tragedy. I had hoped they would be able to give me medication to calm or sedate me. I could not have been more wrong.

Unbeknownst to us, through this most painful moment of our lives, the camcorder stayed on, recording our surroundings aimlessly, but capturing every word clearly as they treated us so coldly, ignoring my cries as I begged for them to let me hold my baby.

> *"No eye has seen, no ear has heard,*
> *and no mind has imagined*
> *what God has prepared for those who love him."*
> *~ 1 Corinthians 2:9*

Use your mobile tag reader
for a video of the
aftermath of the accident.

The way that we see it

Holding cold, wet hands

A tree decides to shrink

The sun decides to drop

Dimming lights flicker on

How to continue at a dead end?

The irony of the flower

Putting curtains over tinted glass

And still ending up sunburnt

But when it becomes our turn

To reach for the sun

We're lost beneath the stars.

They say anything is possible

A crevice beneath our feet

The sound of rainfall becomes music

The echoes of dreams become scars

The roof now under our heads

When dreams become reality

And reality becomes a dream.

~ Blake Scalise

~ *Chapter Eleven* ~

"Patience permits us to cling to our faith in the Lord
when we are tossed about by suffering as if by surf.
When the undertow grasps us we realize that we are actually
being helped even as we cry for help."
~ Neal A. Maxwell

Fred and Kelly finally found a ride for the kids, so Fred left with them all and they headed back to the resort. The road was so steep that the car couldn't make it up the hill with all of them inside. Everyone had to get out. The kids were terrified; it just kept getting worse.

A light rain began to fall. I knew instantly that this perfect light rain had a meaning. It was God's baptism of Brooke. They would not let us go to Brooke.

With the rain, we would never be able to make it up the cliff. A boat came; they told us they would take us in it and they encouraged us to leave. I couldn't go. It was harder than anything I have ever had to do in my life. There was no way. The pain of leaving my baby behind was unimaginable. At that moment I hurt so much that all I wanted was to be with her. I threw myself into the ocean, hoping to float away and find Brooke. With help from the coast guard, George pulled me into the boat. The boat took us away. I sobbed. I knew I was leaving behind not only my precious Brooke, but my life as I knew it. I was certain I would never again be the same woman.

Kelly sat at the top of the hill by herself after Fred left with the kids. She wouldn't leave; she wanted to be there for me. A woman, part of the family that had witnessed the accident, came to her. She said she thought Kelly should get medical attention; Kelly explained that she was waiting for us to come back up. The American woman told Kelly that she thought we were gone and then found her a ride back to the resort. Employees there immediately drove her to get medical treatment for the wounds on her arms and legs.

The kids had gone back to the condo with Fred. Emma was screaming hysterically, overwhelmed by the shock of seeing Brooke drive off the cliff. Fred struggled to care for her, as well as his other two children and Blake, Paige and Little George. He tried to settle the younger ones by getting them to watch TV while he worked to calm Emma. They did not even have access to a phone to call anyone, so Blake got on the computer, reaching out for prayer from friends and starting the difficult task of notifying others of Brooke's death.

We walked into the condo, the atmosphere more somber than imaginable—a house full of dazed people. I immediately went into the room where Brooke had been staying and started to go through her things. I smelled her clothes and held them tight to me as I sobbed. All I could think at that point was, "God, help me. How am I going to do this?" I had to be strong for my other kids—they needed me—but I hurt so much I wanted to die.

We hadn't been there long, so we were surprised when the police came back to get us. They told us they were going to take us to another station where they would be bringing Brooke. Thankfully George was there for me and helped me function. We left with them.

At the station, there were no chairs or anything like that; it was pretty much just a small shack. Too weak to stand, I sat on the ground. They asked us a bunch of questions for the police report. We waited. Over an hour went by and we sat there, dazed. After what seemed an eternity, they finally told us that we were not going to get to see Brooke. They explained that she was being taken to the only morgue in the country, five hours away. They told us we needed to go to the morgue to see her, but her body would not be there until the next day.

Once again, they took us back to the resort. By then Kelly had gotten back. We hugged and we cried. For the first time, we went through details of all that had happened. I didn't know where to start or even what to do. I went out to the patio and called my mom and my sister. Both of them already knew from my call to Sean. I called Briana from work and my boss, Scott. George and I took Blake, Paige and Little George into our room to have some private family time. We did our best to answer their questions. Together, we all cried. Kelly gave me a sleeping pill. She and George reassured me they would handle everything and encouraged me to go to bed.

George worked with the embassy and Kelly worked with lawyers to see what we needed to do to claim Brooke's body and bring her back to the states. Fred, Kelly, and Emma all started packing our things. As hard as it was, Emma packed Brooke's belongings. In the meantime, as if it were a bad joke, the airline called to tell me they had found my bags and were sending them to the resort.

They woke me a few hours later when some detectives arrived to interview me. The detectives spoke with each of us separately, and then reassured us they would be looking into the actions on the part of the tour operator.

We were informed that we needed to wire four thousand dollars to claim Brooke's body. We would have to do it by an international wire, and it would take seven days for the money to be available. They would not release her body without the money. We were told that, in order to handle this, we needed to go to the embassy and to the morgue in San Jose, which was five hours away. Our options were to drive the five hours (we knew we were not in a mental condition to do that) or to charter a small plane. As much as we did not want to put them through any more, we had no choice but to take the children with us, as they would not be permitted to leave the country with Kelly and Fred. I called my mom and Scott to update them. My mom and I both worried that if I left Costa Rica to return to the states, Brooke's remains wouldn't make it home. We decided I shouldn't leave the country without her, so I prepared George and the kids. Although I didn't know where we would be staying, we probably wouldn't get to leave for seven days; we would wait for the wire to clear and Brooke to be released. I called Scott and told him the situation; he let me know that he was working with our company's Human Resources Department to see what could be done.

In the meantime, in the states, Sean suffered such a serious breakdown that he was taken by ambulance to a hospital and admitted. His family was not even permitted to be with him. He has no recollection of two days of his life. Overwhelmed with grief, he suffered pain beyond words at the loss of our child. Being two thousand miles away and helpless was more than he could handle.

The resort did everything they could to help us. They worried about how safe we would be in San Jose, since none of us speak Spanish fluently, and the big city is very different from the resort area we were in. The resort decided to send a woman with us to act as our translator and help us find our way through the city. So the next morning, George and I left with Blake, Paige, Little George, and our translator, taking a small plane to San Jose.

The flight took less than an hour but scared all of us, especially the small children. They weighed our luggage and each of us before we got on the single engine prop plane. We flew through the mountains, encountering a lot of turbulence on the way, convincing us we would be joining Brooke sooner than expected. We honestly feared the plane would wreck. When we landed safely in San Jose, we were relieved, but completely lost as to what to do or where to start.

We planned to head to the morgue first and debated whether to rent a car or take a taxi. The woman from the resort did not think it would be safe to drive a car. It seemed very unsafe there and we were all scared, including our translator. I dreaded what we were about to do and how awful it would be for the children. I tried to prepare myself mentally for the horrid experience in front of me. Seeing my daughter and claiming her would be shocking enough, but doing it in a scary city at the only morgue in the entire country—a country that does not embalm bodies—had me sick to my stomach. I wasn't sure how I would survive this.

We were about to leave in a taxi when my phone rang. My boss called to tell me that he and Barbara in our Human Resources Department were handling everything. He pleaded with me to trust him, to go back into the airport and take the first available flight home to our family. They reassured me that no matter what it took they would make certain Brooke was looked after and get her home to us as soon as possible. He explained that the insurance companies have intermediary companies they deal with and the seven-day wait for the wire is not an issue when insurance is involved. I thanked God for sparing us that experience. We quickly headed back into the airport to start our journey home.

We waited in line at the airport at the American counter and then explained what had happened. They took us to a private office and helped us with the arrangements. There were no flights left on American that would get us home that day. Fortunately, the manager at American was able to rebook us on a Delta flight that was scheduled to leave in only an hour. I can't describe my relief over avoiding the additional horror we had been about to encounter with the young children. Without the help of FIS, my employer, we would have been stranded with three children in a large, dangerous foreign city for seven more days, making our nightmare unimaginably worse.

While we were fortunate to be moved to the Delta flight, none of our seats were next to each other, since the flight was full. We spoke to the woman at the gate, but there wasn't much she could do. She told us to talk to the flight attendant when we got on board. It was so hard to hear the words coming out of my mouth as I explained the heinous story. There was no way this was my life. I openly sobbed.

In the end, we at least got some seats together. Little George and Paige sat with me on the first flight, while Blake and George sat together. We landed wherever our layover was. I only remember going through immigration and being questioned about why we left with six in our party and were returning with five. I lost it, and George explained. We went through the same exercise to get seats together on the next flight. On both flights, I cried nonstop, still unable to believe this nightmare was real. Everyone around us knew something awful had happened; several people told us they were sorry and offered their condolences, even though they weren't quite sure for what.

I barely remember our drive home from the airport. We pulled into our driveway at almost midnight, and all of my family was waiting for us—my parents, my sister, my grandma, George's mom, my aunts, uncles, cousins, and friends. Even our family from out of town had come to be there for us when we got home. Together we cried, and they offered us all the love and support they could. My parents spent the night. Blake and his grandpa slept on the couch and Paige slept with her grandma in Brooke's room.

In the days that followed, many, many people were there for us. They all wanted to help, but weren't quite sure what to do. My grandma and my Aunt Cheryl unpacked our suitcases, did the laundry, and put everything away where they imagined it should go (months later I was still finding things in strange places). People dropped off food left and right; everyone kept telling me I needed to eat. The phone rang constantly. Everyone felt so helpless and didn't know what to do.

Sean came to see the kids. Broken, visibly crushed and in a state beyond shock, he had suffered a complete nervous breakdown, and had to have at least two male adults with him around the clock. You could see the wear on both his brother and his dad. He had expected to have the most joyous month of his life, getting married on July 25 and honeymooning in Mexico the next week. Sadly, it ended up being the most horrid month ever with the loss of his daughter less than two weeks before.

We had to go meet with the funeral home and start making arrangements for the service. I dreaded even setting foot in the door. My stomach churned and I feared I would get sick as I tackled one of the hardest things I have ever had to do in my life. My parents and George were there to support me; Sean's family was there for him.

Pastor Curt from church joined us as well, helping give us the needed strength and prayer. I had my ideas of how I wanted to honor Brooke, and Sean had his. I knew we had to have a special service for Brooke. She was so extraordinary and rare. We had to recognize her uniqueness. We also needed to be sensitive to the many kids who would be attending. I wanted to have the service at home and then a church service the following day, making it a celebration of her life as opposed to a morbid funeral. Sean and I grieved very differently; he wanted a more traditional funeral with the casket and an opportunity for people to pay their last respects. I was adamant that I didn't want anyone to see her body. Initially, I contemplated having her cremated in Costa Rica, but I knew that would not be fair to Sean—and I feared that, after what we had witnessed firsthand, it was possible that it would not even be Brooke's remains they sent home.

We couldn't agree on anything. Both devastated, we took our emotions and anger out on each other. We ended up screaming at one another across the conference table at the funeral home. Finally everyone intervened. Pastor Curt advised us to each think about a few things over the next day. He explained to us that it was natural for us to grieve differently, and that feelings are not right or wrong. It was tough to make such difficult decisions and we were all deeply emotional. The whole planning process was awful.

It took awhile, but with guidance from Pastor Curt, we eventually compromised. We decided to incorporate the few things that were most important to each of us and to give in on those things that were not as meaningful. Really, the problem was that we did not want any of it—no parent would. We just wanted to wake up and have our baby back.

More than anything, I wished that we could turn back time, that we had never gone to Costa Rica. I played out scenarios in my mind. What could we have been done differently? "What ifs" consumed all of my thoughts. I wished we had known more then about the dangers associated with ATVs. I wished we had not ridden ATVs at all, but unfortunately we did.

Brooke loved to live life to its fullest, and on every vacation, she looked forward to the activities. She had driven ATVs at a friend's farm, and had even ridden them just a few weeks before, at church camp. Our expectation of the tour was far different than how it actually ended up being. The tour was supposed to be on beaches and dirt roads, led by guides who clearly understood that our group included several young children. The owner of the company was highly recommended. We paid sixteen hundred dollars for what we thought would be reputable, safe tours. We were not provided a route map, which I later learned is a regulation required by the Costa Rican Governent. However, it is not enforced and the tour operators know this. The adventure tour company ower did not indicate that we would be in dangerous environments, nor did he provide any waivers for us to sign regarding risk. We definitely never imagined that we would be led at a high speed up a narrow road with a 90-degree turn with less than a few feet of room for error—a turn that, if missed, led off a cliff 260-feet high. Never would we have ever fathomed that a tour like this would have led to Brooke's tragic death.

> "They cry unto the Lord in their trouble,
> and he brings them out of their distresses.
> He makes the storm calm, so that the waves are still."
> ~ Psalm 107:28-29

~ Chapter Twelve ~

"The true meaning of life is to plant trees
under whose shade you do not expect to sit..."
~ Nelson Henderson

*I*n the days that followed, my family and friends helped me pore through pictures and memorabilia to display at the house for our celebration of Brooke's life. I had boxes and boxes of the artwork and school projects I had saved over the years, all the way back to her very first papers. My friends and family spent days working to creatively display photos and the many special pieces Brooke had created throughout her life.

The support was amazing; many people I love pulled together to help prepare for the day we would honor Brooke. George took charge and handled most of the arrangements. He was my rock—there for me every time I needed him and every night when I'd finally crash hard. Being with Blake and Paige reminded me I still had so much to be thankful for. I felt secure when I was with them, knowing they gave me hope and a will to live. I also knew Brooke's spirit lived on in them, too. Several of my closest friends, from all over the country, came to be here with me. Their overwhelming love touched my heart, and helped me gain strength to face the hardest days a mother ever has to endure.

Kelly and Emma had come from Columbia to help, and to return Brooke's luggage, which they had brought home from Costa Rica. Right away, they put the suitcase in Brooke's room. Drawn by the need to feel close to her again, I snuck into Brooke's room by myself, opened the suitcase and went through her things. I held them to me as I sobbed, taking in the smell of her as I never had before. As I picked up each piece, I remembered when she wore it. I held the jacket that she and I had gone looking for that last night together. There was so much to do to make this celebration reflect what Brooke stood for, and fortunately, there were even more people willing to help in any way that they could. My creative cousin Kristy took the lead on directing everyone's efforts on what was to be displayed; my close friend and neighbor Debbie took over planning for the refreshments and food, all of which she was able to get donated. Brooke's closest cousins and friends were here to help through it all, and being with them always made me feel better. I could feel her energy through them and all they shared.

I focused on planning the church service and who would speak to pay tribute to Brooke's life. The pastor asked me to pull together Bible verses and songs for the service. The afternoon that I was work-ing on this, Brooke's close friend Courtney, who lived next door and had always been like an older sister to Brooke, called me to come up to Brooke's room. She was holding Brooke's pink Bible open to where

Brooke had circled and noted her favorite Bible verse. In addition, a piece of paper lay on the nightstand by the bed with every word of

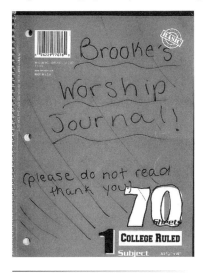

the song *I Can't Wait to See You Again* written out. It seemed like Brooke was telling us exactly what she wanted.

We continued to go through Brooke's things, amazed by what we found. Her worship journal sat in her room, unopened. I had never opened it because she had written "please do not read" on the outside. Inside the journal, she thanked God for always loving her. She wrote, "I will help spread the word about you to people because I know that is what you want me to do." Over and over she thanked God for coming into her life, and mentioned wanting to go to church more. She wrote of her love for her family, saying that we all meant the world to her, but, right there in front of us, was what we needed to see. In her own words, Brooke told us that "most importantly, You God are in my life."

New discoveries filled the next few days. People kept shouting, "Oh my gosh! You have to see this; you won't believe it!" We were all touched by what we found. It seemed as if she had left messages for all of us. The most recent was a letter she had written to God in a journal during

Dear God,
Wow! I had so much fun at Camp today. I'm really starting to understand the different ways to worship you. But, if you could please help be better understand your story that would be great. My goal is to read the whole bible by the time I'm 13. I also really want to go to church more and also get baptised. Soon. Please let every one in my family know that I really miss them but am having a great time. They all mean the world to me and I know it may not always show but I do. Most importantly you, God, are in my life. Thanks for always being there. I LOVE you sooooo much and I know you love me too. Thanks for letting have a chance of experiencing life with you. Please help everyone in the world be healthy & happy!

Amen

the last week of June, just a few weeks before her death. She wrote, "God, thank you for everything, I know you are here for me every second of the day. You still love me even though I have sinned. I'm sorry I don't go to church

> God,
> Thank you for everything. I know you are here for me every second of the day. You still love me even though I have sinned. I'm sorry I don't go to church a lot. Please I don't go to church a lot realize that we were made for you. Also, do the same with my aunt. My cousin Tommy just got married to a great girl named Kelly. Please let them have a happy marraige.
> I ♡you!   Amen
>
> *journal*   6/2009

a lot. Please let my mom realize that we were made for you. Also, do the same with my aunt." I couldn't believe what I was reading; it felt as if she was trying to comfort me and help me understand that she was always God's child.

Along with this we found a picture of *The Return of the Prodigal Son* by Rembrandt, on which Brooke had written "God" with an arrow to the man depicting God and then "me" with an arrow to

the son kneeling in front of God. We were shocked Brooke would think this way and would have viewed herself as the child kneeling in front of God. At first I thought maybe it was something they were told to do at church camp in a lesson, so I asked Lauren if she had any idea why Brooke would have done this. She was as dumbfounded as I was.

Much later, a friend looking at the picture discovered something I had missed. Brooke had also drawn and circled a distinctive mark on the back of the head of the son (the person she felt depicted her), a mark in the exact spot and in accurate proportion to what I would later learn was the most severe of Brooke's injuries, and ultimately, the cause of death. Stunned, I moved in a fog for days after finding this, overwhelmed by the magnitude of what it proved.

This all surprised me. Brooke and I were extremely close. She had always confided in me about everything. Our love was so strong. I have many letters that she wrote to me in which she tells me that I am her best friend and we shared a bond like no other. But, as close as we were, I will admit that I was shocked to find out I was not what mattered most in her life. As we pored through what were now the greatest gifts of my life, I found a sheet that she had filled out at school, titled "Explore Your Future." Under "Who do you look up to?" Brooke listed God, Jesus, and my parents. Under "What is important to you?" she had written: "God, my family, and friends are all important to me." As close as we were, and though she did not go to church often, she put God before me. Not many 12 year olds would write this on a school worksheet in a public school. Seeing this and the other documents made me realize how her love for God was greater than even her love for me and that she viewed herself as God's child first. As devastated as I was, it gave me peace knowing Brooke was with who she loved most.

On the worksheet, Brooke also listed her favorite places or environment as the ocean and the mountains. Wow, I was stunned. This described the exact location of the accident, a mountain overlooking a beach so secluded that few could even reach it. I took comfort in thinking that the final resting spot for Brooke's physical body, the place where her soul was lifted into God's arms as she was called home, matched her description of her favorite place.

I could go on and on with details of what we discovered; the pieces of the puzzle of Brooke's life falling in place together, making her real purpose here on earth obvious. I have no doubt that her story is meant to be shared; to be told over and over to inspire and help others.

In the midst of all the planning for the services, George came up with a wonderful idea to help us and countless others. Knowing Brooke's vibrance, he suggested we start a foundation in her honor. He and my best friend Tammy quickly filed the preliminary paperwork needed to get the Brooke Scalise Foundation started. My family and I agreed that we felt this was an excellent way for us to keep Brooke's spirit alive and follow through on the things that were most important to her. George had grown close with Brooke, and obviously had been positively influenced by her. His recommendation could not have been more appropriate as the ideal means for us to honor Brooke and what she stood for. I can never thank him enough for starting the foundation. Our neighbor Jim helped George get the website up and running; together they started a beautiful thing in her honor.

Originally, we listed the purposes of the foundation as: to raise money for college scholarships for children in need, fund youth church programs, provide food to homeless shelters, and make donations to youth sports teams. After further consideration, we decided that God really mattered most to Brooke. Tying together the things that best represented Brooke, we settled on a new purpose. The foundation strives to use her story to inspire and increase the faith in other children her age by offering church camp scholarships to those in need, along with creating a correlating faith-based camp that teaches the many attributes that Brooke demonstrated in her daily life. I know Brooke is happy with this decision. Attending church camp the last two summers of her life had a significant impact on Brooke by helping her grow even closer to God.

"Simply the thing that I am shall make me live."
~ William Shakespeare

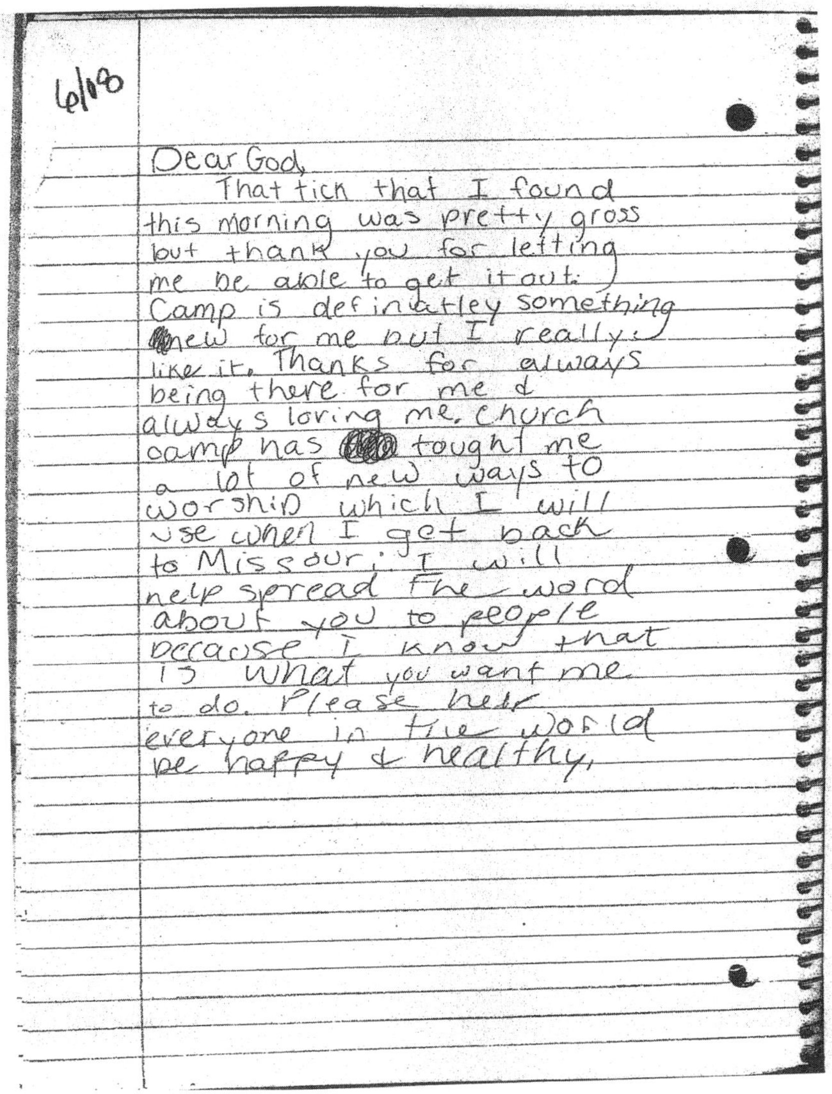

6/1/08

Dear God,
      That tick that I found
this morning was pretty gross
but thank you for letting
me be able to get it out.
Camp is definatley something
new for me but I really
like it. Thanks for always
being there for me &
always loving me, church
camp has ~~also~~ tought me
a lot of new ways to
worship which I will
use when I get back
to Missour. I will
help spread the word
about you to people
because I know that
is what you want me
to do. Please help
everyone in the world
be happy & healthy,

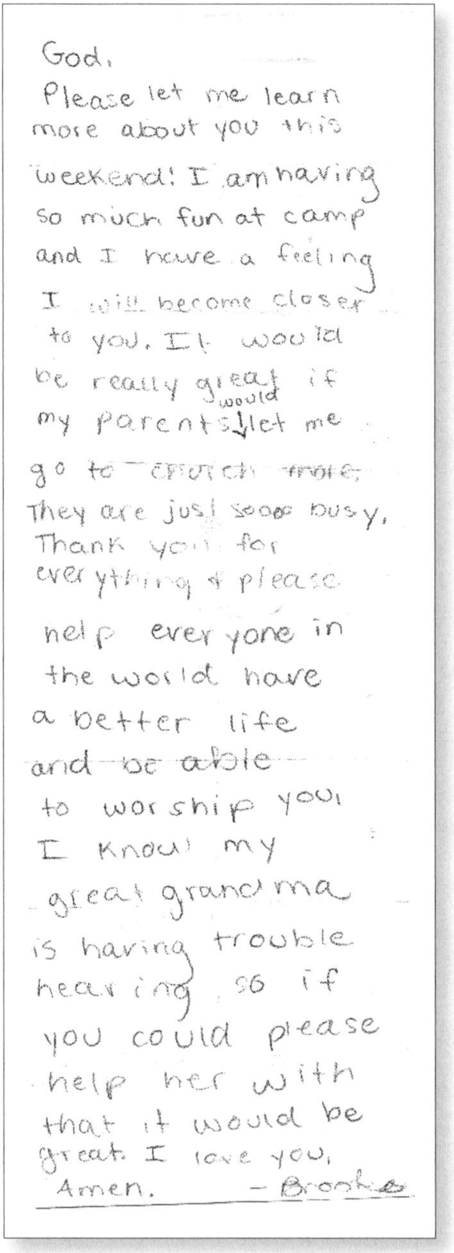

God,
Please let me learn
more about you this
weekend! I am having
so much fun at camp
and I have a feeling
I will become closer
to you. It would
be really great if
my parents would let me
go to church more.
They are just sooo busy,
Thank you for
everything & please

help everyone in
the world have
a better life
and be able
to worship you.
I know my
great grandma
is having trouble
hearing, so if
you could please
help her with
that it would be
great. I love you,
Amen.   — Brooke

~ Chapter Thirteen ~

"Yet what we suffer now is nothing
compared to the glory He will give us later."
~ Romans 8:18

Brooke's remains were scheduled to arrive here on July 16, and arrangements were made for the funeral home to get them from the airport. Sean wanted to be there and ride with her body. The thought of the hearse and casket made me sick; I knew I couldn't face it. Based on my beliefs, I didn't think it held any significance to Brooke. Sean called me to ask if I was sure I didn't want to go, saying that this was our little girl. I knew for sure. He asked Blake and he, too, said it wasn't something he could handle.

After her arrival, I got a call from my cousin Tommy. A friend of his, who worked at the airport, was there when the flight landed. He said that the employees at Lambert Airport knew Brooke was a child who died needlessly in Costa Rica. They were saddened by the story and deeply affected by the experience of witnessing the arrival of her remains. They prayed for our family and handled her coffin with dignity and respect. To me, this mattered.

Sean called me again, as he rode in the hearse on the way back to the funeral home. He was extremely emotional and talking so strangely, as if he were really with her. I couldn't take it; anxiety consumed me. I took a Xanax, which I was depending on more and more to survive.

Sean's doctor had explained to his family that it was important for Sean to see Brooke's body; he needed this experience in order to accept that this was real. Since he had not witnessed the accident, he struggled to comprehend that she had really died. For me, I didn't think it would matter at that point if I saw her, but I hadn't decided for sure. I had been there to witness the accident and it still didn't feel real to me—nor did I think it ever would.

The funeral home could not allow the viewing the first night Brooke arrived; they needed time to prepare her body, knowing she had been in a third world country, where procedures are not up to the standards here in the United States. They agreed to a private viewing for family the next day.

Kelly and George, both traditional Catholics, decided they wanted to see Brooke to pay their last respects and say their final goodbye. Emma and I rode with them to the funeral home, since I needed to provide a picture of Brooke and explain how she did her hair.

Sean and his family were still there when we arrived. Sean was in shock and heavily medicated, as he cried to hold Brooke's broken body like I had done in Costa Rica. Knowing how badly Sean needed strength from the Lord, Pastor Mark from church stayed there by Sean's side through what I am sure was one of the most hearbreaking experiences he has had to witness.

Blake, Emma and I stood in the parking lot distancing ourselves from the horror inside, as Kelly and George went in to say good-bye. I stared at the sky and talked to Brooke in Heaven to occupy my mind until I could flee. George and Kelly returned in less than five minutes. I asked if they thought I should go in and see Brooke, too. I knew I didn't want to, but I was also scared not to, for fear I might regret my decision after it was too late. They felt at peace because they had paid their last respects in the way they had been taught, but they did not recommend that I see her. They both said she looked nothing like herself, which I had known she wouldn't. Brooke was a child so full of life; her soul exuded from her.

I felt confident that Brooke was with me spiritually, and I sensed her presence often. I no longer felt any tie to her physical body, so in the end I opted not to view her remains. I didn't want to let that image burn into my mind, a decision I am thankful that I made.

"The destiny of man is in his own soul."
~ Herodotus

"This is a time in your life when you must learn to let go:
of loved ones, of possessions, of control.
In order to let go of something that is precious to you,
you need to rest in My Presence, where you are complete.
Take time to bask in the Light of My Love.
As you relax more and more,
your grasping hand gradually opens up,
releasing your prized possession into My care.
You can feel secure, even in the midst of cataclysmic changes,
through awareness of My continued Presence.
The One who never leaves you
is the same One who never changes:
I am the same yesterday, today, and forever.
As you release more and more things into My care,
remember that I never let go of your hand.
Herein lies your security, which no one
and no circumstance can take from you."

~ Psalm 89:15; Hebrews 13:8; Isaiah 41:13

from the book "Jesus is Calling" by Sarah Young

~ Chapter Fourteen ~

"You Lord, give perfect peace
to those who keep their purpose firm
and put their trust in you."
~ Isaiah 26:3

*D*ue to Brooke's influence, we did attend church on occasion. For at least the last five years, we had considered Calvary our church and had gone a handful of times each year. The year before the accident, Sean had started to go more often which allowed Brooke to become more involved in the youth group. She loved it. She had been asking to be baptized for several years, but she was younger than the recommended age at our church. Not completely understanding the depth of her relationship with God, I thought we should wait as suggested until she could understand what it meant and the commitment she was making. It was important to Brooke and I wish we had listened. She asked about it often; I was going to schedule it in the summer of 2008, but we were going to be out of town during one of the mandatory classes. We had planned to do it the next time the classes were offered.

I am convinced that, deep down, Brooke's soul knew her life here on Earth would be short and that's why she felt the need to be baptized sooner. Even though it wasn't done in a formal service, I feel confident that her strong commitment to God showed that she had certainly been baptized already. In addition, I was sure the light rain that fell as the EMS workers finally made their way to her was actually God confirming her baptism.

The symbolism of the service had meaning to Sean, and he wanted it done at our church. The pastors agreed that, in Brooke's case, there was no doubt that she had clearly committed her life to God, so we didn't need to worry that she had not done it in a ceremony. It was certain that she was God's child. However, to help Sean find peace, they performed the ceremony, even though it was not common practice. They made sure we understood it was being done for him, not for Brooke.

Knowing how much soccer and the Glavin Select Team meant to Brooke, Sean wanted her to wear her soccer uniform for the baptism. The team uniforms had been ordered a few weeks before, but they

had not arrived yet. Honestly, I didn't see how we could get it in time. But Tony Glavin and the team manager, Angie, worked together to make it happen. Not only did they get Brooke's uniform for the baptism, but, on the day of the open house, Tony personally presented both Sean and me with our own Glavin jerseys, bearing Brooke's name and number six, nicely framed. Again, everywhere we turned, others tried to do anything they could to help us.

On Monday, July 20, 2009, we held the open house. Throughout the entire house, we displayed photos, along with Brooke's journal letters, artwork and drawings. I had saved everything over the years, so what we displayed ranged from the first pages she colored as a toddler to the last letter she wrote to God, only a few weeks before her death. I wanted to make sure that all the guests, even those who didn't know Brooke, left feeling touched by her life.

Brooke's Uncle Jeff, Sean's brother, spent days poring through collections of photos and videos of Brooke. He created a video of Brooke's life that showed off her true spirit. We had it playing on TV monitors in several areas throughout the house. It included crazy videos that she and the Fantastic Four had made together, several of which I had not seen until after she passed. I finally learned what Brooke and Lauren really did when I wasn't home! The videos were so silly; they helped make people laugh and lightened the mood amidst all the sadness.

At one point, I went downstairs and saw at least fifty kids intently watching the video, both crying and laughing.

Hundreds and hundreds of people came through the house that day. We had people scattered everywhere, upstairs and downstairs, inside and out. I don't think we had less than a hundred people here at any time, and it was nonstop from two in the afternoon to nine at night. I could see the immediate impact Brooke had on others as they read her journals and viewed the memories from her life.

The long, emotional day completely overwhelmed me; at best, I was semicoherent from shock or Xanax or, more likely, the combination of the two. Sean seemed like a complete zombie, which I am sure his doctor intended, based on the dosage of Xanax they were giving him. He was physically present, but not mentally. Honestly, I would say both Sean and I were pretty out of it. My mom had accidentally taken an Ambien, thinking it was another pill she had intended to take. Mom remembers nothing from the day, which is probably best.

I did find some peace in knowing the day was exactly as it should have been for Brooke. I had declared it casual, not wanting it to feel at

all like a funeral. I wore a casual sundress, along with a corsage Teresa had helped Brooke make me for Mother's Day several years ago. The carnation was made of Kleenex and sat on top of a heart made from pink construction paper. On the heart she had written, "I love you, Mom." It was perfect. It brought back good memories.

George wore his swim trunks, navy with big blue flowers on them. Brooke had lived in her swimsuit, so he said he knew that if she had been there physically that is what she would have worn. He was right, so I didn't argue. He did put on a nice blue, button down shirt that matched well, and he felt good. Throughout the day there were kids in the pool, kids on the trampoline, and kids in the yard, kicking the soccer ball into the net, which is exactly how Brooke would have wanted it.

At the end of the long day, as night was settling in, the Fantastic Four and Courtney asked everyone to come outside. I knew them well enough to quickly grab my camera. As they stood hand in hand in their sundresses, together, they counted to three and then took off running, screaming, "We love you, Brooke!" as they jumped in the pool. That, too, was perfect. I took a picture of them jumping in, and then another of the Fantastic Four as they stood in the middle of the pool, arms around each other, the bottoms of their dresses floating freely in the water. We all laughed, thinking how appropriate this was for Brooke. It was a nice way to end the emotionally draining day.

Later, when I looked at my pictures, the picture I took of the Fantastic Four in the pool had a perfect orb in it, reassuring us all that Brooke was right there, beside her best friends. In the thousands of pictures I have taken over the years, this was the first orb I had ever discovered; the first of what soon would become many. Some theories claim orbs are caused by the energy of the spirit while some theories claim the orb is the spirit. Orbs are energy and energy is spirit.

On Tuesday, July 21, 2009, we had a private baptism for Brooke in the Warehouse—the Youth Area of Calvary Church where Brooke loved to be. I felt sick. I was not sure how I would ever make it through this. Sean's immediate family attended, along with my immediate family, George, Teresa, the Fantastic Four, Courtney, Kelly and Emma. I walked in and saw the coffin in front of me—a small, extremely narrow white coffin, very different from what we usually see here in the United States. I don't know if it was my anger and hatred for the country that it had come from or just the fact that my baby was inside it that made me think how much I disliked it. I tried to take my mind elsewhere, to happier memories, and not to see the cold wooden box that sat in front of me.

Pastor Curt did the baptism. Because he knew how much I was against a viewing for those who preferred not to see her, he explained to me ahead of time that he would open the casket quickly to sprinkle water on her, but that he would tell us before he did so. Anyone who wanted to look away would be able to. I really thought I was going to get sick. My sister left the room early in the ceremony, unable to stay through it. My dad couldn't enter the room at all, so he waited out in the hall. I kept my eyes closed for a lot of it; I feared I would catch a glimpse that would haunt me forever. At exactly the moment when Pastor Curt opened the casket, the air conditioning in the building kicked on, and we heard a loud boom in the ceiling. I felt better; it was the sign that I needed.

My mom and Brooke's friends unexpectedly caught a glimpse of Brooke's profile from a distance, but they were okay with it. From what everyone said, she looked much better than the day of the viewing at the funeral home. My mom described her as looking angelic. They all said she looked pretty as her physical body was viewed for the last time. I am still thankful that I held my eyes tightly closed.

After the baptism, Becky (Lauren's mom) and the Fantastic Four took Paige shopping for a dress for the church service. My family and I went home. I can't remember exactly what we did in between the services, but I am sure I took another Xanax.

Still in shock, and unable to comprehend that this was really happening, I intentionally arrived back at church no sooner than necessary. I dreaded the entire event. We sat down in the front row, uncomfortably close to the coffin I resented. I prayed for God to give me strength to get through the day.

Little Paige walked in and ran up to me. She looked adorable in her turquoise blue dress with matching shoes and headband. She made me smile and feel happy for a moment, which I desperately needed. The flowers that had been delivered to the church looked beautiful. In the obituary, we had asked that flowers be sent to the church, purposely limiting the amount at the open house to keep it from feeling too much like a funeral—but in the church they seemed appropriate.

Sean had draped an Italian Flag over the casket. I didn't know he was going to do this, and I wasn't sure if it represented Brooke's favorite soccer team or her heritage. As long as it made him feel better, I suppose that was all that mattered—just like my Mother's Day corsage that I was wearing again.

The pastoral staff spoke about Brooke and what a special child she had been, and what an amazing relationship she had with Christ. Uncle Jeff put together a condensed video of photos of Brooke's life that we all enjoyed. Together we sang Brooke's favorite Christian song, *I Can Only Imagine* by Mercy Me, and then the Beatles' song, *Let It Be*. We watched a crazy Brooke and Lauren video in which Brooke proudly demonstrates her love for life and her signature rhythmless dance moves, giving everyone a feel for her fun, good-natured personality.

We were all deeply touched by the eulogies. The Fantastic Four (Kristen, Lauren and Gina), stood together and with great strength each spoke about their friendship. Ms. Spomer, Brooke's fifth-grade teacher shared what Brooke was like as a student. Becky, Lauren's mom, touched on how Brooke changed her life. Coach Jeff reminisced about the many years he had spent as Brooke's soccer coach. Kelly talked about her memories from the last days in Costa Rica. Teresa, Brooke's "other mother," enlightened us with stories about Brooke's early love for God and what it was like for her to love Brooke for twelve years. Teresa shared with us that she felt like God had been trying to prepare her for this when, for the first time in seven years, the flowers that Brooke had given her did not bloom.

The tribute to Brooke was exactly what I had been striving for; I worked hard to try to keep it as uplifting as possible, expecially with the number of children in attendance. Regardless, there is no easy way to accept the loss of a child and many guests struggled to hold it together. Men, women and children all openly sobbed. The children made it hardest; I felt angry that so many suffered needlessly. It wasn't fair.

Immediately following the service, a long line of guests formed to personally offer their condolences. I wasn't prepared for this and contemplated what to do. I wanted to bolt from the church and the coffin as fast as I could, but I feared that would be inappropriate. Many people I had not seen in years made their way up to the immediate families to hug us and share their sympathy for our loss.

In the meantime, the kids lingered nearby. Brooke's younger cousin Gabe stood near the casket for as long as his parents would let him, visibly distraught and in wretched pain. I felt hopeless watching him, knowing I couldn't bring Brooke back or do anything to truly ease his pain. His six-year-old brother, Mason walked up and put his arms around him trying to offer comfort and support crushing the hearts of those that watched.

After a few hours, the line finally ended. It was over. I wasn't sure what I was feeling. *Was I relieved, or sad because at least the service kept me feeling close to her?* Although I hated the casket and what it represented, I was scared to walk away from it, and even more afraid of the future. We went back to the house and I felt better. My closest family and friends were all there for me; I enjoyed their company and support. To my surprise, I actually laughed several times that evening. It was a gorgeous, unseasonably cool night and we relaxed together outside. Later, as my friends started leaving, telling me they knew it had been a long hard day, I was disappointed and didn't want them to go.

"I will not show you what is on the road ahead,
but I will thoroughly equip you for the journey.
My living Presence is your Companion each step of the way.
Stay in continual communication with Me,
whispering My Name
whenever you need to redirect your thoughts.
Thus, you can walk through this day with your focus on Me.
My abiding Presence is the best road map available."
~ John 15:4-7

from "Jesus Calling: Seeking Peace in His Presence" by Sarah Young

Hi, I'm Lauren. I met Brooke on the first day of kindergarten on the bus and we have been like sisters since. Brooke is one of my very best friends and I'll never forget her. She changed my life and many others. From just hanging out to sliding down her mom's stairs through Saran Wrap, we always had something to remember. All the crazy things we did made my life more interesting. I always had a crazy story to tell my sister and my parents about me and Brooke. Brooke was always so joyful and full of action which made our relationship stronger. Throughout this experience I realized that life has hardships but that's how life is and sometime soon we will all reunite with Brooke. Knowing she is in a better place satisfies me but I miss her dearly. Brooke will always be in my heart.

Then, speaking for all of us, we love Brooke and we miss her already. Even though things may be different we will always be the Fantastic Four and we can't wait to see her again.

Friendship That Last's Forever

The world seemed to stop spinning, our bodies trembling, our faces streaked with makeup, and the cool wind making our skin tingle, but yet, right then and there it was a golden moment. My golden moment has the misery of a loss, an impact on my life, and memories that will last forever.

When I found out about the death of one of my best friends, Brooke, the world seemed to spin full speed, leaving me behind in a daze. I couldn't believe that this had happened to me. I had never expected something like this to occur in my life at this age. It was a nightmare. There was going to be an open house in her home to celebrate her life and to share memories with the people she touched and inspired in her lifetime. When the day of the open house came, thoughts raced through my head about how I was going to keep myself together, facing all of Brooke's close friends and family. I sulked into Brooke's house and my ears were instantly filled with the muffled sound of people's steady sobs into each others arms. The words "I'm sorry" being mumbled replayed in my head over and over again. We needed to focus on the joyful memories of Brooke, not just the sorrow of her loss.

I met up with Lauren, Gina and Courtney, my friends that still remained at Brooke's house, as people began filtering out as the day came to an end. All of us were bouncing on the trampoline and decided that we needed to bring back Brooke's fun and crazy personality. Then the idea of jumping into the pool, with our dresses, jewelry, and makeup on, struck us. We gathered all of Brooke's family members and told them to meet us by the pool. All four of us stood by the pool with the coolness of the water making our body's quiver just looking at it. We gripped each others hands as if we were glued together forever. We gazed into each others eyes with a look of nervousness and excitement as we slowly counted to three. We all shouted three and jumped into the icy pool. The crisp breeze nipped at our skin that was beginning to wrinkle. The starry sky showed its face for the first time that night as the stars danced in the sky. As we splashed and kicked around, the scent of lingering smoke from a bon fire mixed with chlorine filled our noses. At that moment life seemed to slowly come to a halt and things became clear once again. Brooke was right there with us when we all jumped in the pool and she will always be with us no matter what.

When I look back at that moment my mind is filled with the incredible times that we had with Brooke. The golden moment that I shared with my friends will last forever in my mind. I learned that friendship is like two rings that are interlocked to each other. No matter how hard you pull they will never come undone.

Because I believe that Brooke will always be with us, the moment in the pool with my best friends will always be golden. When a golden moment fills your life you know it's a golden moment because all of your worries vanish, your thoughts come to a stop, and the moment is glued to your mind forever.

By Kristen Hemmersmeier

Hi, I'm Kristen. I met Brooke in the first grade and she's been one of my best friends ever since. Brooke was an incredible person that words don't even begin to describe. She was the most full of life individual that I have ever met. Brooke was always making the best of every moment that she had with people and she was constantly putting others fisrt, no matter how hard it was. Brooke never cared what anyone thought of her. She could wear the most outrageous outfit and run and dance and fall in front of a big crowd and not care one bit. That's one of the many reasons she is friends with everybody she encountered. I think she was the most random and clumsy yet most amazing person. Even during the few years of her life, she managed to turn so many eyes to Christ. She loved God with all of her heart and mind and that is what made her such an incredible friend. You could talk with her about Christ and never feel awkward or embarrassed. She just had such a remarkable relationship with Him that changed my life as well as many others. Brooke lived her life to the fullest, always doing things to the extreme, like sliding down stairs in buckets or sleeping on her trampoline. Every moment you spent with her would fill your heart with happiness, joy, and plenty of funny stories to tell people. But Brooke is in better hands now and I can't wait to see her again. I loved Brooke like a sister and I know she will be in our hearts forever and ever.

Hi, my name is Gina. Brooke and I met in kindergarten and we have been best friends ever since. I will miss all the things we did together like shopping, cooking yummy food (mostly brownies and Mac and cheese) and TP-ing, but I will mostly just miss Brookie.

Nothing was ever kept between us. We told each other everything. I will miss our long talks on the phone that went on for hours and hours, going over my minutes, which my parents were not happy about.

I will never forget the fun trips Mr. Sean took us on like to Wisconsin and to Mark Twain Lake. I had the best time tubing with Brooke.

I love how Brooke never cared what people thought about her. She just always wanted to have fun, like when we ran through Frontenac Mall, dancing.

I am so thankful for having Brooke as a friend. She taught me to live life to the fullest and to always have fun. I will love Brooke forever and we will always be friends.

~ Chapter Fifteen ~

"Courage is not having the strength to go on;
It is going on when you don't have the strength."
~ Theodore Roosevelt

The days that followed are somewhat of a blur, but I know we still had a lot of family and friends around for a time. I felt like I kept reliving the pain of the realization of Brooke's death, over and over again. Each time I woke up, I would forget that my life had changed. For a few seconds I felt normal and then, like someone punched me, it would hit me and I would ache in agony. The pain that radiated through my body was so great that no amount of torture could hurt worse.

As the shock slowly wore off, the depression set in. I spent most of the day in bed. I rarely answered the phone. I didn't really want to talk to anyone. Our elementary school follows a year-round schedule, so school had started. Paige had already missed a few weeks. It was time for her to go back. My heart ached for her, but in the end, I think it was good to do something normal.

Each morning, I would get Paige off to school and go back to bed for the rest of the day, then force myself to get out when she came home. I dreaded going anywhere. I couldn't handle the fact that, for the other people out in the world, life just moved forward as usual. My life was destroyed. If I went to the grocery store or the bank, and someone smiled at me and told me to have a nice day, I wanted to scream back that I would never again have a nice day; my daughter was dead. It was just so hard to comprehend that while my world had been shattered, the world around me had not.

The funeral home kept calling to ask when they could proceed with the cremation. I kept delaying it. Sean was still calling them and wanting to go there to see her. Apparently, it happens often, and I can understand they can't have people just stopping by, wanting to see their deceased. The apprehension that we were feeling was a normal part of the grief process. They started charging us a nightly fee to motivate us to proceed. Then the funeral director finally found a polite way to tell me that this was part of our denial. So, reluctantly, we took the final step.

The next day, when they called to tell us we could pick up the urn, once again I felt sick. George and I met Sean at the funeral home. When they carried the urn out to us, it was in a clear plastic bag. It seemed insensitive and Sean was offended by it. For me, getting the urn ended up not being as difficult as I expected, but for Sean it was devastating. I felt connected to Brooke spiritually, so I knew she was with me. We left to bring the urn home. As we stopped at one of the three stop lights on our short drive home, I noticed a big, dirty old dump truck in front

 of us. Proudly written on the back of the truck were the words, "The Lord Is Our Strength." Exactly what I needed, exactly when I needed it! That's God—you can count on Him to be there. I snapped a picture of it with my cell phone.

The uncanny coincidences continued. A few days after we came home, for some reason I picked up the book I had been reading on vacation, *Holding Fast*. I was shocked at the connection.

Obviously, I had stopped reading when Brooke died, but I stopped at exactly the point in the book where the body of mountain climber Kelly James had been found and his wife, Karen, spoke of having to bring his body home and get her family back to Texas from Oregon. She went through everything, exactly, that I was living through right then when I was reading it. She described pulling into the driveway with all her family and friends there, surviving the impossible task of planning the funeral, the support, the discoveries and how she was eventually able to find peace.

I never read books like this; I get too emotional and can't handle it. My mom rarely finishes or buys books. It was unbelievable that she had actually purchased this book and gave it to me to read, and that I was reading it exactly when I was.

For quite some time after Brooke's passing, I had no appetite at all and no desire to eat. George continually encouraged me to eat, but I worried that, if I did, I would be sick. I was still spending most of my time in bed. George came in one night and told me he had gotten Chinese food for dinner, and he left some in the kitchen for me. He asked me to please try to eat.

After a while, I went out into the kitchen to put the Chinese food away so it would not spoil. I grabbed one of the fortune cookies and decided it would be something bland and small to eat that maybe I could keep down. I ate it, then, out of habit, read the fortune. It read, "Your luck will soon be at a high point." I was so angry I tossed the piece of paper across the counter and started to walk away.

I had a funny feeling, though, and suddenly remembered something from the book I had been reading. After Kelly passed away, Karen opened a fortune cookie that said, "I miss you."

Thinking of the book, I picked up the small discarded piece of paper and decided to look at the other side. When I turned it over, I couldn't believe my eyes. The first two numbers on the back were 7-13, in that order. July 13 was the date Brooke died.

| Your luck will soon be at a high point. | 7 13 28 34 37 40 |

The chances of this were so remote—one in several million, I imagine. I wondered what this meant. *Why was God telling me that my luck would soon be at a high point when I was at my lowest point ever? Could it be that He was referring to the spiritual discovery that would eventually result from my experiences? To the new sense of purpose I was starting to feel?*

"Don't go through life; grow through life."
~ Anonymous

Brooke's last school photo, Spring 2009

Brooke in San Francisco, 2009

Meghan, Mom, Dad, and Me
June 2009

Meghan and Brooke
June 2009

Avellanas Beach, Costa Rica (Angel Beach)

Avellanas Beach, Costa Rica (Angel Beach)

Flamingo Bay, Costa Rica

Aerial view of Flamingo Bay where the accident occured. The solid yellow line represents the road we traveled on during ATV tour. The broken yellow line represents where Brooke missed the sharp turn and the path she followed.

~ Chapter Sixteen ~

"There is nothing that the body suffers
that the soul may not profit by."
~ George Meredith

In the weeks that followed, my family and I did our best to face the tragedy. My mom felt heartbroken, as we all did, but at the same time, so thankful that she had gotten to spend the evening alone with Brooke on the night before we left for vacation. They had gone shopping and grabbed a quick bite to eat, and Mom had taken Brooke to get her hair cut. My mom was suffering, not only from the loss of her dear, beloved grandchild, but also because of the agony I was going through. She hurt for me, too. She wanted to help ease my pain. She felt hopeless knowing there was absolutely nothing she could do.

Suffering from his own sorrow, George did everything he could to be there for me and offer support. He too, was haunted by the traumatic flashbacks of the accident and what he had witnessed. He explains it as losing two people he loved that day; he lost both me and Brooke. As we stood on the beach, lost and consumed with agony, I looked him in the eye and told him I would never again be the same woman. He knew that to be true; Jennifer as he knew her had died along with Brooke. He felt all his hopes and dreams for us being yanked away from him in one short moment. He feared how this would affect us.

Blake's strength amazed me. He worried about his dad and was resilient to help Sean survive. Blake explained to me that he had experienced something unique. Almost immediately after Brooke's physical death, he felt that she passed her spiritual strength on to him.

From the very beginning, when they first went back to the condo in Costa Rica, Blake dug deep within himself to get through this. Alone and unable to reach out to anyone by phone, he turned to the computer and posted a PowerPoint presentation on YouTube, asking for prayers to help him survive. Blake created a simple PowerPoint presentation, white letters on black background, which he entitled, "My sister…In Loving Memory…Heaven's the Place to Be."

The PowerPoint read:

My sister Brooke…
12 years old
Died of a fall off a cliff on an ATV
Just an hour before I typed this…
Please God, help me
And please people, show your support
This is so hard to think of
And kills me inside
Rest in Peace
Brooke S******
1996 – 2009

Knowing that I worry about the dangers of giving too much information online, Blake didn't put her full last name.

Being the avid paintball player he is, Blake immediately thought about starting a Christian paintball group. He researched it further and found that there already was one. When he went to the site within a few hours of the accident, they were already praying for him and sending messages about how they needed to help him. They had seen Blake's posting on YouTube. This had such an impact on Blake, knowing that young teenage boys all over the country were praying for him, giving him the support he needed to go on, sending him emails and dedicating songs and prayers to our family.

In adition, Blake sent a message to Brooke's best friend Lauren that read:

"Please believe me, it is terrible. I know you don't, but it's all true.
My grandparents are all there at my mom's house. My dad had a

nervous breakdown from it and he is in the hospital but he will be ok,
but yeah Brooke is for sure gone. Please talk to her, pray to her, she will
hear you. Sorry to tell you this. Also, please tell all friends about it so
they know too. And if you know Brooke's password for MySpace, I think
you should make a message on her main page about her. She didn't
deserve it. She was a great person. Thanks Lauren."

Blake had moments that were harder than others, like the
Nickelback Concert we all went to, where in the past, his sister
would have stood beside him. But each time Blake had a really hard
breakdown he felt better and even stronger from it. He went back to
school and remained enrolled in the three honors classes as planned.
He knew he could get through it. He spoke with Brooke often and
let her guide him. He wanted to be baptized as soon as possible. The
ceremony was touching, knowing that Brooke was with him and
proud of his new commitment to his life with God. We felt Brooke's
presence in the church that evening and to see her energy in the
photos was comforting.

Blake's faith has never faltered; he has never questioned how or where Brooke is. From the very beginning, he has remained confident she is fine. He consoled me often by reminding me that whether we live 13 years or 90 really doesn't matter; it is all a blip in comparison to eternal life, and to what Brooke now knows. Although it took me longer to get there, I do feel the same way now. I understand that there is a much bigger plan that we are all a part of.

One evening Blake came into my bedroom to talk with me. I was sleeping in bed, as usual. He told me he had been talking with Brooke while he was in the shower, praying for her to give him direction on how to help Sean. Blake was crying as he explained to me that she answered him. All of a sudden, the words to a song in Brooke's favorite childhood book, *I Love You Forever,* popped into his head, and he had started singing them in the shower.

> *I love you forever;*
>
> *I like you for always.*
>
> *As long as I'm living,*
>
> *My baby you'll be.*

Sean sang this to Brooke all the time when she was little. We hadn't read the book in years, but Blake was convinced Brooke wanted him to give it to Sean. I promised to help find it, so Blake and I started looking everywhere for the book. I looked for days, but the book was nowhere to be found.

A few days later, one of Paige's friends from Teresa's, Ellie, asked Paige to spend the night. When Ellie and her mom, April, came to get

Paige that evening, we sat out on the deck and talked for a few minutes as the girls played. April works for hospice, so we talked about dealing with loss and how she personally has received some shockingly clear signs from patients after they have passed.

April was acting a little strange, and I could tell she wanted to tell me something. Finally she said, "You know, I have something I want to tell you about. My friends all told me to hold off until you are stronger, but I just feel like I need to tell you now."

She went on to say that she had something to return to me. Last year at Christmas, Paige had packed a large gift bag as a present for Ellie. She had made all kinds of drawings for Ellie and, to be honest, I wasn't really sure what else Paige had packed in it, and obviously Brooke hadn't known, either. April explained that she had been meaning to return a book she found in the bag. She knew it was special because we had written a personal inscription in the front with our love. Paige had given Ellie Brooke's favorite book, *I Love You Forever.*

I began to cry. At first, April had no idea what was going on. I shared with her the story of Brooke's sign to Blake. It seemed as though Brooke not only answered Blake's prayer, but also let April know how much we needed the book then.

As for Paige, she struggled with grasping the concept of death over-all. Her world had been turned upside down, instantaneously when a day filled with joy and laughter collided head first with catastrophe. Paige knew from the the terror she witnessed in those very first horrifying moments that she would not be seeing Brooke for a long time. However, this was the first death that Paige had encountered so she had lots of questions. Reading children's books about Heaven and the loss of loved ones helped comfort her, as well as coloring pictures and writing letters to Brooke.

Witnessing the effects Brooke's death had on Paige was heartbreaking. Paige and Brooke slept together every night and Brooke was like a second mother to Paige. Realizing how quickly life can change, Paige began to fear that something would happen to Sean or me. She was terrified there would be more tragedy and when she couldn't reach one of us, she would get upset and make comments like, "I just know my mom is dead."

Paige tried to comprehend exactly what happened to Brooke and asked very detailed questions. She wanted to know if Brooke had boo-boos or was crying, what she looked like, etc. We started attending Annie's Hope, a support group for the family. One night when we were getting settled for bed, she started talking about the support group. She said, "Some people lost their moms, some their grandmas, and some their whole family. It's not really fun to lose someone." A few minutes later, she asked who made Brooke die. And then she commented that she hoped she lived her whole life. Another time when we were going to sleep in Brooke's bed, she grabbed my arm and pulled it tight around her and said, "Momma, please promise me you will keep me so safe and not let me get killed by the bad guys like Brookie."

Paige suddenly became interested in Angels, saying she wanted to become an angel like Brookie. That first Halloween after Brooke passed, Paige of course had to be an Angel. When asked by a clown at a restaurant what type of balloon she wanted, her reply was no longer a dog, but instead an angel halo and wings along with flowers for her sister.

Paige talks about Brookie daily and tells me often how sad she is and how much she misses her. Paige likes to talk about Brooke and the special times they shared. Together we watch home movies, laughing and crying at the memories we treasure.

For the longest time, my dad could barely walk in my house. He couldn't handle looking at the pictures and the mementos I had displayed everywhere. Life didn't seem fair to him; he felt both anger and guilt, feeling that he should have died instead of Brooke, because of his age. The grief books I studied referred to this as "survivor's guilt." What Dad was feeling was common with grief. Besides, for society in general, the needless death of a young, innocent child is always impossible to accept. Within a few weeks of Brooke's passing, as he struggled to work through his grief, he shocked us all by getting a tattoo, something he had sworn he would never do. He designed it himself: Brookie's name with angel wings around it in her favorite

color blue. He said he wanted his angel with him at all times, and that he wanted her name to be the first thing he saw in the morning when he woke and the last thing he saw at the end of the day.

My sister doesn't show her emotions as much as some, so she wept mostly in private. I felt best looking at pictures and being in Brooke's room, but Meghan was more like Dad. She avoided coming here as much as she could at first. Meghan held it all in, but whenever the flood gates opened, it was bad. She and her boyfriend JD had been staying at our house while we were in Costa Rica. Later, I found some clothes she left in my closest. When I told her what I found, she told me to throw away one shirt; she didn't want it. It was the shirt she had been wearing when she found out about the accident, a memory she didn't want triggered.

Meghan and Brooke were like sisters. They both knew when Brooke grew up and they were adults together, that they would be close, and hang out as best friends together. Brooke constantly called and talked Meghan into spending the night. For years, Meghan spent more time each week at our house than she did at my parents'. As Brooke got older, Meghan became her confidante—the person she went to if she couldn't come to me—or if she was upset with me. Because of Brooke's maturity, they had long ago become best friends.

"Have I not commanded you?
Be strong and courageous;
do not be afraid, nor be dismayed:
for the Lord your God is with you
wherever you go."
~ Joshua 1:9

~ *Chapter Seventeen* ~

"Nothing in life is to be feared. It is only to be understood."
~ *Marie Curie*

One of the hardest things for us all was facing Brooke's thirteenth birthday, August 4, only three weeks after her death. It was important to us that we celebrate it, and in nothing short of Brooke style. While I was thankful that—oddly enough— she, Lauren and I took the opportunity to celebrate so early on our trip to San Francisco, I was still devastated as the day approached. Ironically, Brooke had used her thirteenth birthday as her deadline for when she wanted to finish the Bible. She also said that when she turned thirteen she would start eating meat, which she had not done in over five years.

Great anxiety filled me in the days leading up to her birthday. The night before, I went to bed and prayed for the strength to survive it. I fell asleep early, while George lay next to me, still awake, watching a movie. In my sleep I heard the phone ring—it was my office line and it rang just once. George woke me and asked me if I had heard it. I said yes, and asked him what time it was. He gave me the most startled look, and replied that it was exactly midnight—as in twelve-zero-zero—on the day of Brooke's birthday.

I told him right then that the call was just Brooke, letting me know she was okay and trying to give me comfort. I went back to bed without even checking the caller ID. The next morning, I got up to see what it said. Of course there was no message, the phone only rang once. The caller ID confirmed the call at exactly 12:00 on 8/4/2009 from Progress West Hospital, the hospital nearest our house, where Brooke and I had gone to the ER for minor medical emergencies like stitches and bad allergic reactions. I took a picture of the caller ID from different phones to prove that it had happened.

The phone call lifted my spirits and helped me through the day. We invited about fifty of Brooke's closest family and friends over to celebrate her thirteenth birthday as she would have wanted. My best friend Rhonda, her fiance Brian, and Sean's brother Jeff all worked hard to help us make it special. Both sides of the family (Sean's and mine) joined together, united in this. The kids swam, we barbequed, and everyone wrote a personal note to Brooke on a balloon. We played her favorite Christian song, *I Can Only Imagine,* on the speakers outside

as we released the fifty blue balloons to her and watched them disappear, gradually turning into small dots in the sky. They floated up in what seemed like slow motion as we all stood by watching, crying and hugging. The sky was cloudy, but the clouds parted as the balloons drifted into them. We were able to see them for the longest time; we couldn't believe it. The children colored several large crosses and a huge mural in the street for Brooke, wishing her a happy thirteenth.

Originally the forecast called for rain and the day was cloudy, but as the day went on it turned out to be a beautiful day. Brooke's closest friends, all on the Glavin soccer team, were going to have to leave early for practice, but fortunately, practice was cancelled. Everyone joked that Brooke must have pulled some strings from above!

We sang *Happy Birthday* and enjoyed the traditional birthday cookie cakes—Brooke's favorite, watched a special birthday video Uncle Jeff had made, listened to her favorite songs, and then held a candlelit vigil around the pool as we prayed. Several of us noticed that only one star was out, shining down brightly from the sky above. As we all stared up in amazement, George broke the silence by pushing me into pool— fully dressed, I might add—claiming that Brooke would have wanted

him to, which was definitely true. He was kind enough to join me, along with several other fully dressed adults. Of course, all the kids jumped in, but most of them were already in swimsuits.

Although we shed a lot of tears, we closed the day at peace, feeling we had celebrated the day as she would have wanted.

We were happy to find orbs in many of the photos taken that day. Best of all, they were in pictures from multiple cameras.

"Angels are speaking to all of us –
some of us are only listening better."
~ Anonymous

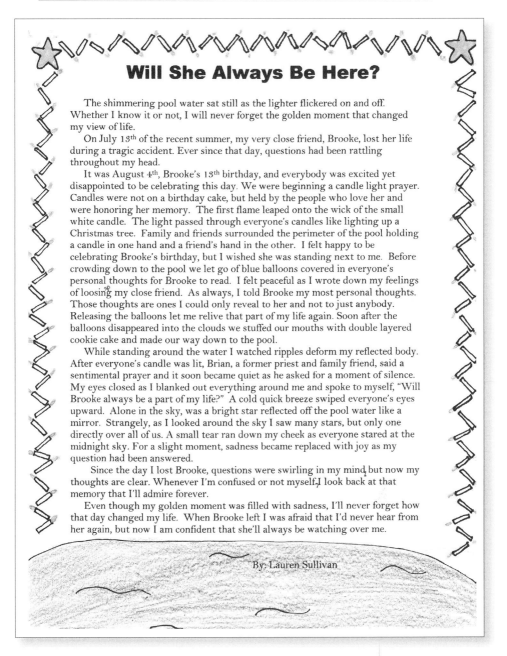

Will She Always Be Here?

The shimmering pool water sat still as the lighter flickered on and off. Whether I know it or not, I will never forget the golden moment that changed my view of life.

On July 13th of the recent summer, my very close friend, Brooke, lost her life during a tragic accident. Ever since that day, questions had been rattling throughout my head.

It was August 4th, Brooke's 13th birthday, and everybody was excited yet disappointed to be celebrating this day. We were beginning a candle light prayer. Candles were not on a birthday cake, but held by the people who love her and were honoring her memory. The first flame leaped onto the wick of the small white candle. The light passed through everyone's candles like lighting up a Christmas tree. Family and friends surrounded the perimeter of the pool holding a candle in one hand and a friend's hand in the other. I felt happy to be celebrating Brooke's birthday, but I wished she was standing next to me. Before crowding down to the pool we let go of blue balloons covered in everyone's personal thoughts for Brooke to read. I felt peaceful as I wrote down my feelings of loosing my close friend. As always, I told Brooke my most personal thoughts. Those thoughts are ones I could only reveal to her and not to just anybody. Releasing the balloons let me relive that part of my life again. Soon after the balloons disappeared into the clouds we stuffed our mouths with double layered cookie cake and made our way down to the pool.

While standing around the water I watched ripples deform my reflected body. After everyone's candle was lit, Brian, a former priest and family friend, said a sentimental prayer and it soon became quiet as he asked for a moment of silence. My eyes closed as I blanked out everything around me and spoke to myself, "Will Brooke always be a part of my life?" A cold quick breeze swiped everyone's eyes upward. Alone in the sky, was a bright star reflected off the pool water like a mirror. Strangely, as I looked around the sky I saw many stars, but only one directly over all of us. A small tear ran down my cheek as everyone stared at the midnight sky. For a slight moment, sadness became replaced with joy as my question had been answered.

Since the day I lost Brooke, questions were swirling in my mind, but now my thoughts are clear. Whenever I'm confused or not myself, I look back at that memory that I'll admire forever.

Even though my golden moment was filled with sadness, I'll never forget how that day changed my life. When Brooke left I was afraid that I'd never hear from her again, but now I am confident that she'll always be watching over me.

By: Lauren Sullivan

Use your mobile tag reader to see a video of Brooke's Birthday Celebration.

The days before the pain

Life was sincere

Given these hardships

I know that you're still here

Rain fell upon

Us with no end in near

The days went by

Stolen from us

Left with tears

So young, yet so near

No one deserves this...

No end in sight

The past too far gone

Why can't she come back

Her time brought to dawn

My life dissolves among the time

Without her here

Just come back to me

Come back home

~ Blake Scalise 2011

~ Chapter Eighteen ~

*"True wisdom lies in gathering the precious things
out of each day as it goes by."*
~ E.S. Bouton

As the weeks went by, my depression continued. Each day, for months, I found myself wandering into Brooke's room, which today still remains untouched for the most part. I would spend hours in her bed, clinging to her sheets and pillow as I cried. I would sit in her closet in a daze as I went through her things. For some reason, her closet was the hardest for me, probably because it smelled just like her. I could open the door and her scent came to me, so strong I would swear she was there.

I would look at her hairbrush and sob as I thought that I would never again get to brush her hair. I looked for so many silly ways to feel close to her, all the way down to using her toothbrush and waiting months before I could finally bring myself to wash her sheets.

My mom and I had each requested a lock of Brooke's hair from the funeral home. It took me weeks to face opening the envelope. When I took it out of the Ziploc and held it, I couldn't believe this was the only recognizable thing left of Brooke's physical body. I smelled it and that made me even sadder; it smelled nothing like Brooke, but had an awful chemical smell to it. Instead, I went back to her hairbrush, smelling it and fantasizing about brushing her long, pretty, shiny, blond hair. I kept the brush next to her bed where she left it and held it often during the countless hours I sat in her room, bawling my eyes out.

One evening when my mom was here, she felt ready for me to give her the lock of Brooke's hair that had been set aside for her. She had gotten a special box she wanted to put it in to keep a part of Brooke close by. I explained to mom that it might upset her because it smelled nothing like Brooke. As we talked, I offered to give her some of the hair from Brooke's brush since it smelled more like her. I ran up to Brooke's room to get it and came down screaming my head off. I couldn't believe it; her hair was gone. I worked to calm myself down and then it hit me. The cleaning lady had come that day. I am sure she thought she was helping me by saving me from doing an impossible task. Since we all grieve so differently, she didn't understand.

I immediately ran outside and started going through the dumpster in search of Brooke's hair. Fortunately, I found it. I had panicked; this was so unimaginably important to me. I put the hair away safely in my jewelry box and the brush in my drawer. I longed for just one more opportunity to touch Brooke's hair—to smell it, the smell I know so well—the scent I still close my eyes and imagine.

It is the little things, like being able to brush your child's hair, that we often take for granted in our hurried lives. These things seem so normal and inconsequential. When we have the opportunity, we don't take the time to appreciate it the way we should. Trust me; once you know that, in this lifetime, you will never have the chance to do it again, you will always wish you had done it more. Very few can grasp the magnitude of what I would be willing to sacrifice to create one more lasting memory with Brooke, even just a moment together. The two things that mean more than anything, our most valuable assets in our existence, are time and people. At the end of the day, all that really matters in life are the people you love and the time you spend nurturing those relationships.

My whole outlook on life had changed, as it had for many of those closest to Brooke. We no longer fear death, but, in a twisted, inexplicable way, actually look forward to being reunited with Brooke. Even her friends no longer fear death. It is different because someone we love so much that we can't wait to be with, waits for us on the other side. I had always feared death because I did not want to leave my kids. It is different now; I feel divided by having children in both spaces.

I now know that our time on earth is short and we have to live for each moment. We need to appreciate every second we have and be sure to let the people we love know how special they are, because we never know when it will be their last day or ours. I live out my life, learning its lessons, fulfilling my purpose here on earth, and looking forward to the day when my family will all be together again.

I have always experienced some apprehension over the inevitable loss of my elders, however, I don't think I truly grasped the enormity of what will transpire. As we age, it is a matter of fact that we will experience more and more loss. Many people we love over our lifetimes will leave the physical world before us. In my case, I certainly pray that I have survived the worst of it with the loss of a child. I do not believe there could be anything worse. I believe the hardest part is over. Every parent's biggest fear is to outlive his or her child. There isn't much left to fear. My entire outlook on death has changed. From this point forward, the death of anyone I love won't be as sad, because I will think of that person being reunited with Brooke. I know they will be together. Not everyone can grasp this, but those in my shoes do.

My mom can relate; she looks at this life as what we have to do until we reach our real, eternal life, together again and reunited with Brooke. Mom actually commented to me the other day that she felt so bad for Blake and Paige because they are so young and still have so long to live. I knew what she meant, but I know others would have been confused. She feels sorry for them because they have so long before they get to go home to Heaven and be with their sister again.

Even though Brooke is physically gone, I do what I can to still feel connected to her. I appreciate anything that evokes a memory or feeling associated with our intense love. For instance, dreams became important to me, and such wonderful experiences.

Unfortunately, you cannot force yourself to dream, so I would always wait eagerly for the next time I would see Brooke in my dreams. A few of the dreams felt so real that I just knew she was with me.

In my first dream, less than a month after she passed, I sensed Brooke standing beside my bed. She looked down and smiled at me with a tenderness that touched my heart. She looked radiantly beautiful in the blue dress she wore to her cousin Tommy's wedding. Her beautiful blue eyes sparkled as she gazed at me, allowing me to feel her peace and tranquility. She whispered to me as she shook her head and smiled, "Mommy I am fine. Don't worry about me, I promise I'm fine. I will never leave you, Mommy, I love you so much. I will always be by your side." She bent down and she hugged me. The hug was so real that I felt the pressure of her against me. Then, the most amazing sensation flowed through my entire body, creating a deep sense of warmth and joy. I suddenly sat up, startled by the experience. The TV, set to a channel it had not been on previously, loudly played the most beautiful song:

> *When I think back on these times*
> *And the dreams we left behind*
> *I'll be glad 'cause I was blessed*
> *To get to have you in my life*
> *When I look back on these days*
> *I'll look and see your face*
> *You were right there for me*
>
> *In my dreams I'll always see you*
> *Soar above the sky*
> *In my heart there'll always be a place*
> *For you for all my life*
> *I'll keep a part of you with me*
> *And everywhere I am*
> *There you'll be*
> *And everywhere I am*
> *There you'll be*

Well you showed me how it feels
To feel the sky within my reach
And I always will remember
All the strength you gave to me
Your love made me make it through
Oh, I owe so much to you
You were right there for me

In my dreams I'll always see you
Soar above the sky
In my heart there'll always be a place
For you for all my life
I'll keep a part of you with me
And everywhere I am
There you'll be

'Cause I always saw in you
My light, my strength
And I want to thank you now for all the ways
You were right there for me (you were right there for me)
You were right there for me always

In my dreams I'll always see you
Soar above the sky
In my heart there'll always be a place
For you for all my life
I'll keep a part of you with me
And everywhere I am
There you'll be
And everywhere I am
There you'll be

There you'll be

I woke George and told him what happened. As the song continued to play and the credits of a movie rolled on, I asked him to hurry and figure out what the movie was so I could find the song. I got up for some reason and left the bedroom. As I walked out into the great room, which has floor to ceiling windows, the room glowed the most beautiful orange. I witnessed the most dazzling sunrise I have ever seen. A sense of peace came over me and I knew Brooke was fine. I went back to bed. When I told my mom the story, she said even people on the radio were talking about seeing the most gorgeous sunrise ever that morning. We later found the song: *There You'll Be,* recorded by Faith Hill.

I had another dream where Brooke came to me; this time she spoke to me more in my mind. She told me, "Mommy, I worry about Blake. You need to talk to him and tell him he has to start focusing on health and exercise. If he doesn't he is going to have problems with his heart." She begged me to caution him and make sure he understood that it was serious, that he needed to worry about his health, specifically his heart. I told Blake about the dream and, within a few days, Blake met a girl who he was very interested in. He felt motivated to get in shape and start a rigorous exercise plan. He lost almost twenty pounds in a matter of months. He has been exercising and in shape since.

In another dream, Brooke and I walked down an old gravel country road. She stepped in front of me, turned around and started walking backwards. She placed her hand gently on my wrist and looked in my eyes in a manner that penetrated my whole soul. Her lips turned upward in a smirky smile and her genuine happiness flowed from her. She promised me, "You don't need to worry, I am happy. I like it better here, Mommy. Heaven is where I want to be." She then reassured me she was always with me, it was just different, but we would always be together and she would never leave my side. I watched her walk off ahead of me and slowly fade. I woke feeling a sense of pride and warmth coming from my heart. Slowly, my lips turned upward, I smiled the same smirky smile, feeling tremendous peace.

Each of these dreams felt so real. Most dreams feel foggy and then fade, but to this day I can still vividly remember every detail of these. I would later learn that our loved ones come to us in our sleep and use these dreams to share important messages. In the dream state, our subconscious minds are more open to these experiences. Others report feeling a loved one's embrace in a dream, a dream so real that they couldn't shake the feeling afterwards. After one dream like this, I immediately knew the difference.

"You know as well as I there's more…
There's always one more
scene no matter."
~ Archibald McLeish

~ Chapter Nineteen ~

"What is faith? It is the confident assurance
that what we hope for is going to happen.
It is the evidence of things we cannot yet see."
~ Hebrews 11:1

*O*ffering condolences is very awkward and uncomfortable for many. Some of my friends knew just what to say to me. Others extremely close to me couldn't call me or talk to me at all. They knew they were emotionally unable to get through it, and were afraid of upsetting me if they broke down in front of me. Everyone grieves differently, but in our family we very much keep Brooke's spirit alive and talk about her constantly. If a friend gets emotional, it doesn't bother us. As Blake said, it shows they care.

Although no one could really do or say anything to make it truly better, a simple, "I am sorry, there is just nothing to say other than this is awful and I wish you weren't going through it" or "Brooke is so special" helped most. It was more upsetting when someone ignored our loss and didn't comment at all. This happened not because people didn't care, but because they struggled to find the right words to offer their sympathy appropriately. I didn't take it personally when this happened. I, too, have lived through those awkward moments when someone I cared for experienced great loss and I just didn't know what to say.

My good friend Nicci in Columbus (the friend that gave birth to her daughter Maddi just a few hours after Brooke was born) helped tremendously. She had gone through a shocking loss less than a year before Brooke's passing. Nicci, her husband, John, and their two kids,

Griffin and Maddi, were in Tennessee with relatives on vacation. Nicci and John had gone for a run one morning as they were training for a marathon. After finishing five miles, Nicci couldn't do anymore. John wanted to run a few miles further, so he went on and Nicci strolled back to the hotel to have breakfast with the kids and John's family. When John didn't return after quite awhile, his brother called his cell phone. Oddly, a woman answered. When Nicci heard the "who's this" conversation, at first she thought it was a joke. But as she watched the color drain from her brother-in-law's face, she knew something was wrong. They asked to speak with her, and a doctor informed Nicci that when they found John, it was already too late.

At the time, I really couldn't imagine anything worse than what she was going through. I felt both shock and panic for my friend and her family; I had a knot in my stomach that wouldn't go away. They had to do what at the time I considered to be an inconceivable task— transporting John's remains home from out of town, in addition to having to get the rest of the family home safely from Tennessee to Ohio.

I remember trying to leave messages for Nicci and struggling with what to say. Did I want to comment that I was thinking of her; or would that make her sad since I was referring to her loss? I now know that we worry too much about struggling with the right words to use. Really, a grieving friend only needs to know that you are there for them and sorry for what they are going through. Words of encouragement don't matter at that point, so there is no need to try to put a positive spin on it. Early on, there is only darkness and it takes time for light to begin to shine through.

Having friends like Nicci, who also suffered catastrophic circumstances, helped. I grew closer to friends like her. We could talk at a different spiritual level and share what we were going through. I have a dear friend Stacey who also has faced some real adversity. Diagnosed with cancer—Hodgkin's Disease—in college, Stacey has survived a difficult journey, too. Not only is she a cancer survivor, she also went on to have three beautiful children despite concerns that the radiation had made her infertile. She lost both of her parents and can relate to the struggles people go through when facing life's challenges. We can talk for hours in deep conversation, deeper than we could process before we experienced these hardships. I migrated to the friends and family who had the strongest faith during this time. They helped lift me when I needed it. They helped me see the flicker of light ahead.

Reaching out to other parents who suffered tragedies like mine brought a great sense of comfort as well during this time. In early August, a nine-year-old boy who lived in our community, Danny Bampton, was struck and killed by a car in a tragic accident. It was just a few weeks after Brooke passed, and although I couldn't offer much, I called the mother, Lisa, and told her I understood her pain. I just wanted her to know I knew what she was going through and I was praying for her family. I invited them to dinner and most of their family came. It had only been a week since Danny's death then, and my heart broke for them as I saw the shock they were all still in. I think it helped them to see a family that was going through a similar loss, but a few weeks further into the grief process. They could see what the next few weeks would bring.

When Rick and Lisa Bampton arrived at the house with three of their children, they introduced their daughters as Lauren, Kristen and Meghan. Blake and I looked at each other and smiled—Lauren and Kristen, two of Brooke's best friends, and Meghan, my sister who was so very close to Brooke. When I told Pastor Mark about it at church that week, he just laughed and said that he liked to explain that as God's way of showing off and letting us know He has a hand in everything.

I also had several parents who had lost children reach out to me. One mother, Kim Schlau, lost two of her children in a negligent situation when a state trooper crossed the highway median at speeds in excess of 100 miles an hour, responding to a nonemergency call, and hit them head on. Worse yet, he was suspected of texting while driving. It helped me to discuss the grief process and see how other bereaved parents pulled through, although they, too, had endured the weight of an incomprehensible pain that made them think they would never feel whole again.

The circumstances of what and who we were able to relate to changed altogether. It is hard to explain, but until you have walked in someone's shoes, you just aren't in a position to fully comprehend what they are going through. You certainly shouldn't judge them. For instance, several months after Nicci's husband John passed away, I remember calling her to see how she was doing. She sounded very upbeat and told me she was doing so much better. She had gone to see a medium and now she recognized all the signs her husband was giving her. She knew he was beside her and the kids all the time. It was really a turning point for her.

A few weeks later, another friend asked me how Nicci was doing, and I told her I didn't think she was doing very well at all. I said that Nicci was in such denial that she was actually trying to communicate with John.

I had never been to a psychic or a fortune teller; I just didn't believe in them. Yet when I was in my darkest place, about five weeks after Brooke passed, Gayle, George's mom, gave me the book *We Are Their Heaven* by Allison DuBois. Outside of the movie *Ghost* and Nicci's story, this was my first exposure to a medium. I learned that a medium is someone who has been blessed with the ability to communicate with those on the other side. The TV show, *The Medium*, is based on the life of Allison DuBois, the author of the book.

After reading the first chapter, I already felt better. That chapter focused on the hardest loss to endure—the loss of a child. Allison described her experience bringing through a fifteen-year-old child who had died, and included the mother's notes on the reading and the impact it had on her. The book gave me confidence that Brooke was okay and we would forever be connected. I felt certain that Brooke was still around me often.

I felt a new peace that helped me and I had a better understanding of Heaven. I related to many of the stories in the book, as many of the experiences echoed what was happening in my daily life. When I finished the first book, I went online and ordered Allison DuBois' other book, *Don't Kiss Them Good-bye,* and several other suggested books, including James Van Praagh's *Talking to Heaven* and *Healing Grief,* two of my favorite reads that truly helped heal my heart. I related to some of the books I read more than others, and I had to interpret the information as I saw fit, but the important thing was that light was finally returning to my life. For the first time in weeks, I finally wanted to get out of bed.

As I earlier admitted, until Brooke influenced me otherwise, I was never overly religious. So I will confess that I have never read the Bible in its entirety. I have tried, and while I love to read and I enjoy the many lessons in church, I have a tough time grasping what the Bible says without help interpreting it. I have always considered myself a Christian, but I have always had a few beliefs that I knew might be at odds with the church. For instance, I have always felt that Dale, my father who committed suicide, is in Heaven. I believe he suffered from depression and post-traumatic stress disorder because of his time in Vietnam. Since I do know God is a loving God, I believe he was forgiven. It gave me peace of mind that Allison Dubois and James Van Praagh both wrote of bringing through those who had committed suicide, too.

In the first book I read, Allison discussed how meaningful it was for her to have dinner with a Catholic priest who is a medium. They openly discussed the church's feelings about mediums. The priest explained that different interpretations of the Bible are possible, and that his beliefs still lined up with what was written. He felt that both he and Allison were created in God's image, while the "false prophets" of the Bible are people who pretend to communicate with the dead or predict the future. They discussed how the church acknowledges that mystics truly exist, but fears that evil spirits and the devil may try to come through mediums.

I had a lot to take in, and after I finished reading multiple books on the topic, I finally decided I had read enough. I wanted to step away from it and digest what I had learned. So I spent some time doing that. I thought back to the things my friend Nicci had said to me after Brooke passed, about how much her reading helped her. I reviewed a letter she had written, encouraging me to be open to new experiences that I probably never would have considered before.

After giving it a lot of thought and consideration, I decided that I wanted to do this. I thought about which medium would be right for me. I could tell from the books I read that they are vastly different. I felt very connected to both Allison Dubois and James Van Praagh. After further research, I learned that Allison no longer scheduled readings like this. She focuses most of her time now on solving crimes, since she could no longer handle the demands of both.

The only other medium I considered was Laurie Campbell, Allison's best friend and mentor. In her books, Allison constantly refers to Laurie as the very best medium, one who will never be surpassed by another. I knew from her book that Allison met Laurie Campbell when they both participated in a four-year study at the University of Arizona. Laurie was actually the lead medium in the study and Allison described her own tremendous respect for Laurie and how they went on to become best friends.

When Allison's father passed away, Laurie was able to contact him first. Something led me to Laurie Campbell as the right place to go. The book had described several readings done over the phone for the Arizona study, so I knew I could get a reading over the phone.

When I called to make my appointment, I provided my name and credit card information and was told they would get back to me about scheduling. Several weeks went by and I hadn't heard back. Concerned, I called my credit card company to confirm that the transaction had gone through. I sent an email asking when I would hear about the schedule and expressing my concern that no one had contacted me.

Later that day, I got a phone call from Laurie, the medium herself. She apologized, telling me that there were over a hundred people on the list. As we spoke, her tone changed suddenly.

She said, "Wow, your spirits have known you would do this and they have been waiting; they are ready." Laurie said, "Wow, I have chills. Even without meditating I am receiving a lot of information. Your daughter has blonde hair; she is younger than your son; your son's hair is darker."

I was shocked; I had not expected Laurie to share anything when the call was simply to schedule the appointment, but I found it reassuring.

Laurie commented she understood how much I needed this; she was going to arrange to fit me in as soon as possible. We scheduled the reading for three weeks from our call, on September 28 at four in the afternoon.

Sean was still struggling and seemed so depressed. I could relate and thought it might help him to read the book by Allison Dubois that I had read. I gave him the book, and as he started reading it, I could tell it was helping him, too. I decided to confide in him about the scheduled reading and invite him to be a part of it if he would like. I told him to think about it; either way, I planned to do the reading with Laurie. After contemplating for a long time, he finally decided that he had no choice but to find some peace in his life so he could continue. He decided to join me.

Together, we sat in Brooke's room. The reading took three hours and I took 19 pages of notes. We had a truly amazing experience. Going through my notes afterward, I realized the meaning of many things that I didn't quite understand during the reading. Laurie Campbell's psychic abilities were uncanny. It was interesting to see how Laurie worked her way to Brooke and how the information would come to her. Her accuracy and abilities were completely undeniable, and I have not a doubt in my mind that she communicated with Brooke in Heaven.

The Reading

"Jenn, your maternal grandmother has passed."

"No, my maternal great grandmother."

"I see a June birthday and an April birthday."

"Yes our daughter's is June 9th and mine is April 6th."

"Sean, your maternal grandmother's name is Patricia and she goes by Pat."

"Correct."

"I keep getting something about not being your fault. Jenn, you are one of two children, and have a sister. Sean you are one of two children, and have a brother."

"Yes, you are correct."

"This isn't the first child you have lost, is that right?"

"No, but our son was born prematurely and it was very scary."

"You have a son and a daughter; your daughter's hair is lighter than your son's, and your daughter is younger. I keep seeing a giant "S" [possibly for our last name?]. There is something with breathing difficulty before with this spirit."

"Our daughter did have severe asthma when she was younger. She was taken from the doctor's office once by ambulance to the hospital."

"Jenn, you have experienced depression in your family."

"Correct, my father took his own life after suffering years of depression."

"She was always busy. You are upstairs in your home making this call."

"Yes, we are in our daughter's room."

"I sense the outdoors and there is water nearby; it is a busy day and there is a lot of driving. Everything takes place outside; there are a lot of trees, hills and mountains—lots of green. I sense an abundance of nature and beauty. It is a time of great happiness. There is water nearby. I have a headache, my head hurts. Yes, she was definitely hit or struck in the head, but it happened very fast. But I know it is head trauma. She said

there was nothing you could do about this, do not blame your-self. She says you are really having a rough time with this."

Sean and I just both sat there stunned.

Laurie went on, "I see water and crashing waves and rocks, a place of exploration; this was your first time there. I am getting a sense of joy and much happiness, and that she thought it a great place to be. She said there is sand and it is a simplistic time with a great sense of joy. She said there were some people nearby, a "K" name—Karlee, Kathy or Kelly?"

"Kelly."

Even after all the books I had read regarding readings, I was still shocked by the level of detail and accuracy.

"She flips, there was nothing she could do. Does this make sense to you?"

"Yes, she drove her ATV off a 260-foot cliff."

"Her name is Brooke or Barbara."

"Brooke."

"Brooke said you were terrified, Jenn, and she wants you to know it is not your fault. There is so much pain in each of you, but to her it is just a matter of fact. She said the crossing over was very fast and quick. Brooke indicated something about being stuck. She said it was a straight drop-off, and other areas around it are also dangerous. She said it is very questionable, that other things have happened there before. Brooke was unable to respond, she couldn't change anything. She missed the turn. She said this wasn't the first time, other things have happened there before. Everything felt very quick."

The tightness in my chest from my constant anxiety started to relax.

"Brooke was confused at first when she wasn't able to respond to you; she references the impact and stresses it was a severe accident and other things have happened there before. The

*location is deemed unsafe. The accountability is with the loca-
tion or place. You rented the equipment; it wasn't yours?"*

"Correct."

*"There were no warnings to alert the danger from the turn or
cliff—no signs, no guardrail. There is a lot going on behind the
scenes. This has happened there before; it is extremely sad. It
was supposed to be all about having fun and you wouldn't have
considered it a high-risk environment; there was a great sense
of happiness and joy before the accident. Was Brooke blinded
by the sun?"*

*"No, but we did later learn of a thirteen-year-old boy from
Chicago who had died in Costa Rica a few years before when
he drove his ATV off a cliff because he was blinded by the sun."*

*"Brooke didn't comprehend she was in any danger at all until
the second when there was no ground beneath her. Brooke is
showing me the guy at the back of the group and the shock from
his perspective. She refers to the older male behind her."*

"Yes, that would be George."

*"Sean, you escape through your work and try to keep your
mind occupied. Brooke says she is with you when you are
sleeping. She says something about other people's knowledge;
Brooke says people should be told. She says there is no
accountability and it has already gone back to the same old,
same old. She said this will happen again if they aren't held
accountable. They are not stepping up to accountability; you
have to push for this."*

I knew she was correct.

"Brooke is showing me a lot of hats; does she have a lot of hats?"

Initially we responded "no," but later we realized we overlooked the fact
that her school had just had hat day, where everyone donated a dollar to
raise money for a large tree planted in memory of Brooke.

"She loves music, and shows a piano by her. Brooke says she felt the others above her and there was a sense of falling through air, a sheer drop-off and a sense of an airborne feeling, but then she says she stepped out of her body right away."

Silently I thanked God. It gave me peace to know Brooke did not suffer.

"Brooke is showing me bears and the younger kids (Paige and LG) and she says she watches over them all the time."

That week in our family support group, Annie's Hope, Paige and Little George made stuffed bears in memory of Brooke.

"Brooke will always be part of the family. She was very excited that day. After the accident her mind went right to you, Sean, since you were not there. She says that you think things would have been different, Sean, if you had been there, but that is not true. Brooke keeps showing you (Sean) so busy, just trying to stay busy. Brooke senses too much pain between you two (Sean and me). Sean, you want to blame Brooke for being on the ATV, but it was just about freedom and fun for Brooke. There was no recklessness on her part and she shows all the arrows pointing to the tour company. Brooke shows a huge wedge between you and Jennifer. Sean, you keep beating yourself up for being the father, her protector and she says you feel like you should have been there to protect her. Your thoughts are different because you were not there. The feeling of the separation was very diffi-cult for Brooke, too. She can feel the hysteria and anxiety of everyone's pain. Sean, you are a very protective person and you have anger about her being on the trip and on the ATV."

It was surreal; I knew Brooke was speaking to us directly.

"When Brooke points to her dad she shows you feeling a lot of anger, but there is so much unknown since you weren't there, Sean. She says for you, Jenn, it was different because you bore witness to this and have a different kind of pain. 'What ifs' can eat you up inside. The arrow is pointing to the person who

owned the ATVs. More children have died there because of this and other things have happened because of their misuse and misconduct. It is all about profit. She says the place you were staying at recommended them; you did not plan ahead to use them. There is a feeling of being misled. Brooke says your anger should be channeled to the tour operator and she believes there is more with other children."

I was not surprised by this. I already expected as much and felt myself being pulled to pursue further investigations and possible criminal charges.

"You should know Brooke had a wonderful time on vacation. She is very calm about all of this." I could hear the smile in Laurie's voice and sense her admiration for Brooke coming through, as she said, "It is as if Brooke is the adult, and you two are the kids. You are both going through your own hell. Jenn, Brooke can feel your anger the minute it happens and how much pain you were in, and the nightmare you went through to get home. Sean, Brooke knows you are consumed by thoughts that if you had been there it may have been different. When Brooke shares the feelings she senses in her dad, she feels so torn up inside. Those people should have been responsible. Brooke puts a block of wood between the two of you (Sean and me). You need to channel the energy towards the people who were responsible for what took place. Brooke was totally oblivious that the turn was there, she had no idea. It was reckless that the people took you where they did."

I understood, and agreed completely.

Laurie said something about Brooke's heart and how Brooke was ecstatic that day. "Brooke says she did so much that day. She was at such a high and having so much fun; she says she saw this as a sense of freedom. Yet there is terror in everyone and she can feel it."

In a tender, loving voice, Laurie said, "Brooke is a beautiful child. She has a big heart, but is also a rebel in her own way."

I could picture the smile on Laurie's face as she shared this.

"Brooke is full of laughter and on the trip enjoyed many laughs and had so much fun there. She is at peace and looks in on your lives. Brooke can be around you all anytime she wants. The depression and sadness affects those here, but not Brooke. For Brooke the accident was extremely quick and sudden—there was no way she could do anything about it. The people need to be held accountable. She said she looked to make sure there was nothing mechanical that caused the accident, but it was more about the location than anything. It really comes to fault with where she was and the fact that the location was very improper. It was a place of great tragedy, a set up waiting to happen."

Again, this confirmed what I had already suspected.

Laurie described Brooke as a high achiever, a bright light and very funny with a wealth of knowledge. She said, "Brooke has knowledge beyond her years. She is known for drawing people to her and has a heart of gold. She keeps showing that she hugs Sean and is by him outside. She shows herself sitting under a tree reading a book as he searches for answers outside. Brooke has a lot of Sean in her. She shows much love for her mom."

I wished we could go on forever. I felt close to Brooke and didn't want our session to end.

"Brooke is showing me balloons in the sky and a garden you made for her, does this make sense?"

"Yes, we let fifty balloons go with notes to Brooke on her birthday. I did create a garden area in the yard with an angel and a tree given as a gift in her memory."

"Jenn, Brooke shows you taking charge and doing things. Sean, she shows herself holding your hand like she is a mother to you. Jenn, she is your best friend and you have an amazing love together. She shows Sean feeling so much anger and pain."

I asked, "What does Brooke do in Heaven?"

"She loves to listen to music, she spends time drawing and writing. She has always shone academically and made you very proud, hasn't she?"

"Yes. Brooke was always a Straight-A student."

"Brooke talks of the dog with the long hair. She says the dog can see her and knows when she is there. Brooke is often with you. When you feel her presence you can be certain, it is because she is there."

Laurie continued: "Sean, you keep searching for answers and, Jenn, you are online looking at laws. Sean, you want confirmation that you belong here. Brooke makes it clear you have a purpose on earth. It is odd; Brooke feels like the parent here."

Everything Laurie was saying was true.

"Brooke soaked up every day like a sponge and was so happy with life. She refers to the divorce and understands you outgrew one another, but she emphasizes that you are all still family and must not punish one another."

"Sean, you do your deep thinking at night. And, Jenn, you do yours during the day when you are alone. It is important for you to know Brooke is with you and she hears you. You both get your signs from her."

It gave me peace to think she was there beside me when I would wander into her room in the afternoons and hug her things to me as I prayed for the strength to survive.

"Sean, when you go outside and sit in the woods, Brooke is with you. She shows herself there jumping from rock to rock and she says she answers you."

Sean often wandered out to the woods, even in the middle of the night, to feel closer to Brooke.

Laurie advised us how Brooke would communicate with us and that, when we saw pictures popping up in our minds, a lot of time that is her coming through. She explained the various forms of communication and how you cannot expect them to be as obvious as loved ones on the other side just talking to you.

> *"Brooke keeps talking about her writing and says she left many precious gifts for you."*

> *"Sean, she has more of a mother's or sister's relationship with you than a daughter's, and when she shows you in the forest, it is definitely like you are the child."*

Then Laurie mentioned she knew I gave Sean the book by Allison DuBois, and shared that the more we understood, the better. She explained how grief can be a block and often we are more open to spirit communication in the dream state. She explained it was important that when we had a dream to share it with everyone as there could be messages for others. She spoke of George's great sadness and how he was affected, and how Sean felt like an outsider because he was not there. She stressed to Sean it didn't matter that he wasn't there, what mattered is he gave her life.

Laurie said Brooke was showing her lots of photos and there was something with a black and white photo. (That day I had just put a black and white photo of her on my desk and had been staring at it intensely for the longest time. A few days later, a black and white photo of her showed up in a random folder that did not have family pictures. I noticed, and opened it. It wasn't a photo, but a quick video that Brooke had taken of herself, in which she smiled at me, real big, and raised her eyebrows and gave me this unbelievable look.)

Laurie told us something would happen with a bird. (My friend Robyn came into my life soon after and has become so important to me.) She spoke of the emptiness Sean felt inside and how lost he was and she explained that there was no emotion as painful as what we were going through. She told us we were both like Brooke's children, that Brooke was the one that is so wise.

She explained that Brooke wanted Laurie to see the width of a tree and writing on the tree. (A few days before, my sister had a dream—the vivid type—that involved Brooke showing her a trunk of a tree with carvings in it. In the dream, Meghan told her how much she missed her and Brooke asked why and told her not to.)

Laurie explained that Brooke had found wholeness, a sense of peace there in Heaven. She said she kept showing her a symbol, something Japanese or Asian, that she explained like the pi sign. She referenced how learning was something Brooke embraced and how she was well behaved and paid attention in school. She said she was a pleasure for teachers and her friends were all good kids.

> *Laurie then asked, "Sean, do you carry something around in your hands, something small and dark, maybe a cell phone?"*
>
> *"Yes, I carry Brooke's cell phone with me."*
>
> *"There is a picture of Brooke smiling on it that you stare at intently and Brooke wants you to know she stares back at you through it."*
>
> *"Yes, the main screen is a picture of Brooke smiling that I often stare at."*
>
> *"Brooke shows herself listening to her iPod, which is light pink."*
>
> *Sean said, "No, her iPod is silver."*
>
> *"No, she is showing me a light pink, rectangular thing she listens to her music on. It is a light pale pink, not a hot pink." (In the back of my mind, something made me think she was right. We moved on from there, but, as soon as the call ended, I opened the drawer to the nightstand next to Brooke's bed and, sure enough, there was the light pink iPod case that I forgot I had bought her quite awhile ago.)*
>
> *"Jenn, you feel her around you all the time, and Sean, you have a different feel; you focus with intensity and are struggling to believe it is real. Brooke is on a path; she is with you. Sean is processing it in a bit of a different way. No matter what, know that you are her love and her connection—she will always be connected to you. She wants you to live a life of joy. You need to*

work on your relationship with her and become open to doing the things that help you get signs and have faith that she is with you always. Meditation can help you connect. You must understand that love is all-continuing; we do not die."

I asked, "Who is Brooke with in Heaven?"

"She is with her family. There is an 'M' name, a Marian (my dad's mom, who passed when Brooke was three or four, was named Marian) and then there is a male with a "J" name, a John."

My Grandma, Marian Albrecht (my dad's mom), passed away when Brooke was three. My friend Nicci's husband, John, had passed away less than a year before Brooke. Nicci had prayed constantly for John to take care of her. John's daughter, Maddi, was born only a few hours after Brooke, so there had always been a connection. When I told Nicci this, she sobbed, saying she knew they were together.

Laurie also said Brooke was with Lindsey. This one stumped me for some time. But as I put together a memory book for Blake as a baptism gift from Brooke, I could not decide how to word the dedication. I flipped open a few books on my desk to see how others had done it, and I am certain I found the Lindsey she mentioned. *We Are Their Heaven* is dedicated as follows:

> *"To those who live and those who live again,*
> *especially little Lindsey Whelchel*
> *who died young, but touched many."*

I researched Lindsey Whelchel and found that she had died in an automobile accident when she was about the same age as Brooke during their family vacation. Her parents established a foundation to help others dealing with grief.

Laurie then spoke of my dad's tattoo and knew it was in the shoulder area. She explained how our loved ones walk into our world all the time and how we need to find the door to go into theirs. She spoke of guided meditation tapes and how doing those would help. She explained that not all communication would be in words. She explained how it was different for Brooke, as she was around us all the time. She said Brooke is happy, but in a different way than we can understand. If we could relate to eternal life and knew how soon we would be together again, and if we understood we would be together forever, we also would be at peace. She told us that we were not alone and that Brooke is with us. Laurie advised us to be patient and open to new experiences.

Laurie said that, at first, Brooke was confused when she passed over, and didn't understand that, no matter how loud she shouted, we couldn't hear her. She spoke of Brooke's love for animals and again talked about her passion for drawing and artwork, as well as reading and writing, and said in Heaven this is what she did. She said Brooke was busy writing intensely and showing a lot of colors floating on paper.

Laurie also mentioned that we needed to watch to see handprints on something and to expect the unexpected, but to be careful what we wished for. She spoke of how she had had spirits rearrange her furniture at night! She explained that we had to be open and how open space was required for the spirit to come in. If you weren't open to it, then you could block their ability.

> *Sean said, "I have been asking Brooke for some direction and I was hoping she would give me a response today."*
>
> *"Yes, Brooke shows you in church contemplating this very thing. She keeps showing your feet firmly on the earth, telling you that you belong here and have purpose; do not question your life. You are considering a move and changing either where you live or work. You are considering a big change in your life and that is okay. You are going through personal transformation and guidance that is very personal to you—Sean. You need to change your direction and walk away from your feeling of comfort. Things have changed in your life; expectations have changed and Brooke shows herself behind you pushing you forward and pushing you out a door, away from where you are. Brooke stresses that it is time for a change."*

There were a few other specific personal things that she shared that I will not elaborate on here, out of respect for Sean's privacy.

> *"Sean, you shouldn't look at the aftermath of what happened. You need to welcome life after death experiences and work to take comfort in other people who understand and can bring you comfort. Brooke stresses that you really need to just have time. Time to yourself is important. She keeps showing you alone, wanting you to know you need time on your own. Brooke also stresses it is important that the two of you (Sean and I) come together and love each other. You are still a family even though you are divorced. She said her family is what is most important to her. Jenn, Brooke knows you are trying to bring about 'good' in life and she wants you to know she hears you."*

> *I asked, "Laurie, how do you see Brooke?"*

> *"She is somewhere between twelve and thirteen, and while she has the enthusiasm of a young child, she has the wisdom of an adult somewhere between thirty and forty. Trust me, Brooke is fine. It is all about your acceptance and you must make every day count. You need to treat every day like it is your last and find your passions in life. It is important that you help other people and set goals for yourselves that are ten years out. You must understand that it is your energy that welcomes them, but know they are always with you and you can feel them differently from moment to moment."*

After three hours, Laurie told us how precious Brooke was and what an amazing child she is. The tone of her voice resembled love, and I could tell Brooke had really gotten to Laurie. I had no doubt we spent the last three hours communicating with our daughter.

When the session was over and Sean and I discussed the experience, we felt some disappointment at first. Although we knew that almost everything she said was completely accurate, we had both gone into the reading with expectations of what we wanted Brooke to say to let us know it was real. We had each picked a few things, and when they weren't mentioned, we were disheartened. As I gave more thought to this over time, I realized that what I was looking for was minor. I wanted her to tell me that she knew I had gone back to San Francisco and let go of some of her things over the Golden Gate Bridge, as a tribute to our love and the great fun we had experienced there together. I wanted her to know I stood in the very spot where she and I had once before stood hand in hand, staring out at the gentle beauty of the rolling mountains, in awe of how they blended into the vast ocean below us. The memory, so important to me, held little significance in comparison to the things she needed to tell us. Besides, she probably experienced beauty far greater than this in Heaven.

I quickly came to understand that this was Brooke's time, and I believe she made this all happen. Brooke had very important messages to share with both Sean and me. She wanted us to quit being upset and angry with one another, and to remember that, no matter what, we would always be family. She wanted Sean to stop questioning his life and to spend some time alone to heal. She wanted me to fight for accountability and change as a result of the action and learn more about the past negligence. And, most importantly, she wanted us to know she had not left us, that she was always by our sides. Our souls would always be joined.

"Some things are true,
whether you believe them or not."
~ Nathaniel Messenger

July 28, 2009

Dear Jennifer,

Where does one start? I have thought so much about you over the past couple of weeks. Losing John brought a pain I could only have imagined. But losing a child must bring something completely indescribable.

There are so many things I want to tell you. Things I have felt and experienced over the past 10 months that I am so sorry someone I love and respect must also endure. Some of this may sound like babbling but I hope you'll bear with me.

First and foremost, when I heard about Brooke I immediately asked John to help her as I know he will. Although with as crazy as John was, Brooke was probably thinking "stranger danger, stranger danger!" but seriously, I know he will make her laugh and show her the joy of Heaven.

I know that, no matter what anyone says, you will question why Brooke was on that ATV and why this had to happen. Don't waste your time or your energy with that one! There is no answer to that question that we can ever understand. As simple as it sounds, only God knows why.

When John died I asked myself so many times: Why didn't I keep running with him so I could have helped him? Why did I leave him alone? Why did this happen? I didn't stay with him because I wasn't supposed to. John was meant to go be with Jesus that day. I know that now and I truly feel John and God spared me from having to see him die. Jenn, please don't blame yourself. Let Brooke give you that grace. She wants that so very much.

So many of your friends will be there for you during this horrible time in your life. As time passes some of them may not come around as much. They are uncomfortable and don't know what to say. Forgive them. Those who you are closest to will always be there for you. We love you and would do anything to help you now and in the future.

What bothered me most after John died is that I didn't feel his presence. I would have thought that, with as close as we were, he would have come to me in some way. A dream, a sign, anything. But I noticed nothing. A few weeks later I decided to see a psychic. I had never done anything like that before and had no expectations. It was the best thing I could have done. She told me things that made me feel that, without a doubt, she was communicating with him.

She repeated phrases that only John would have used and even described the setting of where we were running that morning. She brought to my attention things that happened shortly after John died. Signs that John was sending me that I wasn't paying attention to. Look for the little things, Jennifer. She is there. I promise.

Something that really caught my attention was when Teresa, the kids' babysitter, spoke at Brooke's service. She talked about the flower Brooke gave her several years ago. It had bloomed every year but this one. She thought that maybe that was Brooke's way of preparing her. I believe that. John wrote me a letter for our 19th anniversary that was exactly one month before he died. In the letter he told me how much he loved me and that he would give me everything. He said, "I cherish every second that God gives me with you on this earth." I think maybe we know subconsciously when we are about to leave this earth and we want to help our loved ones.

I think I told you the other thing that really shook me was the picture in Brooke's video of her wearing a shirt that says Live Your Life. That was a message to you and Sean, Jennifer. She so very much wants you to live your lives and not let your sorrow pull you under. The happiness she is experiencing with Jesus is unlike anything we can imagine. Her only sadness is knowing what her loved ones are going through on Earth.

I read something recently that I try to remember every day. It said, "Happiness is a choice." As we struggle with situations we find ourselves in we can be depressed and anguished or we can choose to be happy. As a tribute to all John gave me I am going to do that for him. I will be happy. The deep sadness I feel from his loss will never go away but I have promised him I will choose happiness. I hope you can get to that point as well.

Lastly, I recorded two songs for you that I hope help in some way. The first one is by Leona Lewis. "Footprints in the Sand" was John's favorite prayer/poem, but it is so impactful. The other is "Prayer" by Celine Dion. I've had this on my iPod forever but never really noticed it until I heard about Brooke. When I hear it now, I think of Brooke running around Heaven with other kids her age playing soccer and being so unbelievably happy and carefree.

Remember I am always here for you 24/7. I love you and hope you can have peace.

Love,

Nicci

~ *Chapter Twenty* ~

"Even the saddest things can become, once we have
made peace with them, a source of wisdom and strength
for the journey that still lies ahead."
~ Frederick Buechner

I still had no answers as to the exact cause of death, and though I am not sure why, I needed to know every detail about her injuries. I was searching for answers to my questions: Did she suffer and feel pain? Was she alive, listening to me scream for her when they would not let me near her?

I called the embassy time and time again, searching for information, anything they could give me. They really were not very responsive; they explained to me that things just moved slowly in Costa Rica. I pushed for the police report and updates on the status of criminal charges against the tour guide, but I got the same standard answer that things there didn't happen the way they did in the United States. They never gave me much beyond that understatement.

I finally started making my way through the tons of cards and letters that arrived daily. In addition, someone told me about the online guestbook for the obituary, and pulled it up on the computer for me to see. The posts were touching and appreciated. I noticed several from one family, who mentioned witnessing the accident. They had posted over and over, giving me their contact information in case I wanted to call them. I was surprised to realize that they were the family from Florida who had been walking up the road at the time of the accident. They own a condo at the top of the hill.

It took me a few weeks to call. I knew I needed to know what they saw, but I didn't really want to know. The embassy could tell me nothing, so reluctantly, I called. I spoke with each of them who had been there that day—Larry, his wife Grace, and their fourteen-year-old daughter, Samantha. Larry told me how much he had been hoping I would call. He was so understanding and sympathetic. Clearly, this had affected him and his family; they were extremely upset about it. He told me that this tragedy would be with them the rest of their lives.

Larry explained he was a police officer in Florida, only a few hours south of my corporate office. At the time of the accident, they were walking up the road from Flamingo Beach to their condo at the top of the hill. Samantha had been walking backwards, looking at her mom. They had just passed the turn, the point where Brooke would drive off. Even walking near it raises fear, and Samantha asked her mom what she would do if Samantha fell off. Grace joked that it would sure be a shame because she had such a hard time when she gave birth to Samantha. As she was saying it, the ATVs started to come by. This wasn't unusual, although it always surprised them on the steep road. Only this time would be different; they witnessed Brooke miss the turn and drive directly off the cliff. They were devastated. Larry told Samantha to run up to the police station at the top of the road and get help.

Since Larry is a police officer, he knows CPR and has emergency medical training. He prayed he could help and took off to find his way down to Brooke. When he had almost reached her, he saw two construction workers walking away from Brooke. They had been working at a house nearby, on the point, and came running when they heard the accident and Emma's first piercing screams. Larry told them that he could help, that he knew CPR, and continued to rush to her. They stopped him and told him, no, that there was nothing he could do—they were certain. I kept asking him if he was sure, and why they said that. He explained to me that based on the extend of head trauma, her death was instantaneous.

Larry told me that they stayed in Flamingo for several days after the accident and that every day, he walked the beach and studied the cliff, wondering if there were any way she could have survived it. He told me that he felt certain, no matter what the circumstances, it would have been impossible.

We all spoke about Brooke; I told them more about her life and mine, as they told me more about theirs. Samantha actually reminds me a lot of Brooke. She also shares a unique relationship with God that just comes from within. It is a shame that the memory of what Samantha witnessed will haunt her forever, but from the moment it happened I knew for sure their souls were connected—united in the strangest of ways.

I asked lots of questions about whether Brooke tried to stop or turn, whether she screamed, and anything else they could share that would help me understand exactly what had happened. They explained that there had been a loud revving sound, as if possibly Brooke had mistakenly hit the gas instead of the brake. She showed no signs of trying to stop. Almost immediately, they heard a loud noise which most likely had been the impact of the ATV as it crashed below.

We discussed the road and how, unbelievably, this dangerous site has no rails to guard it, no signs indicating caution—nothing. Even more shockingly, the Flamingo Beach tourist police station is just a few hundred feet up the road, visible from the site of the accident. If it

is fairly common for ATV tours to drive up the road, why have the tourism police never stopped it? Why do they allow this, and why have no warning signs been put up to prevent this type of accident? Samantha explained how even driving their car up the road scares her. The tourism police obviously drive by there often and know the danger it represents. Why haven't the police stopped tour

companies from doing this? Why don't they focus on safety and protecting the lives of tourists—which is the reason the Tourist Police (Turística Policia) was established.

The Meholicks and I agreed to stay in touch, and we certainly have. They returned to Costa Rica over Thanksgiving and tended to the accident site. They planted flowers around it and placed the most beautiful arrangement there as well. Of course, they sent me pictures and went there daily during their trip to pray.

I met Samantha and Larry in January when I went to Florida on business. They drove up to meet me, and it was a touching experience. I was surprised by how much this torments Larry—he is a police officer

and often deals with tragedy. He said this is different since Brooke was a child; he often struggles with thoughts about what would have changed if he had jumped in front of the four-wheeler or pulled her off as

it drove by. I told him not to be so hard on himself; as much as we wish that were possible, there is no way he could have reacted that fast. Although we are barely more than strangers in the ordinary sense, our ties together are so deep we feel more like family.

Larry went back to Costa Rica the week following our visit and sent me more pictures. He faces his own nightmare in Costa Rica with its ensuing legal battles. While he emphasizes that their situation in no way compares to ours, I still consider it terrible, and indicative of the corruption in Costa Rica. After buying his dream condo, a place he hoped to retire to and an investment he would use as a vacation rental property until then, he has basically had it stolen right out from under his feet. After he paid 98% of the condo's value to the developer, the developer leveraged the title illegally and then went bankrupt. Larry's dream condo, practically paid for in full, now belongs to a bank.

Larry has offered me the use of their condo if I ever want to return to Costa Rica—as long as the legal issues resolve in a way that he still retains the right to occupy it. Right now I have mixed emotions; I am not sure if or when I will return. Flamingo Bay is a beautiful place. At this point, I do not know if I am capable of seeing it for the beauty. I typically seek out ways to feel close to Brooke and our many memories, but for now I consider it too dangerous to even think of.

"Character is not made in crisis–it is only exhibited."
~ Robert Freeman

Use your mobile tag reader
to see a video of
the Costa Rica Memorial Service.

~ Chapter Twenty One ~

"Only he who keeps his eye fixed on the far horizon
will find his right road."
~ Dag Hammarskjöld

The English-language newspaper in Costa Rica, *A.M. Costa Rica*, ran a story on Brooke's needless death, as well as a follow-up story about the foundation we started in her honor. As a result, Americans in Costa Rica reached out to us, offering their condolences and willingness to help in our time of need with an outpouring of love that astounds me to this day.

Don Hopkins, originally from Arizona, moved to Costa Rica in 1996 and is currently residing in Flamingo Beach with his wife, Babe. I received an email from Don telling me how touched he was by Brooke's story and how it had deeply affected him and his wife. He had visited the foundation website and was happy to see that Brooke was deeply rooted in her Christian faith. Sadly, they had lost their son unexpectedly just two years prior and could truly feel my pain—something only a bereaved parent can relate to. He committed to being our "prayer warrior" in Costa Rica.

Over the past two years, Don and Babe have done so much for our family. They, along with Pastor Brett Clifford, and other members from the Community Beach Church held a memorial service for Brooke on her birthday. After reading her favorite passages from the Bible, they laid fresh flowers next to a permanent concrete cross engraved with Brooke's name and birthday at the accident site. Afterwards, they sent me photos and a video of the remembrance which was beautiful to watch, but was also almost scary as they stood in that dangerous spot and I worried about them being so close to the edge. There are no words to describe how thoughtful it was of them to hold this ceremony, especially on Brooke's birthday.

Following the memorial service, three individuals from the Costa Rican Tourism Board, Instituto Costarricense de Turismo (ICT), approached them, stating they were simply writing a report and wanted to know if it was the site of the accident. The timing was curious; however, because an article I had written about the incident had just been published in *A.M. Costa Rica* a few days earlier. Don proceeded to speak with the officials about the need for installing a guardrail there so that other lives could be saved. Unfortunately (but not surprisingly), they remained unresponsive. Therefore, with the strength he's found through his own loss and knowing the emotional turmoil I was facing, Don Hopkins, with the help of his employee Wilbur, took it upon themselves to personally construct a wooden guardrail at the site. Without the resources to build one that would truly stop an ATV, the handcrafted barrier is more symbolic than anything, but the strength of the love behind it is obvious.

Although the Costa Rican government is oblivious and uncon-
cerned, U.S. citizens residing there continue to witness the country's
negligence and lack of accountability, and thankfully, they do care. *A.M.
Costa Rica* published a letter written by Craig Salmond, an American
citizen who currently lives in San Jose. Craig spoke adamantly of how
failure to accept responsibility is a national pastime in Costa Rica, and
Brooke's death exemplified this. He spoke of the reasonable expectation one would have for safety on a tour like this—that someone taking
a tour would expect to have the risks explained to them or at least sign
a waiver indicating such risks. In our case, we had no warning. No
written information was provided whatsoever and we certainly didn't
sign a waiver. Craig addressed the fact that there is zero-regulation in
Costa Rica with regards to safety and because tourists are not informed
of this, they are clueless to the real dangers they could be facing when
signing up for these tours.

Fed up with the system and intent on getting justice for Brooke,
Craig made an incredible offer—if our family wished to pursue legal
action against the tour operator, he would provide an attorney and
personally pay for it. I did not see this article and most likely would not
have, but apparently Craig and I connecting was part of the plan.

Rob Woodrow, a complete stranger from Perry, Missouri (less than
100 miles from my home) who now lives in Costa Rica, read the article
and forwarded it to me through the foundation website. I replied,
thanking him and letting him know that I planned to take Craig up
on his offer. Rob forwarded my email to *A.M. Costa Rica* who, with my
permission, published it and then put me in touch with Craig so that
we could begin our mission together.

Craig's help has been tremendous and, undoubtedly, more than I
could have ever imagined. He has lived in Costa Rica for three years
and during that time, has witnessed complete negligence on the part of
the country as it continues to fail in protecting tourists from dangerous situations such as ours. As we began taking action, it was clear
that we were headed for a battle and I cannot even fathom having gone
through this without Craig's assistance. I tried contacting the embassy

for follow-up and copies of the many pending documents regarding Brooke's case, but they did not respond to my requests. More than six weeks after the accident, I still had nothing. I began struggling with the fact that I was not able to get close to Brooke after the accident. The cause of death was important to me and I wanted the autopsy because I did not know if she had been alive initially and I did not understand the extent of her injuries. My anxiety level continued to increase as I was also forced to wait for the criminal investigation and police report. I could not reach the lead detective and he would not respond to any calls or emails. Each time we tried, we heard the same story—that he was supposedly "out of the office for another week or two." Even though it required him to travel to another part of the country, Craig took matters into his own hands and went to visit him in person. The embassy continued to remind me that, unlike the United States, Costa Rica moves very slowly in these cases.

When I did finally receive the autopsy and police report, they were written in Spanish. Obviously, I could not easily translate two lengthy, detailed reports so I turned to Craig who proceeded to have them officially translated for me. When the translated autopsy report arrived, I felt sick. I knew I had to read every detail so I waited until the kids were at school when I could be alone. From the very first page, I was shocked. I had received only the one autopsy report—the one for Brooke—but right there on the cover letter which was from the medical examiner to the embassy there was reference to four more autopsy reports for Americans. I read every page and studied the diagram of Brooke's body which indicated each injury she sustained. I began to imagine how each one may have happened. I struggled with how long the fall took—*what was she thinking on the way down?* I became consumed with whether she had felt pain and decided to seek out medical guidance.

I turned to the doctor who had cared for all three of my children from the very beginning. He helped me understand some of the terminology used in the report and provided me with his interpretation. He said it was evident that Brooke had fallen headfirst because her skull took the brunt of the impact. The instantaneous brain damage meant that she felt no pain, and that faster than within the blink of an eye, her physical body shut down. As awful as it was, I felt peace knowing her death was instant. As I moved through this stage of grief, I had an obsessive need to know every detail. I studied all the rules about the speed of falling, including Newton's Law of Gravity and Galileo's Law of Falling Bodies, in an attempt to determine how many feet she fell per second and the duration of the fall. According to the law of gravity, it takes one second to fall the first 32 feet and each second after that is accelerated an additional 32 feet. Since the official reports described the cliff as being between 200 and 300 feet, I estimated that Brooke's fall took roughly between three and a half to four seconds. It saddens me that I had to go to these lengths in order to find some sense of peace in knowing that my baby was not terrified for long.

It wasn't until mid-September that the police report finally arrived, but I was relieved because both Craig and I had feared that it could potentially disappear, as things are known to do in Costa Rica. The report contained the results of the investigation into the wrongful death of Brooke. It provided information on William Huyling Fonseca, the operator of the adventure tour company, and identified Glory Yomafra, S.A., as the formal owner of the ATVs. When I followed up with the embassy for information about when the government would pursue the criminal charges, they made it very clear they would not help me anymore and that I needed to retain a lawyer. They were then kind enough to send an email warning me how hard it is to find a good attorney in Costa Rica and explaining what to do in case I needed to file a complaint against any attorney I'd hired. Fortunately Craig assisted me in obtaining the information that for whatever reason I was not able to obtain from the Embassy. Craig actually had to travel to other parts of the country to obtain the information that I have been advised should have been made available to me all along.

Although there are regulations that require tour operators to be licensed and insured, based on what I am told, these regulations are rarely enforced. The tour operators by law are responsible for disclosing risks, providing a route map, and having a waiver signed. Our tour operator clearly did not comply with these regulations but to the best of my knowledge there have been no repercusions for his actions. Last I checked, Williams Tours was still in business in the same general area (Flamingo, Tamarindo, Brasilito, Playa Conchal) offering adventure tours ranging from fishing to ziplining, to ATVs.

The final outcome of the criminal investigation into Brooke's death was an order for dismissal, based on the conclusion that no crime was attributable. From the legal point of view, her death was accidental. The dismissal notes that there is liability for Brooke's death on the part of the company that we hired, but not to the criminal extent. Therefore, if we opted to pursue the case, it would need to be filed in civil claims court. I am uncertain if the tour company operator suffered any consequences whatsoever for operating his business without a proper license and being uninsured, although I have been told that seldom is anything done to enforce these regulations.

A civil suit is unlikely to result in the changes I had hoped for, so basically it is pointless to proceed. Creating awareness is most likely the best thing I can do to save lives now. Fortunately there have been some positive changes, such as our government's more serious warnings for the risks of travel to Costa Rica at www.state.gov. The U.S. government has an obligation to keep us informed of the dangers present in other countries so we can make educated decisions on where we travel.

Now that I am aware of the dangers, I have done a fair amount of digging. I have been shocked at the information I have been able to find. This information includes a list I was able to find that provides details of the non-natural deaths of U.S. Citizens Abroad.

DEATH OF U.S. CITIZENS ABROAD

U.S. Citizen Deaths From Non-Natural Causes:

Sec. 204(c) of P.L. 107-228, the Foreign Relations Authorization Act for Fiscal Year 2003, mandates that, to the maximum extent practicable, the Department of State collect and make available on the Department's Bureau of Consular Affairs Internet web site certain information with respect to each United States citizen who dies in a foreign country from a non-natural cause.

The information required is: (1) the date of death; (2) the locality where the death occurred; and (3) the cause of death, including, if the death resulted from an act of terrorism, a statement disclosing that fact. Whenever possible, a more specific cause of death is provided (e.g.,Drowning-Ocean, instead of Drowning. The information on the web site must be listed on a country-bycountry basis, and must cover deaths occurring since the date of enactment of the legislation on September 30, 2002, or occurring during the preceding three calendar years, whichever period is shorter. The information is updated every six months.

Important Note: The following table should not be considered a statistically complete account of U.S. citizen deaths in foreign countries during the reporting period. The table includes only those deaths reported to the Department of State and for which information available to the Department establishes the death was by a non-natural cause. Most American citizens who die abroad were resident abroad. In some instances, it does not occur to surviving family members to inform the nearest U.S. embassy or consulate of the death. The report may not include some deaths of U.S. military or U.S. government officials.

To accommodate privacy concerns the table omits identifying information. The table excludes countries where, during the reporting period, no deaths met the above criteria.

According to this site, the top three countries in terms of number of deaths are: Mexico, Iraq, and Costa Rica. The non-natural deaths in Iraq are 244, mostly terrorist- and war-related in a country 437,072 square kilometers in size with a population of 31,600,000. Costa Rica, 236 non-natural deaths in a country 51,100 square kilometers in size with a population of 4,500,000. These statistics make it obvious Costa Rica is a "paradise" with risk.

2001 – 2010 Costa Rica Non-Natural American Deaths

Date	City	Cause of Death
12/14/10	Jaco, Puntarenas, Costa Rica	Vehicle Accident - Other
12/11/10	San Jose, Costa Rica	Vehicle Accident - Other
12/5/10	San Carlos, Alajuela, Costa Rica	Drowning
10/21/10	Paquera, Puntarenas, Costa Rica	Suicide
10/21/10	Santa Cruz, Guanacaste, Costa Rica	Drug-Related
9/24/10	Osa, Puntarenas, Costa Rica	Other Accident
9/23/10	Jaco Beach, Puntarenas, Costa Rica	Homicide
9/23/10	Jaco, Puntarenas, Costa Rica	Homicide
9/15/10	San Jose, San Jose, Costa Rica	Drug-Related
9/12/10	Osa, Puntarenas, Costa Rica	Vehicle Accident - Auto
9/9/10	Puerto Viejo, Limon, Costa Rica	Homicide
9/1/10	San Vito de Coto Brus, Puntarenas, Costa Rica	Drowning
8/31/10	San Jose, Costa Rica	Suicide
8/14/10	San Jose, Costa Rica	Drug-Related
8/6/10	San Jose, Costa Rica	Vehicle Accident - Auto
7/10/10	Golfito, Puntarenas, Costa Rica	Suicide
5/26/10	San Carlos, Alajuela, Costa Rica	Suicide
5/13/10	Guanacaste, Costa Rica	Vehicle Accident - Auto
5/9/10	Costa Rica	Drug-Related
4/6/10	Quepos, Puntarenas, Costa Rica	Drowning
3/24/10	Puerto Viejo, Limon, Costa Rica	Drowning
3/13/10	Quepos, Puntarenas, Costa Rica	Other Accident
3/12/10	Sarapiqui, Heredia, Costa Rica	Vehicle Accident - Other
3/10/10	Quepos, Puntarenas, Costa Rica	Drug-Related
3/5/10	Puntarenas, Costa Rica	Homicide
2/26/10	Costa Rica	Suicide
2/25/10	Tibas, San Jose, Costa Rica	Suicide
2/18/10	Turrucares, Alajuela, Costa Rica	Vehicle Accident - Auto
2/16/10	Grecia, Alajuela, Costa Rica	Homicide
1/12/10	San Rafael, Heredia, Costa Rica	Suicide
1/11/10	Belen, Heredia, Costa Rica	Drug-Related
1/5/10	Quepos, Puntarenas, Costa Rica	Suicide
1/1/10	Santa Cruz, Guanacaste, Costa Rica	Homicide
12/26/09	Liberia, Guanacaste, Costa Rica	Vehicle Accident - Motorcycle
12/2/09	Osa, Puntarenas, Costa Rica	Drowning
11/12/09	Santa Cruz, Guanacaste, Costa Rica	Drowning
10/21/09	San Jose, Costa Rica	Homicide
10/21/09	San Jose, Costa Rica	Homicide
10/15/09	Cahuita, Limon, Costa Rica	Drowning
10/4/09	Parrita, Puntarenas, Costa Rica	Drowning
10/4/09	Parrita, Puntarenas, Costa Rica	Drowning
9/23/09	San Jose, Costa Rica	Other Accident
9/20/09	Liberia, Guanacaste, Costa Rica	Vehicle Accident - Motorcycle
9/6/09	San Jose, San Jose, Costa Rica	Drug-Related
8/26/09	San Ramon, Alajuela, Costa Rica	Suicide

2001 – 2010 Costa Rica Non-Natural American Deaths

Date	City	Cause of Death
8/25/09	Cartago, Cartago, Costa Rica	Vehicle Accident - Auto
8/13/09	Puntarenas, Puntarenas, Costa Rica	Suicide
8/7/09	Osa, Puntarenas, Costa Rica	Drowning
8/3/09	San Jose, Costa Rica	Vehicle Accident - Auto
7/13/09	**Cabo Vela Flamingo, Guanacaste, Costa Rica**	**Vehicle Accident - Other**
7/5/09	Santa Cruz, Guanacaste, Costa Rica	Drowning
5/27/09	Liberia, Guanacaste, Costa Rica	Vehicle Accident - Motorcycle
5/25/09	Puerto Viejo, Heredia, Costa Rica	Vehicle Accident - Motorcycle
5/16/09	Puntarenas, Costa Rica	Drowning
5/10/09	Cuajiniquil, Santa Cruz, Guanacaste, Costa Rica	Drowning
5/7/09	Quepos, Puntarenas, Costa Rica	Drowning
5/4/09	Montezuma, Cobano, Puntarenas, Costa Rica	Other Accident
5/2/09	San Jose, Costa Rica	Suicide
4/16/09	Quepos, Puntarenas, Costa Rica	Other Accident
3/24/09	Osa, Puntarenas, Costa Rica	Vehicle Accident - Auto
3/20/09	Puntarenas, Costa Rica	Vehicle Accident - Motorcycle
3/9/09	Puerto Viejo, Limon, Costa Rica	Drowning
2/26/09	San Jose, Costa Rica	Vehicle Accident - Auto
2/17/09	Parrita, Puntarenas, Puntarenas, Costa Rica	Homicide
2/10/09	San Jose, Costa Rica	Vehicle Accident - Motorcycle
1/31/09	San Jose, Costa Rica	Suicide
1/5/09	San Carlos, Alajuela, Costa Rica	Other Accident
12/24/08	Limon, Costa Rica	Drowning
9/24/08	Esparza, Puntarenas, Costa Rica	Homicide
9/17/08	Guanacaste, Costa Rica	Vehicle Accident - Motorcycle
9/6/08	San Jose, Costa Rica	Homicide
9/1/08	San Jose, Costa Rica	Homicide
8/27/08	Puntarenas, Costa Rica	Drowning
8/14/08	Guapiles, Limon, Costa Rica	Suicide
8/7/08	Escazu, San Jose, Costa Rica	Vehicle Accident - Auto
7/31/08	Aguirre, Puntarenas, Costa Rica	Drowning
7/21/08	Puerto Viejo, Limon, Costa Rica	Drowning
7/4/08	Osa Puntarenas, Costa Rica	Drowning
6/20/08	Puntarenas, Costa Rica	Suicide
6/12/08	Estero Beach, Limon, Costa Rica	Drowning - Beach
5/31/08	Jaco, Puntarenas, Costa Rica	Suicide
5/4/08	Arenal Lake, Tilaran, Guanacaste, Costa Rica	Drowning - Lake
3/1/08	Cocles, Talamanca, Limon, Costa Rica	Drowning - Beach
2/29/08	San Jose, Costa Rica	Suicide
2/13/08	Cocles Beach, Cahuita, Limon, Costa Rica	Drowning - Beach
2/11/08	Santa Cruz, Guanacaste, Costa Rica	Drug-Related
2/7/08	Cahuita Beach, Limon, Costa Rica	Drowning - Beach
2/5/08	San Jose, Costa Rica	Vehicle Accident - Motorcycle
2/2/08	Manuel Antonia Beach, Quepos, Puntarenas, Costa Rica	Drowning - Beach
1/12/08	Liberia, Guanacaste, Costa Rica	Suicide

2001 – 2010 Costa Rica Non-Natural American Deaths

Date	City	Cause of Death
1/11/08	Tamarindo Beach, Santa Cruz, Guanacaste, Costa Rica	Drowning - Beach
1/10/08	Heredia, Costa Rica	Vehicle Accident - Motorcycle
1/5/08	Quepos, Puntarenas, Costa Rica	Other Accident
10/28/07	San Jose, Costa Rica	Homicide
10/24/07	Cahuita, Limon, Costa Rica	Drowning
8/3/07	Huacas De Santa Cruz, Guanacaste, Costa Rica	Vehicle Accident - Auto
8/2/07	Tres Rios De Coronadp, Osa, Puntarenas, Costa Rica	Vehicle Accident - Auto
7/6/07	Baru Beach, Quepos, Aguirre	Drowning
6/18/07	Guanacaste, Costa Rica	Other Accident
6/7/07	Colorado River Mouth, Pococi, Limon, Costa Rica	Drowning - River
5/26/07	San Jose, Costa Rica	Vehicle Accident - Auto
3/24/07	Puntarenas, Costa Rica	Suicide
3/23/07	Cobano Puntarenas, Costa Rica	Suicide
3/15/07	Playa Grande, Guanacaste, Costa Rica	Drowning - Ocean
3/15/07	El Carmen De Guadalupe, San Jose, Costa Rica	Homicide
3/15/07	Playa Grande, Santa Cruz, Guanacaste, Costa Rica	Drowning - Ocean
2/27/07	Playas Del Coco, Guanacaste, Costa Rica	Other Accident
2/7/07	Punta Uva Beach, Talamanca, Limon, Costa Rica	Drowning - Ocean
1/28/07	San Jose, Costa Rica	Vehicle Accident - Auto
1/14/07	Bejuco Beach, Parrita, Puntarenas, Costa Rica	Drowning - Ocean
1/12/07	Montezuma Beach, Cobano, Puntarenas, Costa Rica	Drowning - Ocean
1/12/07	Montezuma Beach, Puntarenas, Costa Rica	Drowning - Ocean
1/9/07	San Jose, Costa Rica	Other Accident
11/3/06	San Jose, Costa Rica	Suicide
9/21/06	San Jose, Costa Rica	Homicide
9/10/06	Cartago, Costa Rica	Vehicle Accident - Auto
9/10/06	Cartago, Costa Rica	Vehicle Accident - Auto
7/21/06	San Jose, Costa Rica	Other Accident
7/15/06	Esterillos Oeste Beach, Puntarenas, Costa Rica	Drowning - Ocean
7/14/06	Poas, Alajuela, Costa Rica	Suicide
6/11/06	Puntarenas, Costa Rica	Drowning
6/11/06	Puntarenas, Costa Rica	Drowning
5/22/06	Parrita, Puntarenas, Costa Rica	Vehicle Accident - Auto
5/14/06	San Jose, Costa Rica	Homicide
4/30/06	San Jose, Costa Rica	Suicide
4/27/06	San Jose, Costa Rica	Other Accident
4/12/06	Puntarenas, Costa Rica	Suicide
4/7/06	Puntarenas, Costa Rica	Drug-Related
3/8/06	Hermosa Beach, Puntarenas, Costa Rica	Drowning - Ocean
2/22/06	Curridabat, San Jose, Costa Rica	Homicide

2001 – 2010 Costa Rica Non-Natural American Deaths

Date	City	Cause of Death
1/29/06	Esterillos Este Beach, Parrita, Puntarenas, Costa Rica	Drowning - Ocean
1/21/06	Barranca, Puntarenas, Costa Rica	Vehicle Accident - Auto
1/15/06	Oreamuno, Cartago, Costa Rica	Air Accident
1/15/06	Oreamuno, Cartago, Costa Rica	Air Accident
1/14/06	San Jose, Costa Rica	Homicide
11/17/05	San Jose, Costa Rica	Drug-Related
9/11/05	Panama Beach, Guanacaste, Costa Rica	Drowning
8/6/05	Tarcoles Road, Puntarenas, Costa Rica	Vehicle Accident - Auto
7/30/05	At Sea Near Guanacaste, Costa Rica	Maritime Accident
7/30/05	At Sea Near Guanacaste, Costa Rica	Maritime Accident
7/16/05	At Sea Near Cabo Velas, Santa Cruz, Guanacaste, Costa Rica	Air Accident
7/16/05	At Sea Near Cabo Velas, Santa Cruz, Guanacaste, Costa Rica	Air Accident
6/23/05	San Jose, Costa Rica	Homicide
6/22/05	San Jose, Costa Rica	Suicide
6/3/05	Limon, Costa Rica	Drowning
5/31/05	Near Puntarenas, Costa Rica	Air Accident
5/31/05	Near Puntarenas, Costa Rica	Air Accident
5/31/05	Near Puntarenas, Costa Rica	Air Accident
5/18/05	San Jose, Costa Rica	Suicide
5/4/05	Near Quepos, Puntarenas, Costa Rica	Maritime Accident
5/4/05	Near Quepos, Puntarenas, Costa Rica	Maritime Accident
5/1/05	Alajuela, Costa Rica	Homicide
4/15/05	San Miguel De Turrucares, Alajuela, Costa Rica	Homicide
4/1/05	Horquetas, Sarapiqui, Heredia, Costa Rica	Vehicle Accident - Auto
3/22/05	San Jose, Costa Rica	Homicide
3/10/05	Matina, Limon, Costa Rica	Homicide
3/9/05	Montezuma, Puntarenas, Costa Rica	Drug-Related
3/9/05	Manuel Antonio Beach, Quepos, Puntarenas, Costa Rica	Drowning
2/26/05	Chiquita Beach, Puerto Viejo, Limon, Costa Rica	Other Accident
2/11/05	San Jose, Costa Rica	Homicide
2/7/05	Bandera Beach, Parrita, Puntarenas, Costa Rica	Drowning - Beach
2/3/05	Barrigona Beach, Nicoya, Guanacaste, Costa Rica	Drowning - Beach
1/16/05	Escazu, San Jose, Costa Rica	Drowning
1/5/05	Quepos, Puntarenas, Costa Rica	Drug-Related
1/5/05	Matapalo Beach, Quepos, Puntarenas, Costa Rica	Drowning
12/28/04	Mirado Jaco Cliff, Puntarenas, Costa Rica	Vehicle Accident - Motorcycle
12/26/04	Puntarenas, Costa Rica	Air Accident
12/11/04	San Jose, Costa Rica	Other Accident
11/21/04	Reventazon River Bed, Siquirres Limon, Costa Rica	Drowning

2001 – 2010 Costa Rica Non-Natural American Deaths

Date	City	Cause of Death
11/21/04	Guiones Beach, Nicoya, Guanacaste, Costa Rica	Drowning
11/19/04	San Jose, Costa Rica	Drug-Related
11/10/04	Jaco Beach, Puntarenas, Costa Rica	Drowning
11/7/04	Cima Hospital, San Jose, Costa Rica	Other Accident
10/30/04	Cocles, Cahuita, Limon, Costa Rica	Other Accident
10/18/04	San Jose, Costa Rica	Homicide
9/15/04	El Coco Island, Puntarenas, Costa Rica	Drowning
8/25/04	On The Road From Zapote River And Samara Beach, Guanacuaste, Costa Rica	Vehicle Accident - Auto
8/14/04	Llorente De Tibas, San Jose, Costa Rica	Homicide
8/4/04	Puntarenas, Costa Rica	Drowning
7/12/04	Santa Cruz, Guanacuaste, Costa Rica	Other Accident
7/4/04	Mata Palo Cape, Puntarenas, Costa Rica	Maritime Accident
6/26/04	Puntarenas, Costa Rica	Homicide
6/14/04	Ciudad Neily Hospital, Puntarenas, Costa Rica	Vehicle Accident - Auto
6/5/04	Langosta Beach, Tamarindo Guanacaste, Costa Rica	Drowning
4/19/04	San Jose, Costa Rica	Other Accident
4/15/04	Escazu, San Jose, Costa Rica	Vehicle Accident - Pedestrian
3/27/04	Near Bijagual Waterfall, Turrubares, San Jose, Costa Rica	Other Accident
3/19/04	Bijagua, Alajuela, Costa Rica	Other Accident
3/17/04	Puntarenas, Costa Rica	Suicide
2/6/04	On The Road In La Garita, Alajuela, Costa Rica	Vehicle Accident - Auto
12/23/03	San Jose, Costa Rica	Suicide
12/17/03	Highway 150 Mtsw North From Melia Cariari Entrance, Belen, Heredia, Costa Rica	Vehicle Accident - Auto
12/8/03	Nicoya, Guanacaste, Costa Rica	Drug-Related
11/21/03	Potrero Beach, Santa Cruz, Guanacaste, Costa Rica	Drowning
11/17/03	Guapil Beach, Puntarenas, Costa Rica	Drowning
10/27/03	Playa Naranjo, Puntarenas, Costa Rica	Homicide
10/3/03	San Pedro De Montes De Oca, San Jose, Costa Rica	Drug-Related
9/10/03	Near Murcielago Island, Guanacaste, Costa Rica	Drowning
8/25/03	Calle Blancos, San Jose, Costa Rica	Homicide
8/16/03	Cacao Villas, Limon, Costa Rica	Vehicle Accident - Auto
7/25/03	Hotel Presidente, San Jose, Costa Rica	Other Accident
7/10/03	San Vito De Corredores, Puntarenas, Costa Rica	Air Accident
7/10/03	Coto Brus, Puntarenas, Costa Rica	Air Accident
7/8/03	Puntarenas, Costa Rica	Suicide
7/1/03	Escazu, San Jose, Costa Rica	Other Accident
6/24/03	San Jose, Costa Rica	Suicide
6/9/03	Puntarenas, Costa Rica	Suicide
5/31/03	Dominical, Puntarenas, Costa Rica	Vehicle Accident - Auto

2001 –2010 Costa Rica Non-Natural American Deaths

Date	City	Cause of Death
5/16/03	Coco Island, Costa Rica	Other Accident
4/12/03	Esterillos Beach, Puntarenas, Costa Rica	Drowning
3/22/03	Lomas De Ayarco, San Jose, Costa Rica	Other Accident
3/19/03	Highway To Nicoya, Costa Rica	Vehicle Accident - Auto
2/28/03	Piedra La Chancha, Puntarenas, Costa Rica	Drowning
2/10/03	San Jose, Costa Rica	Vehicle Accident - Pedestrian
1/23/03	San Jose, Costa Rica	Homicide
1/19/03	Puntarenas, Costa Rica	Drug-Related
1/15/03	Atenas, Alajuela, Costa Rica	Vehicle Accident - Motorcycle
1/4/03	San Pedro, San Jose, Costa Rica	Homicide
12/27/02	San Jose, Costa Rica	Vehicle Accident - Auto
12/7/02	Alajuela, Costa Rica	Suicide
11/16/02	San Jose, Costa Rica	Suicide
10/7/02	San Jose, Costa Rica	Suicide

My research into the dangers in Costa Rica helped me uncover many horrors, like stories of Americans who went missing more than five years ago and have never been found, their families offered little or no assistance from the Costa Rican Government or the U.S. Government. I have also discovered unimaginable statistics about human trafficking, a crime that is, sadly, quite common in Costa Rica.

A Sister's Grief Over The Loss Of Her Twin At Sea

By Lisa Herrington
Twin sister of Laura McCloud Vockery, presumed lost at sea

I am the identical twin of an American citizen lost July 29, 2005, in your paradise. I am greatly saddened by the communication and cooperation and lack thereof with Costa Rican officials. My main concern, as I am sending you this, is that many American tourists that are persuaded to come to your country, are in awe of the paradise aspect, but are not in the least thoroughly educated with the death trap and the illegal activity that is quite apparent there.

For instance, a charter boat called King Fisher I takes my sister out to the Pacific sea and it is not even authorized to be three miles off shore. (Three Costa Rican locals were on this boat along with my sister's husband Mark). She never returns to her

Laura McCloud Vockery (L), and Lisa, her twin, the writer of this report (R).

family in the U.S. I, as an American and a U.S. citizen, have great value for life, for this is not the case everywhere, I have learned.

Is this a safe and frequent measure taken by the locals there? to take a vessel out on this sea illegally? I will not come to your country unless it is to make positive identification of my sister, who is my identical twin, and lost in the "paradise" there, just enjoying Costa Rica, and paying money to support your country.

I am frightened of what I hear goes on there by others that have made it back safely and alive and by what I read in your paper on a daily basis, just to have a clue if my sister is still there. I wish your country luck and success, but I do not respect it, for it has taken part of me, my twin, who lives in me forever.

"We will never forget them, nor the last time we saw them... as they prepared for their long journey and waved good-bye and slipped the surly bonds of Earth to touch the face of God.
~ Ronald Reagan

~ Chapter Twenty Two ~

"Believers, look up – take courage.
The angels are nearer than you think."
~ Billy Graham

Other than the kids, only one thing kept me from slipping into the deepest of depressions—Brooke continued to send me reassurances that she was okay. Some of these messages completely shocked me. I had not expected communication like this with our loved ones in Heaven or the joy it would bring me. She made it clear to me that her soul had gone on, but she was with me constantly. Some of these messages are so boldly obvious that I am surprised by them. But I believe the good Lord knew I had to have them to survive. I won't be able to share all of the stories because there are too many, but I will share some of the significant ones.

One of the first things happened just a few days after Brooke's death. I was on the phone one morning, and my TV turned itself on. Stunned, I kept saying over and over again, "My TV just turned itself on." I was so shocked. The next night, while Brooke's Uncle Jeff and Sean worked on the photo video for the service, Jeff's TV did the same thing. Our smoke detectors at home all started beeping from low battery. We tested the batteries, but they were fine.

We held a small service at the house for my family on Saturday and Pastor Curt helped us pray. As we prayed, the smoke detector in Brooke's room started beeping. Paige ran up and entered the room, shutting the door behind her as if she wanted to be alone with her sister. The alarms didn't stop; they were beeping constantly and fresh batteries didn't help. For days we had a counter full of smoke detectors that had all been removed because, no matter what we did, they beeped continually. Sean came by one morning and l could tell by the look on his face that he was perplexed. Completely bewildered, he asked why all the alarms were down—I told him. He proceeded to tell me that the alarms at his house were doing the same thing.

Sean showed me Brooke's phone, and the day before she passed, Brooke received a text that read, "Hey It's Me JESUS... if you deny me on Earth, I will deny you in Heaven." It was forwarded to her from Gina, but I had never seen it before. I wasn't surprised by it at all.

I gave Becky (Lauren's mom) the book *We Are Their Heaven* and asked her to let me know if she thought it would help Lauren. Becky called and told me that it appeared Brooke wanted Lauren to read it, because, in the bag with the book, somehow, completely inexplicably, was Brooke's library card, making it clear to Becky what Brooke wanted.

At the end of August, Blake was outside with his friends Johnny and Michael, jumping on the trampoline. They all came running in to tell us that, while Blake's phone was locked in his pocket, the voice command prompt asked, "Did you say call Brooke?" A few days before that, George and I had been sleeping when the alarm clock went off right at midnight. It was George's alarm clock, which we never used or set. The process for setting the alarm was complicated and not something that could have just gotten bumped.

About a month later, when George and I were getting ready to go out, both the TV and the DVD player in our room came on. Both remotes were across the room. Four days later, the alarm went off again, this time when I was having a really rough night and in the process of crying my eyes out. This became a regular occurrence; George wasn't so sure how he felt about it.

We actually got in a dispute one night when he spoke about unplugging the clock. I was upset because I felt the clock was one of the main ways Brooke connected with me, but he was not as comfortable with the signs as I was. Typically, the signs occurred in twos, just to make sure we had no doubts. For example, the dishwasher that had never before beeped started beeping, while at the same time, a smoke detector would go off. I am not sure Brooke intended the signs or if they resulted from the possible energy her spirit emitted when she was present. Either way, none of these things had ever happened before and now they were not just happening to me, but to Sean, too.

One thing we had noticed is that our dog, Kingie started acting strange. There were a few occasions I would find her in Brooke's room standing and staring at a spot where there was nothing. She would turn her head side to side as she watched as if someone stood before her. I had been told by others that dogs could actually see spirits so I wondered if she was sensing Brooke. A week later, my mom and I were sitting on the stairs in the foyer talking. Kingie started walking circles in the foyer and behaving as if she was following someone. Mom and I couldn't believe what we were seeing and watched in shock. This went on for at least 5 minutes. She made the little whiny noise and then a bark like she makes when someone is teasing her. Finally she walked to the front door and stood there and stared out the door as if she was watching someone walk away.

In mid-November, I took my first long business trip to California— I had a lot of anxiety over it. On the trip one night, as I headed back to the hotel with Briana and Jeannette, friends from work, we got into a deep discussion on the Book of Revelations. I explained that I didn't really understand it. We stepped into the elevator at the hotel, continuing our conversation. We pressed the button for the fifth floor and the elevator door shut, but the elevator didn't move. We just sat there. We pressed the button again, then started pressing the Open Door button, but nothing happened.

We were the only ones on the elevator, so I joked with them that it was Brooke and we should just give it a minute. We waited and waited, then finally Bri pressed the Open Door button again. This time it worked. The doors opened onto the sixth floor, the top floor. We all looked at each in confusion. The light over the elevator door had the second floor light on, not the sixth. We had gone up six floors, but never felt the elevator move at all from the lobby. We never pressed six, and nobody waited for the elevator on that floor. We felt like we had entered *The Twilight Zone.*

Later that night, we all went to dinner at Summit House, a cozy English Inn with fantastic views overlooking Orange County. Soft, classical piano music played in the background. All of a sudden, I couldn't believe what I was hearing—the Beatles' *Let It Be* rang in my ears. I stopped the conversation and asked if they heard what I did. Immediately Briana recognized the song from Brooke's funeral, a song that stood out as different from the genre that played throughout the night. We all looked at each other and smiled.

In late November, I went to lunch with a friend whom I hadn't seen or spoken with in over two years. From the moment we met, there was a connection that we joked about as being soul mates, yet circumstances prevented us from ever exploring our true feelings for one another. Even though we didn't stay in contact, the connection still existed. Fortunately, he has been blessed with a good life and has been successful in many ways. He is a hard-working, thriving businessman, who does a good job balancing his career and personal life. Although he works extremely hard, he manages to have lots of fun and enjoy life. He has been most fortunate that he has not yet had to suffer the loss of a loved one. He told me years ago when we met that he had never been to church. My conclusion was that he never had a reason or opportunity to find God in his life. In short, he had very little faith. After Brooke's passing, I wondered if my pull towards him was different than I imagined and I played an even bigger role in his life—that I could help him understand life is eternal.

When we met for lunch, I shared my story and all I had been through with him. I told him about the undeniable signs I had been given and I asked him to trust me as a friend that they were real. I hoped my story would help increase his faith. I assured him, I knew for certain that life is eternal. He enjoyed hearing what I had to say and admitted to me at one point that the hair on his arms was standing up.

After we had spent several hours together just catching up, the fire alarm in the restaurant went off. He looked at me a little shocked as he asked, "Is that the fire alarm?" I just looked at him, smiled and said, "Welcome to my world." Although he is a friend I am not in touch with often, I believe he was affected that day and hopefully inspired to live life differently. I told him that through faith, we find the needed strength to survive life's adversities. Loss of loved ones is inevitable, and someday he will need to find the strength to survive it. I hoped my words encouraged him to see things differently than he had before.

I won't deny that at times, all of this has been quite overwhelming, but I am learning to be patient and trust in God as the events of my life play out as a perfectly choreographed production. I have come to accept the realization that each piece of the puzzle that represents my life was created, predetermined, to fit with the next. Even to me, some of the coincidences seemed so unbelievable that I find myself in awe. I once read a quote that I liked, both because of its simplicity and its intuitiveness: "Coincidence after coincidence is no longer a coincidence." I know this is certainly true in my life.

For years I have kept a journal, logging happy memories I shared with the kids and making sure that someday they would know how proud I was of them. I always envisioned that, when I was ill or after I passed, the kids would read my deepest thoughts and happy memories of them. I will never forget the day, a few months before our trip to Costa Rica, I came home to find Brooke sitting in my office, crying, reading my journal. I asked what she was doing reading my journal and she said, "Aww, Mommy, thank you for all the wonderful things you said about us. I love you so much." I look back now and think how happy I am that she had the opportunity to read it and know the depth of my love for her.

Based on the letters Brooke wrote and the things she did shortly before she passed, I have to believe that, deep down, her soul knew what was going to happen. Brooke had given me an 18-month calendar that ended in August, 2009. The calendar was made out of colored construction paper with a poem or a story written to correspond with each month. Out of the entire calendar, only one month was on black paper—July, 2009, the month of the tragedy.

Ironically, on that same calendar, she put her birthday on the wrong day. We laughed about it then, but today I think how odd it is that we didn't get to celebrate her thirteenth birthday with her on the real date, though we did, at least, get to celebrate it early. So it wasn't surprising that she marked it wrong on the calendar.

One morning in the beginning of September, my Aunt Nancy called. I had had a bad day the day before, so I was trying to get some sleep, and I didn't really want to talk to anyone. She kept calling again and again, so I called her back. She told me that the night before, when she was at work, she shared Brooke's story with a man she met. A short while later, the man called her over to him. He was with a woman from Chicago who explained that her good friend there had lost her thirteen-year-old son in a tragic ATV accident in Costa Rica a few years ago. He had driven his ATV off a cliff.

I researched the accident. I found the *A.M. Costa Rica* article that reported his death, just like Brooke's. The boy's name was Brian Avery. I contacted the family. They had been on a guided tour in an area of Costa Rica not far from where we had been. The sun was bright, making it hard to see. Brian rounded a turn. There was a large hole in the road and, instead of repairing it, someone had stuck a pole in it. The boy swerved to miss the pole and drove off the cliff.

The *A.M. Costa Rica* article said the cliff was only 60 feet high, and I know the child did require medical care; they tried to save him. The medical resources available in Costa Rica are extremely limited, especially outside San Jose. The medical abilities in the tourist areas are probably one tenth of what they are in the United States. The 911 emergency system in Costa Rica has limited resources; it is not unusual to have long delays or no response at all to urgent calls. After what I have been through, I recommend researching and understanding facts such as these prior to deciding to travel to foreign countries.

The Avery family had relatives who lived in Costa Rica and resources to help, so they did not experience the challenges we did trying to get home. It is, nonetheless, a terrible story. And I hope my efforts will prevent other children from sharing this same fate.

It seems as if I am constantly hearing stories preceded by the words, "You are not going to believe this…" Betsey, the mother of Brooke's good friend Morgan, shared with me that a friend of hers works in the crematory where Brooke's remains had been taken. She was the last person to be with Brooke's physical body and she reassured Betsey that, through the entire process, she prayed for our family. She wanted us to know that she was there with Brooke and cared for her through the end.

My sister had dinner with some friends she had not seen in almost ten years. At dinner, they asked about the blue bracelet she wore on her wrist. She explained that her niece had been killed in an ATV accident in Costa Rica and the bracelet was for the foundation established in her honor. One of her friends could not believe it. She had been on the EMS crew that transported Sean after his breakdown. She explained that she and her coworkers considered it the hardest call they had ever been on. They were so affected by it that they often spoke of that night and wondered how Sean was. However, due to confidentiality issues, they had not been able to check on his status.

Our subconscious mind seems to know what our future holds. I believe I knew something was going to happen to one of my children. I also feel certain Brooke knew her life would be short. Not only did she write these amazing letters to God, but she also mentioned death in many of the cards and letters she made me. She also drew herself as an angel in some of her earliest childhood drawings

A mother's love is so great and her connection to her children so strong, that she instantly feels it inside when her child dies, even before she really knows. I suppose you can conclude that a part of you dies with your child. However, as much as I felt the death of my child at that moment, I still feel the spiritual life of her soul; I feel her presence in my life each and every day. Our souls will never be parted.

"To the ones who can't be here
Words can't express
There is a burning in our souls
An eternal flame of love
Your time here was short
But your love ever reaching"

~ Nick Adams, Brooke's cousin

~ *Chapter Twenty Three* ~

"Peace—
it does not mean to be in a place where there is no noise,
trouble or hard work—
it means to be in the midst of those things
and still be calm in your heart."
~ Unknown

*S*uffering a traumatic loss such as this adds tremendous strain on a relationship. By mid-September, George and I were having trouble. I was heartbroken and I felt like it was inappropriate to laugh or do anything fun during this time of mourning. I did not want to be passionate or romantic; I felt dead inside. As much as I loved George, the pain held me back from being the fun, lively person he had fallen in love with. I wanted to be alone. For whatever reason, that was how I dealt with my grief, which made it extremely hard on George because he was used to being there for me and sharing a close relationship. He felt me slipping away, but had no idea how to stop it.

Our relationship took a turn for the worse over Labor Day weekend. George and I struggled to be happy and in a good mood at the same time. When one of us laughed, the other cried; we grieved differently and what made me feel better made him feel worse and vice versa. It seemed like we were constantly bringing each other down. Determined to pull through this, we left for San Francisco on September 13 for Bridget's wedding. We stayed for a week and visited many of my favorite areas. I hoped to find myself again, while at the same time searching for an inner peace in my favorite, most heavenly places. We first went to Carmel and stayed at the Tickle Pink Inn, a small, quaint hotel with the best views in the area. I spent a lot of time on the balcony, just staring out at the crashing waves and watching the grace of the seagulls as they flew by. We rented a convertible and drove down the coast to Big Sur and let the beauty surround us. I fought to feel alive again and save myself from drowning in the sea of grief that surrounded me.

On our first day, we went to the Target store in Monterey to get a memory card for the camera. I refused to use any memory cards we had for fear of recording over something of Brooke. The store clerk told me I had to check out in the video department. As she rang up my purchases, the cashier commented, "I like your necklace. You are the first person I have ever seen with the same necklace as me." I looked down and touched Brooke's cross necklace, the necklace that I was so thankful to have, and that I had worn every day since she passed. Originally, I was going to put the necklace with her, but my sister encouraged me to keep it—she knew I would need it more than Brooke. I looked at the clerk's necklace, which was identical. She told me how her necklace was special since her mother had given it to her. I looked at her as tears streamed down my face and told her mine was special, too, that it had been my daughter's and she had recently passed. She, too, started to cry and told me how happy she was to meet me. I thanked her and

told her that I knew it was a sign from Brooke, letting me know that she was with me on the trip. I took a picture of the clerk as a keepsake.

We stayed in the city for a few days and traced the many paths that I had gone on just a few months before with Lauren and Brooke. I stood on the Golden Gate Bridge in the very spot Brooke and I had once stood, and released a few of her personal belongings off the bridge in a tribute to her. Had it been up to me, I would have scattered Brooke's ashes at the same place, but Sean had every right to have his say in that and he did not agree. If he had ever gone to San Francisco with Brooke, I know he would have felt different, but I can appreciate that on some things, I had to compromise.

Bridget's beautiful wedding was held at the Legion of Honor, a museum that overlooks the bay and the bridge. Bridget had taken Brooke, Lauren, and me there, back in June. My mind drifted back to memories of that day, but then the beauty of my special friend, whom I have loved for thirty years, helped my heart beat and reminded me joyfully that I was alive.

It was such an honor to be seated next to the bride at the reception, and the day was exactly what I needed. I needed to feel the joy and love of the wedding, and to be reminded that I could feel such immense happiness again. We danced the night away. We all had a wonderful time together and it felt so incredibly good.

"Death is not the greatest loss in life.
The greatest loss is what dies inside us while we live."
~ Norman Cousins

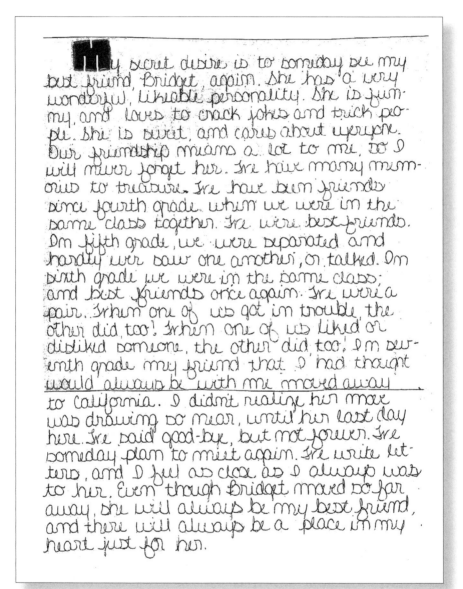

My secret desire is to someday see my best friend, Bridget, again. She has a very wonderful, likeable personality. She is funny, and loves to crack jokes and trick people. She is sweet, and cares about everyone. Our friendship means a lot to me, so I will never forget her. We have many memories to treasure. We have been friends since fourth grade when we were in the same class together. We were best friends. In fifth grade, we were separated and hardly ever saw one another, or talked. In sixth grade we were in the same class; and best friends once again. We were a pair. When one of us got in trouble, the other did, too! When one of us liked or disliked someone, the other did, too! In seventh grade my friend that I had thought would always be with me moved away to California. I didn't realize her move was drawing so near, until her last day here. We said good-bye, but not forever. We someday plan to meet again. We write letters, and I feel as close as I always was to her. Even though Bridget moved so far away, she will always be my best friend, and there will always be a place in my heart just for her.

~ Chapter Twenty Four ~

"Courage is the price that life extracts for granting peace."
~ Amelia Earhart

Life continued to go on, and I knew I needed to learn to figure out how to move forward in light of what I had been through. I went back to work shortly after the trip to San Francisco. I was ready and it forced me to get out of bed every day, which was a huge start.

I stayed busy with the kids and tried to do things that made me feel close to Brooke. I saw her friends often and loved to be with them. I spent a lot of time on photo albums and laminating everything Brooke ever made. We attended memorial services held at Brooke's school, planned fundraisers for the foundation, attended our support group for grief counseling (Annie's Hope), hosted youth events for the foundation, cleaned the highway for the Adopt A Highway program, and I started redecorating the house. My doctor finally broke it to me: I had entered the next stage of grief. I was doing everything I could to stay busy. As a result, I had very little time for my relationship and it continued to suffer.

Holding it all together certainly isn't easy when you are going through a difficult loss. Many marriages even end in divorce after a terrible loss like this. It is hard to love when your heart is shattered. Initially, I wasn't prepared for all the different things that could trigger my sadness. For me, the firsts of everything were the hardest. Simple little things, like the first time I went to the mall without Brooke, the first time I walked into her school, the first time I went back to San

Francisco, the first time I went to each of her favorite restaurants. When I first returned to these places that symbolized Brooke to me, the poignant memories would overwhelm me. Tears would streak down my face, but the liberation of overcoming it made me feel better in the end as I fought to regain control of my life.

My mom was right there with me. She, too, experienced the constant "punched in the gut" feeling when she went somewhere and the memories flooded her. I will never forget the first time I went to the mall. I dreaded it, since Brooke and I loved to shop together. I needed to shop for a dress for Bridget's wedding, so my mom and Brooke's close friends, Lauren and Morgan, all went with me. As we walked by the many stores that we had spent countless hours in shopping with Brooke, we found ourselves wandering in and picking up things that we knew she would like. It didn't seem real that she was gone. Over time, it has finally gotten easier, but I imagine I will always have those moments when something unexpectedly triggers a memory that makes me sad and reminds me how much I miss her.

The most emotional experience was our trip to Brooke's favorite restaurant. It must have been all the Mexican food I ate when I was pregnant, because, even though Brooke didn't eat anything but a plain cheese soft taco, she loved to go to Mexican restaurants with me. A few years ago, we started going to one close to the house called Matador. It was her favorite. She had gotten to know all the employees. They barely spoke any English, but they loved seeing crazy Brooke come through the door and they were all smiles.

It all started several years ago when Blake dared Brooke to say some silly things to the waiter about the stuffed chicken sitting on a counter nearby. Brooke never backed down from a dare and Blake knew it, so his dares could be quite ludicrous. As she looked at the chicken and pointed to him, she asked the waiter in a funny country voice, "Can I take that there chicken on that there roller coaster?" She then pointed to the ductwork in the ceiling. It was just the kids and me, and I was enjoying being silly with them. I laughed, too—it was so stupid it was hilarious, and I couldn't help thinking, as she said it over and over again, that the waiter must have thought she was absolutely crazy.

Blake sat by, laughing out of control, in the cute mischievous laugh that sounds just like his father and uncle. He and Brooke continued to pester our poor waiter about the chicken the entire time. By the end of the dinner, they had named the chicken Charlie.

Charlie became an obsession for Brooke, and we started visiting the restaurant more and more. We would barely be seated before the waiters would come over, laughing with us at the table and drawing pictures of Charlie on napkins. I am not sure if they ever completely understood what was going on, but they had fun nonetheless. I took Lauren with us once, and she and Brooke were just crazy. Lauren and Brooke wrote a song about Charlie and danced as they sang it to equally crazy Miss Spomer, the fifth grade teacher that Brooke just loved. Over time, each of Brooke's best friends went to Matador with us and Charlie became famous at school.

Completely out of my mind and loving it, I took the Fantastic Four, Blake and Paige all to Matador for dinner one Friday night, as their sole adult escort. The girls had rehearsed and were excited about performing as they went back in the kitchen to dance and sing "the Charlie Chicken song." That same night, the girls dared Brooke to eat a spoonful of the hot green sauce at the table. She did and Lauren videoed her as she

threw up in the bathroom after. Oh, the joy of children!

In 2008, Lauren and Brooke had a joint birthday party for their twelfth birthdays. Lauren's older sister Emily and Kristen's older sister Paige helped plan a scavenger hunt throughout the area we live in. It was an absolute blast as each team raced through the list of silly tasks, each of which had to be photographed or videoed with the team camera. It involved crazy things like asking the cute boy who worked at Hollister for his phone number, buying a goldfish at Petsmart, painting your face with makeup at Sephora, riding a two-by-four like a horse at Lowes, and, of course, taking a picture with Charlie the Chicken at Matador.

Now, we didn't eat there that day, but each group had to run into the restaurant and take a group photo with the chicken. Imagine how nuts everyone there thought we were with this chicken fetish. So it became Brooke's mission to get the restaurant to let her have Charlie. She begged them every time she went. Consistently, they would tell her they were going to get her one. But again,

with the language barrier, I am not sure what they really thought she was asking. We started frequenting the restaurant—thankfully, I love Mexican food. One week, we dined there four times.

Finally, after almost two years of trying, the owner gave Charlie to Brooke. Only Blake, Brooke, Paige and I were there that day, so she couldn't wait to tell the girls. The staff at the restaurant all signed Charlie's Corona bib for her and she walked out, still stunned from the victory. No doubt about it, my daughter was going to be as determined and persistent as her mother. Lauren came over that night to see Charlie and the next day Brooke took him to school.

On two occasions after the conquest, we took Charlie back with us to Matador to visit while we dined. The other customers in the restaurant had to be so confused when the staff hovered over us to say "hi" to the stuffed chicken. After Brooke passed away, I looked at Charlie proudly displayed in her room and I knew where he belonged. I gave him to Lauren, knowing it was what Brooke would want.

I think it was around October that Becky, Lauren's mom, shared her plans with me. Charlie would sit proudly on top of their family's Christmas tree. I loved it; it was so Brooke, it was so Lauren. Becky decided to really make it special. She helped us through the hardest holiday ever, our first Christmas without Brooke. She had a Charlie Chicken Christmas Party and invited all those who were closest to Brooke, the people who understood the crazy story behind the chicken. Our families all came together to lean on each other to get through this tough time.

The tree was not a kids' tree in the basement like you might imagine. This was their family tree, a huge tree in their great room, beautifully decorated, and Charlie sat proudly at the top. He wore a Christmas bib that Becky had made for him and he was glowing with special lights that she had shopped diligently to find. The menu consisted only of chicken: each family brought a chicken dish. The whole thing was so random, and completely Brooke. It was perfect.

With all those happy memories, going back to Matador, Brooke's favorite restaurant, was the hardest. Just Blake, Paige and I went. It took us months to work up the courage. We went in and everyone was instantly excited to see us. I knew I needed to tell them; Brooke wouldn't want them to think that she finally got Charlie and they didn't matter to her anymore. With the language barrier it was tough, but I gave the waiter a memorial card from the service. It had a picture of Brooke along with the dates of her birth and death. The waiter's eyes immediately filled with tears, and we all started crying. He left the table. Soon he and another employee were on the computer, pulling up the Brooke Scalise Foundation website. When we left there that day, I wasn't really quite sure what to say. Blake, being the strong young man that he has grown into, said to me that it comforted him when people cried, it showed that they cared. I couldn't have agreed with him more.

"We have come from somewhere and are going somewhere.
The great architect of the universe
never built a stairway that leads nowhere."
~ Robert A. Millikan

~ Chapter Twenty Five ~

"Everything you see happening
is the consequence of that which you are."
~ David R. Hawkins

We made it through Thanksgiving, barely. The holiday was hard on all of my family, and of course, on Sean's as well. Jeff sent out a mass email first thing in the morning, telling everyone how thankful he was for his time with Brooke. The holiday tradition at Grandma Seuss's house (Brooke had named her this when she was little because she couldn't say Mary Sue and liked Dr. Seuss) was to see how many pranks they could pull on one another, and how badly they could aggravate Grandpa Ron in the process. Brooke used to joke with Grandpa Ron and tell him he had COPD, Crabby Old People's Disease.

The email read:

> On this Thanksgiving morning, I can only think of one thing.
> This was the day that Brooke and I loved to play jokes on
> one another more than any other day. Most people do
> April Fool's Day, we did Thanksgiving. There was the one
> Thanksgiving that she sprayed about a whole bottle of
> Grandma's perfume in my car. I got her back by putting a
> dirty diaper under the car seat in the car. (That one back-
> fired because even though Sean had the car that day, it was
> Jenn's and she got very angry.) There were potatoes put in
> tail pipes and dog food put in your Thanksgiving meal plate,
> and on and on and on. I will never forget those days!!

I will however take today and do what we are supposed to do on this day and think about the things that I am THANKFUL for in life. Today, I will say that I am most thankful for the 13 years that I was able to have Brooke in my life. What a great ride!!!

Thanks and God Bless,
Jeff Scalise

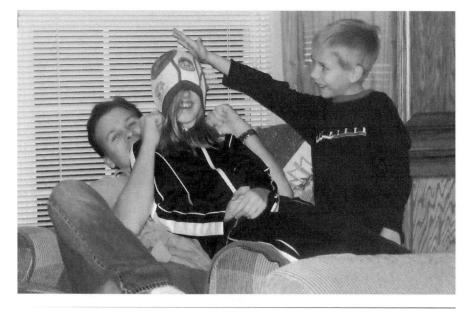

For my family, it was a pretty somber day. We were all quiet and found ourselves crying a lot. My sister, who was born on Thanksgiving Day, typically planned a huge birthday celebration for herself. She would count down to it for months. This year, for the first time ever, Meghan didn't want to celebrate. There was no party.

Fortunately, during these tough times, our signs from above continued. By now, it was common for various alarms to be making noises in the house. George's alarm clock went off all the time when I was lying in bed crying or we were in bed talking about Brooke. George was really starting to feel uncomfortable about it. His birthday was coming up, and he wanted a new alarm with a dock for his iPhone, so reluctantly, I bought it for him. It took a few days before he plugged it in, but the first time I walked into the room and saw the old alarm disconnected, I was so upset. It had become a consistent way for Brooke to communicate with me; it helped me feel close to her. But I knew nothing would keep us apart; she would still be near me always.

Around that time, my mom found information online about the St. Louis Bereaved Parents group that she thought looked helpful. They had a weekly meeting that my mom started attending and also held an annual Celebration of Life for the holidays in which all the children who had passed were recognized. Honestly, I didn't want to go; I felt a ton of anxiety over it. It was obvious this was important to my mom though, and she wanted Brooke to be a part of it. Mom and I grieved differently, and I knew this would help her so I agreed, despite my concerns about how I would handle it.

The event was held at Shaare Emeth Congregation. As soon as we walked in the door, I was overwhelmed with darkness as I took in the proud display of hundreds of local children who had died over the years. Most parents were much further into the grieving process than I was. So many of the pictures seemed dated, with hairstyles and clothing from years ago. I realized that someday Brooke's pictures, too, would appear this way, since there would never be another.

My mom noticed a child just standing there, staring at Brooke's picture. She was talking to it and wouldn't walk away because she was so drawn to it. Mom asked if I had a foundation bracelet with me. I did, so she gave it to the little girl.

We proceeded into the chapel for the Celebration of Life. In the room full of hundreds of people, the atmosphere was somber. The guest speaker was a mother whose teenage son had been killed in a car accident while driving with a friend who was under the influence.

As the service continued, they showed a picture of the child who had passed from each family attending. As the child's picture was displayed, the family lit their candles until, in the end, the room was completely aglow. Many families have made this their holiday tradition in remembrance of their loved one who had passed.

It was just too much for me to handle. I bawled, out of control, the entire time; my sobs resonated throughout the large room. I couldn't breathe. It took everything I had to not run from this nightmare. George and Mom both tried to comfort me, but there was no calming me at that point. I couldn't leave soon enough. As the service concluded I immediately scurried towards the exit.

As difficult as it was, I am so thankful we attended the service. It soon became obvious that being there was part of the plan, as the events of my life continued to unfold.

The following Saturday, we received another touching email sent to the Brooke Scalise Foundation website. The email read:

I accompanied a dear friend of mine to the candlelight vigil on Tuesday night where my seven-year-old daughter, Logan, took a keen interest in Brooke's photograph. She was given a Brooke Scalise Foundation bracelet that night and hasn't taken it off since. She wore it to school and was invited to tell her class about the bracelet and about Brooke. The children did not understand; however, Logan's teacher did and told Logan that it was beautiful that she was wearing Brooke's bracelet... especially since we didn't even know her. Logan, too, has a very deep relationship with God although I think she's been to church maybe twice in her entire life. Also from a divorced family, Logan is wise beyond her years and journals, as well, often writing about God (which floors me because I'm not sure where she's learned it from). We moved from St. Charles County two (2) years ago into Webster Groves so we know the area well — my ex lives there still so Logan visits there every week. I finally visited this website... it has taken me awhile because I've tried to distance myself a bit from this story somehow knowing that I would be deeply touched...and I was right. Logan has inquired about Brooke so much since Tuesday that I felt it only right to learn about who she IS (I say "is" because it is so clear that she's still here, reaching out to complete strangers and moving us in ways we could never have imagined) so that when Logan is asked again about her bracelet, she can share Brooke's truth and her smile and her love for God. Logan has the same Halloween costume, as well, which she proudly wore last Halloween (she decided to be "Very Bat Girl" this year... it was last year that she "sported" the "Wonderwoman/Superwoman" costume), and as I looked through the photos posted on this website, I found myself in a complete tearful mess. I cannot possibly understand this kind of pain and I pray to God that I never will, but I can, for a moment, put myself in "that place" — that gut-wrenching deep hole that I am lucky enough to be able to pull myself out of that I only wish Brooke's family could do, as well. There are no words. I am surprised that I'm even writing this e-mail.

I own C3 Magazine that launched at the end of June and hit the shelves early July, 2009. The magazine is about philanthropy, nonprofits, good deed doers, local/national heroes, etc. Had Brooke seen the magazine, she would've loved it. I did not expect such success right out of the gate and was not staffed appropriately to fulfill the requests from readers so after only 3 issues, I paused to prepare (and staff!) for our huge 2010 "relaunch" issue. I would very much like to discuss doing a feature story about Brooke — please understand that I have been bombarded with touching stories from all across the city since June (it's been unbelievable) and I've had to put on my "game face" just to work through some of the emotions that accompany these moving tales of triumph, loss, and challenge. Brooke's story, however, is one that needs to be told over and over again. I am deeply moved by her life story and it was my junior partner who looked into this website before I. After getting her "thumbs up" (and a very emotional rundown of Brooke's story), here I am, writing to you, requesting permission to run her story. What a great way to launch 2010 and I cannot think of a better way to forge ahead into the new year than bringing Brooke front and center to share her life story with over 45,000 readers... keeping her spirit alive and working towards a better good.

Thank you for putting together such a beautiful website and for sharing Brooke's story with us. This holiday is certain to be a precious one knowing that Brooke is by God's side sprinkling the glitter of His love upon our hearts, hand in hand.

> *Thank you again,*
> *Robyn Obermoeller*
> *Managing Member*
> *C3 Magazine*

Robyn and I met for lunch the following Tuesday and we both left the meeting speechless. Robyn later emailed me, telling me it was the most profound interaction she had experienced to date. She couldn't shake the unbelievable pull she felt towards the cause, Brooke, and everything that was circulating around the entire situation. Robyn emailed me photos of what her daughter Logan had proudly brought home from school that day. Logan is in first grade, and she had asked to skip her recess because she wanted to work on a special project, a Christmas ornament of Brooke and Logan holding hands. She rushed in excitedly after school to place it, the first ornament, on the Christmas tree. As Robyn looked at the ornament more closely, she noticed a few things that she found quite interesting on the—as Logan had written— Brooke Scalise Ornament.

Logan had been saying for days that Brooke was her Guardian Angel. So it made sense that the ornament illustrated Brooke as an angel with a halo over her head. Although Brooke had arms, she had no legs or feet, which Logan explained was because angels didn't need them. Drawn around Logan's neck was a cross necklace. Logan didn't own a cross necklace, and she had never drawn one on a picture before. The girls' hands were stapled together and Logan's wrist proudly displayed her blue Brooke Scalise Foundation bracelet.

The connection between us was unfathomable; clearly God had planned for us to meet. Strange coincidences overwhelmed us, ranging from Logan's soccer jersey—number six, a number she had insisted on having long before Brooke had even passed, to both Logan and Brooke wearing the same Halloween costume the year before, to Logan calling her Brookie without knowing that this was what we called her.

Both Robyn and her partner at the magazine, Kelli, instantly became like family to me. Together, we spent countless hours poring over Brooke's story. They were so involved that it seemed like they had both known Brooke her entire life. They have helped with everything imaginable—the foundation logo, the website, press kits, and videos. Honestly, both Robyn and Kelli have spent as much time on Brooke's causes as I have, which is unbelievable.

Robyn later shared another connection with me. A good friend of hers had been on the EMS crew called to help the father of one of Brooke's good friends. Brooke was close with this family, and over the years, she had spent a lot of time with them. The father, who has multiple sclerosis, had a setback with his health because he became so upset over the accident. This was the first I had heard of this, but I knew immediately who it was.

As Christmas grew closer and closer, I grew more and more depressed. I took the last two weeks of the year off, anticipating how difficult the holidays were going to be for me. Until December 21, I had not even started my Christmas shopping. Mom and I spent that entire day shopping, and surprisingly, I got most of it done. The incredibly emotional day was difficult for us both. It hurt when we walked past Brooke's favorite stores. We were out shopping like always, and I wished she could show us the things she loved so that I could sneak back later and buy them to surprise her, just like I used to do in the past.

Paige continued to stay in good spirits most of the holiday season thanks to a new holiday tradition. Paige had learned from a few friends that they had a real elf who went back to the North Pole every night to report to Santa if the kids they watched over were being naughty or nice. She was so intrigued by this that I immediately set out to find this Elf on the Shelf. She fell in love immediately and the magic of him going back to the North Pole each night seemed to relate to her vision of Brooke's journey to Heaven. She imagined Elfie (as she called him) and Brooke crossed paths in this magical place. Each day Elfie would move and Paige would find him hiding in another spot in the house. It was by far the highlight of the holiday season for all of us. Typically your elf leaves to return to the North Pole to work after Christmas, but Paige couldn't part with hers. Elfie stayed and played with Paige daily until Easter. We think Santa must have asked the Easter Bunny to run him out and send him to the North Pole to start working!

On December 22, I met with the Fantastic Four and had a private Christmas exchange with them, just as Brooke always had. I had worked for months to have professional photo books made for each of them from Brooke. I was really excited to give them their gifts, as each book was designed individually for Gina, Kristen and Lauren, with so many wonderful pictures representing all their most memorable times. The girls gave Paige a baby doll and me a musical snow globe with a silver tree inside. On it, a heart displayed the words, "We never lose the ones we love… they live on in our hearts." Engraved in the base of the globe were the words "Fantastic Four Forever." It was a perfect Christmas present.

I was sinking lower each day, and on December 23, I had one of my worst days ever. I didn't get out of bed, but sobbed, literally, all day. Eventually, I heard a strange noise and got up, looking around to see what it was. At first I thought it was Blake messing with me; the sound was like a heartbeat, getting louder and louder. Suddenly I realized it came from George's new alarm clock, which, of course, was not set. I felt such tremendous relief. It didn't matter which clock was beside me, Brooke would always find a way to reach me. I ran and got

Blake to have him listen. By the time he reached top of the steps, he could already hear it and asked what the heck that noise was. I smiled, laughed and told him what had happened.

Later that day, we gave Teresa her Christmas presents, which included a few items from Brooke—an engraved Merry Christmas from Heaven ornament and Brooke's cross necklace that Teresa had given her. We both let our emotions get the best of us and cried together in each other's arms, thinking there was no way this was real.

On Christmas Eve, Becky, Lauren, Mom, Teresa, George, LG, Blake, Paige and I all went to Calvary for the Christmas service. The service was so applicable to our lives, and I think attending it really helped us all. The play was about a couple on their honeymoon. The wife was upset because the holidays were a tough time for her, since she had lost her mother. It was a strong message about getting through holidays after loss and how important your relationship with God is to give you the strength to make it through.

We spent Christmas Eve with George's family, and I really struggled to hold myself together. My heart literally hurt; I felt consumed by anxiety and was having panic attacks. I didn't know how I was ever going to get through the night, or Christmas Day, or the next week, or the next year, or the rest of this lifetime.

On Christmas Day, my mom and Meg came over first thing in the morning, so we could all be together for breakfast, and Sean came to be with the kids and see them open their presents. It was such a difficult morning for all of us. Sean brought a stocking filled with all of Brooke's favorite treats, placing it and a soft, white, fuzzy Christmas bear next to her urn. By noon, everyone had left and they weren't scheduled to return until four, when all of my family would come over.

I took this time to mourn, spending hours lying in Brooke's bed. I held her baby blanket—her gee gee, as she called it—and her twin doll that was made to look like her. I sobbed and sobbed and sobbed, but I needed it. I tend to keep things bottled up inside, so I needed to let the poisonous grief out of me.

My family came at four and we all spent time talking about Brooke, sharing stories to feel close to her. We all just tried to get through the day. It ended up being one of the hardest days ever on my relationship with George. He didn't seem to completely understand what Christmas was like for me. I spent most of my emotional energy dealing with the emptiness I felt on Christmas without Brooke; what little I had left, I needed to give to Blake and Paige. Christmas really took a toll on our relationship.

I began to dread New Year's. The year before, we had a big party. Brooke and Lauren invited several of their friends and George and I invited several of ours. It was a blast. The girls made playlists of fun dance music, and we hung a disco ball in the center of the great room. We even added strobe lights and a fog machine. I have to say that it was the most fun New Year's I have ever had. We stayed up into the wee hours of the morning, dancing, and singing karaoke all night long. A ton of people spent the night, both kids and adults.

I knew being at home this year would make me too sad, but I wasn't ready to travel too far on a holiday yet. We planned to go to a New Year's Ball at the Hilton with my Aunt Lori and her husband Randal, as well as Meg and JD, and several of their friends.

On December 30, I received a huge floral display from Kelly, duplicating the arrangement Don and Babe Hopkins had put at the cross in Costa Rica. The flowers stood three feet tall and the note on it read, "Since you can't be there to see these in person, I decided to bring the flowers to you." I felt peace; this was exactly what I needed to give me some comfort.

On New Year's Eve, we headed to the hotel early to check in to our room and meet up with Lori and Randal. I felt sad and was doing all I could to snap out of it. I am not sure if I drank more than usual to numb the pain or if it was the Long Island Iced Teas I was drinking, but I was definitely under the influence. George felt upset with me because I was so distant. I hurt his feelings early in the night when I didn't want to dance, but by midnight, we were dancing and doing our best to have fun. Robyn helped me the most. She texted me all night, sharing with me the things she was working on, like the logo and video. Her progress motivated me and gave me the will to smile.

The countdown concluded; everyone hugged and kissed as they screamed "HAPPY NEW YEAR!" George and I broke down in sobs, hugging and crying harder than anyone could imagine. Lori and Meghan did the same. The realization that I was heading into 2010, the first year without Brooke here with me physically, absolutely tore me apart with anguish. I called Paige and Blake to wish them a Happy New Year and that helped me keep things in perspective. Despite my loss and heartache, I still had so much to be thankful for, including the most amazing love for my children. Although my heart was broken, it still swelled with love.

On New Year's Day, I received another unbelievably touching email, this one from a gentleman named Bob Harbert in Costa Rica. I had never before met or heard of him. Only divine intervention can explain it.

The email read as follows:

Dear Jennifer,

My wife Vickie and I moved to Flamingo late August, 2008 into a condo we bought 5 years earlier. I will not forget last July 14th at the Monkey Bar, when Ulrick was grief stricken as he told us the news. I have never been very religious, but I do believe in God. That same day, a long-time Flamingo resident friend, Jo, invited us to the Community Beach Church where we met Don Hopkins and Pastor Brett. We have been drawn to church after 40+ years for unknown reasons... until now, I strongly believe. I had been invited by 2 men to walk with them every morning. Our walk took us way up a hill past Flamingo Beach Hotel. I always lagged behind and for some strange reason I always stopped at a 90 degree turn to see that awesome view with disbelief there was no safety wall there. For months after the accident, I only imagined that may be the spot of the tragedy. I did not know until several weeks ago on our first daily walk since we've been back to Costa Rica. There was Brooke's cement cross. I stepped over the very short and low "guard rail" to place my hands on her cross and pray for her and your family. I have been back to her cross most every day praying for you all. Today I Googled Brooke and found her website reading most every single word. The smoke alarms and phone ringing were very certainly Brooke. I can walk anywhere in many directions, on the beaches, the roads, paths... but something or someone brought me to that curve. Someone kept stopping me there for a breather, after the tragedy and before the cross appeared. Someone brought us to Don, Brett and the church. We got very involved this month helping schools, many young kids here and in helping to spread the word of God to children. Again, we are not that religious, and have never been involved with the church or their special events. One Sunday this past November at church they had sign-up sheets to donate supplies, our time and maintenance help for schools here. I donated gallons of leftover condo paint wondering how I would ever be able to "make good use of it." I couldn't wait to volunteer. I was the very first name signed on 4 days of events. Ask Brett whose name is first! Someone brought us Jo, who brought us to church. The feelings I got from seeing Brooke's cross the very first time were quite sad, inspiring, heart-felt, emotional, traumatic, loving, grief-stricken, mournful, yet empowering. Many emotions. I knew I needed to search for Brooke's name to put a face to my prayers so when I go visit her cross each day I can be closer to her and your family. I touched Brooke's cross to pray that one day, then realized I really needed to find her family to ask permission to do this, so I have not done that since. I just stand staring at her cross and praying aloud. I will continue to visit Brooke and pray every day I can while we are here through next April. I truly believe Brooke brought my wife and I closer to God starting on July 14, 2009. Imagine my surprise, yet total understanding, when I found out today that Brooke's Foundation is in St. Charles, MO. I was born in St. Louis and my wife, from a very religious background, grew up all her life near St. Charles! Brooke is still here, among you, your family and even people she never knew. It's the only explanation for our draw to church after 45 years since we were about 12. A draw to Brett's and Don's church. A draw to walk 2 miles up a steep hill to stop day after day at the exact site where no cross had been. I had begged my friend weeks ago to not walk up that hill, let's just walk on the beach instead. He insisted the hill is better exercise. I'm so glad he insisted, otherwise I may never have seen Brooke's cross weeks ago. Now, I look forward to my early morning walk to visit her and pray for you all. God bless you and your precious family. We will think of you daily.

Bob and Vickie Harbert

When I replied to Bob and told him that Pastor Brett had actually held a service there for Brooke at the cross on her birthday, he had had no idea. I shared the email with Don Hopkins, the American living in the area who had put the cross and guardrail up, who attends the same church, so they could meet one another. Don sought out Bob at church, and the Community Beach Church prayed for our family. They understood the impact Brooke had on their community.

Bob explained to me that even though they had bought a condo in Costa Rica, they do not like living there for more than five months at a time. The high crime, bad roads, bad service, corruption, and lack of security and safety prevent it from being the dream retirement they had expected. They sold everything they owned in 2007 and moved to Costa Rica, but now look forward to leaving and dread going back. Financially, they are not able to afford to move back to the states. They seek out caretaking opportunities here in the states for part of the year, hoping to find work in exchange for a place to live. If they had been warned of the truth about Costa Rica, chances are that they would not be stuck living apart for months at a time just to make ends meet and avoid having to live in Costa Rica year round. After 32 years of marriage and a life spent by each other's side, being separated for months at a time has to be devastating.

Bob told me I could be certain he would visit Brooke's cross almost daily when he is in Costa Rica for five months a year. He feels with certainty that Brooke drew him to the site and pulled him to join a church the very day after she passed. I can't help being touched, and proud of Brooke's influence and ability to inspire. I look forward to meeting Bob and Vickie someday. It is so powerful to see this group of Americans, all complete strangers to each other before, now connected as they share the impact this loss has had on them. Our American ties to one another make us all part of the same family, and their genuine sorrow, along with the power of their prayers and support, has been instrumental in my healing.

Blake's fifteenth birthday was January 6. The night before, George and I stayed up late, talking. We heard my phone ring, indicating I had a text. It was 12:20, now officially Blake's birthday. The text said, "Message to 636-***-**** (Brooke's cell phone number) has expired." It seemed like Brooke wanted to remind me I needed to be strong for Blake's birthday. And then, as if she sent him the perfect gift from Heaven, we ended up having a big snowstorm on his birthday and they cancelled school for the following day!

Things still weren't getting better between George and me. He really wanted me to go to counseling with him, but at the time, I just wasn't ready. I felt like I had already done my share of therapy with the support group we attended and the family counseling we had already been to. I worked to heal my own way. Reading emails and letters from the people who had been touched or inspired by Brooke and working with Robyn and Kelli on the foundation and communicating Brooke's story did far more to help me. In my opinion, that was what I needed at the time.

I hoped that true friends and people who really cared would live their lives differently because of Brooke's story. I felt fulfilled when I knew Brooke inspired others, which happened often—even with complete strangers. This happens in so many instances. In January, on a flight from Tampa to Chicago, I got into a discussion with the man next to me. This gentleman's son would soon be deployed to

Brooke and Sean

Brooke and Me

Angel of Hope, Blanchette Park
St. Charles, Missouri

Blake's Baptism, 2009

(See orbs in both photos)

Afghanistan and he was concerned about it. We spoke for most of the flight and I shared with him everything I had been through with Brooke. By the end of the flight, the man confessed to me that, when he woke up that day he had no faith whatsoever, but that changed for him on the flight. He said that hearing my story changed his life. I found helping others like this was therapy and made me feel better.

Complete strangers had started to play a role in my life. In February, on a flight to Arizona, a man took my bag as I was boarding and put it in the overhead for me. He stood aside to allow me to enter his row, but for some reason, I felt a pull to sit in the row in front of him, in a middle seat at that. Eventually the man next to me, Drew, started a conversation with me. As a chief investigator for a law firm that works with primarily industrial accident cases, he gave me a lot of information to consider. He encouraged me to look into the Honda four-wheeler model that Brooke had been riding to make sure there wasn't a history of fatal accidents that could be due to manufacturer defects. He explained he had been involved in other cases where the four-wheelers actually caused the fatality.

At the end of the flight, the woman on other side of me joined our conversation. She told me she had overheard us and expressed her sorrow for my loss. She told me that she, too, had lost a child, twelve years ago—her 22-year-old daughter. I asked if it ever gets easier, if the pain ever goes away—do the memories fade or stay with you? She reassured me that I will always have my memories and they will always feel like yesterday. She told me that the pain will always be there, but that it will get easier. We all left the plane with tears in our eyes. The man next to me told me he would pray for me and help, and the lady told me to be strong. I understood why I felt the pull to sit in the row I did and I was glad I followed my intuition.

When I had an opportunity that evening, I researched the model of the Honda four-wheeler that Brooke was riding. I was pretty certain that the equipment had not caused the accident. That was addressed specifically in the reading we did with Laurie Campbell and later confirmed by forensic studies. However, researching this information led me to a group that I had not been aware of, up until that point— Concerned Families for ATV Safety (atvsafetynet.org).

When I contacted the group, which is run by mothers who have lost their children in ATV accidents, they already knew of Brooke's accident. They offered their prayers and support. I only wished that their message could have been louder and more widespread, so that it reached me before that fatal day on July 13, 2009. Had there been more coverage of the dangers and risks associated with children under the age of 16 on ATVs, there is a good possibility Brooke would still be with us today.

Concerned Families for ATV Safety aims to let their children's stories reach other families, hoping to spare them from enduring similar tragedies. They want to keep other parents from having to say "if I had only known," the very words I uttered. Brooke's story has since been added to the website.

I want to help spread this message so other parents don't have to experience the nightmare that is our reality. The founder of the group, Sue DeLoretto-Rabe, lost her ten-year-old son several years ago on a Honda 250, the exact same ATV that Brooke had been driving. Sue works full-time, day and night, educating others and calling attention to the dangers of children under the age of 16 driving full-size ATVs. Sue and I eventually worked together with ABC on a segment that aired on the dangers of ATVs. The interview aired on *Nightline, Good Morning America, World News with Diane Sawyer, ABC News Now,* and *Brian Ross Investigates.*

The same thing holds true for travel to third world countries. Had I known then what I know now, I never would have left the resort, and most likely would not have taken my children to a place like Costa Rica. I have always thoroughly researched our destinations and made

Use your mobile tag reader to see the ABC Nightline interview.

decisions based on what I discovered. When Blake and Brooke were younger, we once took a cruise on a ship that docked in Jamaica for a day. We opted not even to take the kids off the ship; we considered it too risky. I had been there years before when I was younger and I could sense the imminent danger. I was not aware of the danger in Costa Rica until it was too late.

Third world countries (Mexico, Caribbean, Costa Rica, etc.) often have high crime, putting our families in danger. American tourists are often targeted. In the event of a true emergency, medical support is very limited in these countries; they are not prepared or able to meet our needs. If Brooke had survived the accident, chances are the medical support there would have been insufficient to help her survive any trauma. This is true in many countries, but something we rarely take the time to think of.

Tourists should pay special attention to tours and excursions; use extreme caution. I have since been told countless stories where others were put in great danger. Accountability is next to nonexistent in these countries, yet they continue to lure Americans there for the "dream" vacation. Even on a cruise, excursions are dangerous and put families at great risk. While these adventures are fun and kids love them, they can easily result in tragedy.

Be careful not to make the same mistake I did by assuming safety regulations exist in other countries like they do in the United States. Traditional safety regulations, as we know them in our world, are nonexistent in these countries. It seems tour companies often care primarily about profit and think nothing of putting tourists in danger. In the states, safety is a priority. I think back to when I took Lauren and Brooke to San Francisco and Brooke could not take the Segway tour because she didn't meet the weight requirements. Brooke was so upset that I asked the reason for the restriction. They explained that operators needed to weigh that much in order to properly stop and turn the vehicle. We understood, of course, and went on to rent bikes and have a fantastic day.

The restrictions we enforce to ensure safety on tours like this, or at theme parks, etc., are ignored or don't even exist in many countries. Often, profit and greed motivate people in these countries and corruption is very common. Instead of protecting tourists, police more often rob them. I have several friends who have been robbed while traveling in third world countries. The methods used vary, but they can be quite deceptive. Perpetrators single out tourists, intentionally putting them in situations that make them vulnerable. For example, in Costa Rica it is common for a local to wait for tourists to go into a store, to the beach or inside a restaurant and then damage their rental car, maybe cutting the tire. When the traveler returns to the vehicle and leaves, they might go several miles before they notice the flat. When they pull over, the person responsible for the damage to begin with, who has followed the car, pulls up to offer assistance and robs the victim in the process.

Another factor very few of us consider at all is that human trafficking is the third most profitable criminal activity extant. Each year, an estimated 700,000 to 800,000 people are trafficked across international borders; an estimated 70% of them are female and an estimated 50% are children. Most of these victims end up as either sex slaves or labor slaves, a fate so horrendous one can barely imagine it. Human trafficking stats vary significantly due to the covert nature of the crime. Some estimates are as high as two million people being trafficked across borders each year. Sadly, trafficking is quite common in Costa Rica. I have been advised by Americans living there that it is so widespread that there is actually a commonly known market price, based on the child's age. Prostitution is legal in Costa Rica and the country openly promotes sex tourism. Up until just a few years ago sex with a minor under the age of 12 was even legal. As a result, pedophiles from other countries frequent there, seeking sex with minors.

Just thinking about this, knowing that it happens that often, literally makes me sick. Every parent should be aware of statistics and warnings regarding this type of crime before taking their children to a country where there is a greater risk for this heinous offense. Travelers need to make educated decisions about their destinations based on the true risks they will face there. These dangers have not been sufficiently exposed; communication about these risks is critical. I would strongly advise tourists that you cannot research enough. Travelers must familiarize themselves with the threats they may encounter. The government provides some information at www.travel.state.gov/travel. Be advised, though—your research should go beyond this; the travel warnings do not seem to be cautious enough. Bottom line, we can never be too cognizant of the dangers when we travel to "paradise."

"Everyone and everything around you is your teacher."
~ *Ken Keyes*

~ Chapter Twenty Six ~

"Healing does not mean
going back to the way things were before, but
rather allowing what is now to move us closer to God."
~ Ram Dass

Years ago, I visited the Stanley Hotel in Estes Park, Colorado. The spiritual connection I felt when I walked into the park at the base of the Rocky Mountains was one of the most moving experiences of my life. I would go for a walk each morning, and the entire time, feel inner peace and appreciation for the opportunity God has given me on this earth. I prayed out loud to God and thanked Him for my blessed life. I felt like, no matter what, the beauty of this place could make anyone appreciate life. The experience was very unusual for me, so I found it very profound.

In January, George and I started planning a getaway with my Aunt Lori and Randal. The holidays had been unbearable for us, and we had all been through so much that I thought the Stanley Hotel would be the perfect getaway. The others liked the idea of going to Colorado since they had never been there. I longed to feel the spiritual connection I once had felt there. For obvious reasons, I wanted to be as close as I could to Heaven, and since it doesn't get much closer than fourteen thousand feet above sea level, we considered the Rocky Mountains the ideal place. My parents have always loved Colorado and dreamed of someday returning. They had been there twenty-five years before, on their last major vacation together, so we asked them to join us. I was shocked when they agreed. Other friends of the family, Tom and Sherri, planned to go as well. We booked the trip for the beginning of March.

As the trip grew closer, everyone else was getting really excited. Things had gone from bad to worse with George and me; the uncertainty of our relationship made it hard for me to feel the same. We had a really bad weekend in late February and we ended up separating a week before the trip. Fortunately, despite the short notice, Kelly was able to join us in George's place. So on March 4, I left to go to Colorado, while George stayed back and moved out.

We stayed in downtown Denver for the first two nights. They all wanted to go on a train tour, but Kelly and I opted to take in the theater and just relax in the city. George and I were, for the most part, barely speaking. I was so confused by the heartache I was feeling. The immediate loss of George and LG from my life felt like experiencing another form of death. Kelly knew I was hurting and she was a trooper, doing everything she could to be there for me. Despite it all, we managed to have a lot of laughs and a lot of fun, along with way too many bottomless mimosas that started at breakfast and led to martinis before noon.

On Saturday we left early to drive to Estes Park and the Stanley Hotel. The Stanley Hotel stands at the base of the Rocky Mountains, in one of the most picturesque settings imaginable. Oddly enough, though, the Stanley is known best as the birthplace of Stephen King's novel, *The Shining*. There, in Room 217, *The Shining* began. A historical hotel, it opened in 1909 and is recognized as one of America's most haunted hotels.

When I stayed at the hotel the first time, I was terrified to say the least. One TV channel plays *The Shining* continuously. Although I was scared to death, the magnificent views and the sheer beauty of the area made the trip more than worth it; I always knew I would go back. Fortunately, the hotel had added new villas since then. Nuzzled in the hillside, they shared the same great view.

I spoke with the hotel prior to our arrival, and since there were so many of us in one group, I managed to get us upgraded to one of the spacious four-bedroom villas for about the same amount we would have paid for individual rooms. Just what we were looking for, the villa gave us an opportunity to all be closer together. Not to mention that it was gorgeous with vaulted ceilings, tons of windows, large decks along the entire back, cozy fireplaces, a private hot tub and a view that made me never want to leave. I would have been content doing nothing.

At night, we would all relax at the villa and enjoy sitting around together, talking. On Sunday, March 7, 2010, most of the group was watching the Academy Awards. I sat in the big, comfy recliner next to the fireplace and responded to emails. The *C3 Magazine* featuring several pages dedicated to Brooke's story had just launched and I had received several emails about it.

One of the emails I received contained such startling coincidences that I feel compelled to share the entire correspondence:

Date: Sunday, March 7, 2010, 8:01 AM

Dear Brooke's Mom and Dad,

I read your story in C3 Magazine, the opening hauntingly familiar to "The Lovely Bones" book. You meet Brooke right away in the first person. I am so sorry for your loss and the tragic circumstances of her death. It seems impossible and surreal to grasp your explosion of emotions looking over that cliff. We all have our painful story to relate with the loss of a child in our lives, but in the telling we can heal our heart and help others as a legacy to their lives lived.

I read your casual mention of the telephone, and smoke alarms going off as Brooke lets you know she [is] around you always. It has been 22 years since my son died; it's his whispers of love that have been the most healing balm to my grieving heart. From my book and ensuing workshops with Bereaved Parents groups over the past 8 years, I have become somewhat of an authority on communications from loved ones whom have died. Thousands have attended my workshop: Whispers of Love and every year it is standing room only. This summer I present at the TCF national conference held in Washington DC, then w/ BPUSA in Little Rock. Next week Puerto Rico, next month Omaha, and NYC in September.

I have heard many smoke alarm and telephone stories and hundreds of different ways that our kids can slip their spirit so subtly across the veil and connect with our hearts. It's real and it happens a lot. I also write several columns in Living with Loss magazine, one entitled Validations where I share stories of anecdotal evidence of whispers of love. If you have a story to share please send to me.

I am catching up on a gazillion emails and somehow stumbled on your article, and felt compelled to write to you, so I did. You will never be the same again, it is a life long journey of discovery, God Bless you on your journey.

Mitch Carmody

Whispers of Love

If you have lost someone close to you and suffer with that loss, you may have wished for, prayed for, expected and or anticipated some sort of supernatural experience that would validate your belief that there truly is life after death. I believe that somehow our loved one who has moved on in spirit can communicate with us in some form or fashion, and that it can bring us a peace that can be found in no other way. I believe we live in one sphere of existence, our departed loved one lives in another, but we can meet at the seam where our worlds connect. If our love is strong, and we keep all our senses open, it can and will happen. We need to let go of fear of the unknown and our own preconceived notions of what is and what is not real.

I have recently become a grandfather. I cannot believe the depth of love I have for my granddaughter. At this point in my life and in my bereavement journey of almost twenty years I had thought I hit a plateau of acceptance with the death and physical loss of my son Kelly. I had accepted that my heart would never quite feel the intensity of joy that it once had. This child born to his surviving sister has brought that intensity of joy back to my heart. With that joy has come some unexpected blessings and some very special visits from our son.

I think Kelly stuck his foot in the door when his niece, baby Kinsey came to this world. I believe he is lingering real close to us for a while; it has been quite a long time since we felt his energy this profoundly. There were many years of silence or maybe there was too much white noise in the way for us to hear, but we feel so blessed that he continues to surprise us with his visits and everlasting love.

Many, many people have had some form of experience with communication from a loved one who has died. Most people are afraid to tell others fearing that they will be labeled as nuts, gone off the deep end, lost it completely, or just desperate for anything to assuage their pain. I believe that for the most part, people are just still plain afraid of ghosts! Even the word ghost, conjures up thoughts of scary things. We find ourselves using words more palatable to our psyche, such as "a presence," "a spirit," "an angel," "a visitation," "an entity," "'their soul," or "energy field," verbiage that takes away the enigma of darkness that surrounds communication from spirit world. People are scared of things they do not understand and attribute phenomenon like this to some malevolent spirit, rather than whispers of love from our loved one.

Twentieth century Hollywood brought us many movies filled with ghost, specters and poltergeists that seem to continue to haunt the lives of the innocent. From "The Shining" to "Ghostbusters" these movies perpetuate the belief in evil spirits that have a want and need to frighten us. Communications from beyond the grave for the most part in our society has been relegated to Gypsy lore; late night séances with unsettled spirits raising tables and blowing out candles. Eerie, creepy scenarios made to frighten and to entertain.

Some religions have also helped to reinforce urban legends of malicious entities that are bent on plaguing humankind. That demons and evil spirits surround us continually, tempting us, frightening us, and may be even possessing us. Ghost and departed spirits are pigeonholed with demonic spirits and by association become something to fear. Therefore communications with the dead via a medium, a séance or Ouija board is deemed dangerous and viewed as an aspect of the occult. This is somewhat of a paradox as the concept of speaking with the dead goes back to ancient times and most religions are based on prophets who hear voices, have spoken with angels or have had visions of long dead religious icons.

In today's world people report orbs in photos, lights turning on and off, hearing voices, objects being misplaced, a cool breeze from nowhere, doors slamming, phones ringing, dogs barking at nothing, finding a penny, and on and on. Most people have historically attributed these "happenings" to evil spirits or a poltergeist. Possibly, it is just our loved one using what is available to let us know they are around us always. We just need to remove the cloak of darkness and mystery that surrounds after death phenomena and understand it is a fairly common occurrence world wide.

Not until the release of the movie "Ghost" starring Patrick Swayze did a movie create a more believable image of a spirit who left too soon. Spirit communications have been mystified and sensationalized for so long it has become ingrained in our collective psyche as a negative thing, when it is merely love trying to shine through the veil of darkness.

I believe love is more powerful than evil, for evil is merely the lack of love. When we carry light with us, we should not be afraid of the dark, because—there is none. If we study physics, we know that there is no such "thing" as darkness but merely the absence of light. There is pure energy (love) or lack of it. Science clearly shows us that energy does not die, it is only transformed; everything in the universe goes through continual transformational cycles. So does the love that is the essence of our souls and it is transformed to a new existence of light. Spirit is light and loving energy and nothing to be afraid of. It is ignorance that is scary.

There is some speculation that the weight of the soul is 21 grams (the weight of a hummingbird). Soul is love, it is energy, therefore it has substance and that energy continues on. Just as a satellite dish can connect to anywhere in the world and tap into that continual flowing energy field, so can our hearts. We must strive to turn on that switch to receive the signal and possibly even climb a mountain to get better reception. Love never dies. Light attracts light. Turn on your heartlight and spread the light we are meant to share; give the love, and show others we care.

"You are the light of the world.
A city set on a hill cannot be hidden.
People do not light a lamp and then put it under a bushel basket.
They set it on a stand where it gives light to all in the house.
In the same way, your light must shine before all people
so that they may see goodness in your acts
and give praise to your Heavenly Father."
~ Matthew, 5:14-16

Love is the light of the world, the energy that keeps the balance, and what opens doors to spirit. Without love, I do not believe that disembodied spirits could make themselves known to us, but with love they are empowered to do so and our love empowers us to receive it. They use whatever means they can to get our attention to say "Hello!!!! Knock, knock 'pudding head'... it's me, pay attention!" So things go bump in the night, lights go on and off, and society labels it as a ghost, poltergeist, or some evil phantom when it is only our loved one trying to get our attention to simply show us that their love lives on.

They can even enter our dreams and speak to us in such a way that cannot be dismissed as "just a dream." In the dream visitation, it is usually in full color, like watching a movie you can remember it vividly as the day it happened. You can experience smells, emotions, taste the tears, feel the pain, and feel the love. Your mind, body, and spirit react to is if it was real, you remember the experience as it if was real, you do so because it was not just a dream, it was real.

Our bodies react accordingly when we have an experience of some form of after death phenomenon. The joy that comes in recognition of a loved one alive or dead releases endorphins which are the body's opiates that give us a sense of pleasure and/or relieve pain. Even sighing/moaning triggers the release of endorphins, which ultimately helps relieve pain physical and emotional. Deep moaning, as in a physical trauma, or in the intense screams as in childbirth are the mind and bodies attempt to alleviate extreme pain.

Crying and laughing are flip sides of the same coin and laughter also triggers the release of endorphins and we feel pleasure. Sigh away, cry away and allow the laughter; it does help ease the pain. Embrace the love, embrace the light, for with the light comes healing. Our loved ones are with us always, so filter out the noise of life and speak to them from your heart and in prayer. Listen closely with all your senses, for love cannot be denied, it was and is always there… and only a whisper away.

Mitch Carmody

My reply to Mitch was as follows:

So I just read your article out loud to my family, you will not believe this (yes, you will). I brought my family, who has all been in such a bad place since our loss, to the place I felt would be best for us. Years ago I came to the Stanley Hotel, and it was the closest I ever felt to Heaven. (Yes it is the hotel where Steven King was inspired to write "The Shining," but it is sooo beautiful here.) We are at a new part of the hotel, these houses in the hill where we got a 4 bedroom house. My parents, my best friend who was with me in Costa Rica and my Aunts/Uncles. So they are all watching the Oscars, I am working on my computer. I told them I had something I wanted to read to them later, they all told me I needed to read it then, they turned the TV down, and I read your email and your article out loud. When I was reading the part about the "Hollywood" movies, etc. not only are we sitting at the "Shining Hotel" but the Oscars showed a part of "The Shining" during all the horror films. We welcome our connections with the other side and love them actually. Thought you would enjoy that, maybe that is why you felt compelled to email me, I am sure Brooke sent you to me. I have also attached a few email strands that give you a good idea of the energy my daughter has. There is no doubt she is part of a bigger plan. I am so happy to hear that after 20 years you felt your new grandbaby gave back what you lost from the death of your son. I long for that day....

And Mitch replied to me:

Hello Jennifer,

Thank you for responding and sharing while on vacation. I am not surprised at the connection we made. My son was 9 when he died of cancer, before he died we took one last trip to see his cousins and my sister in Fort Collins. Kelly loved "The Shining" (and most horror films), so while out there we just had to drive up to see the "Overlook" or Stanley hotel, he thought that was so cool. We drove through up to the mountains as far as we could go, road was closed, when we got out we saw a pure white wolf who just stared at Kelly from below (very odd feeling). We waded in the Big Thompson, climbed through some cave on the side of the road, great memories for us and last adventure for Kelly.

I am sure Brooke used me to contact you. It has happened before through the years and why I follow through on my compulsion to contact someone, so I am glad I did. The story you sent about Logan is so cool, and again not that uncommon of an experience, although the kids are usually around 5 and under who share things about their "imaginary friend." Once people are given permission to speak about such things, we hear more stories. I may contact C-3 Magazine to share what I am doing in this regard.

It interesting today as well that I received the newsletter for the Bereaved Parents USA of St. Louis. I have been to three national BPUSA gatherings in St. Louis and have made some wonderful friends there, all whom are bereaved parents. I know there is a St. Charles chapter and would expect they may have contacted you. It is a WONDERFUL group. The national gathering this year is in Little Rock, I would strongly urge you to attend if at all possible. It is three days on planet grief and we proudly wear buttons of our ascended children. We are all on the same page, neither a shunned pariah of society nor a pitiful focus but a place to honestly and openly share our story, share our hugs and most importantly share our children. I can certainly give you contact names in St. Louis if you have not been contacted.

Peace, love n light
Mitch

I knew Brooke was there with us in Colorado and that Mitch reaching out to me was a sign she would be with me regardless of where I was.

When we returned, the "coincidences" continued all around me; I found myself amazed by what I was encountering. It was a tough time for me personally and I tried to make changes in the house to lighten my mood. I repainted a few rooms and changed the furniture around, hoping to give things a new feel. The final step was to add a little color to my typically neutral décor with a painting. I decided to take a chance and let someone who didn't know me choose the painting. The colorful abstract painting by Sara Stockstill looked unlike anything else in my home. When they carried it in I questioned the choice and expressed my concern that it didn't feel consistent with my other décor but they encouraged me to wait and give it some time. As I stared at the painting across the room, almost certain the painting was not for me, I noticed the face of a woman.

That evening I asked Blake and Paige to come see the painting and give me their opinions. They both immediately told me they loved all the color. Right away, Paige commented that it was Brookie blue and pointed out the large "B" in it. I was sold and felt that Brooke had certainly been the one to want the painting. She always did try to get me to add more color to the house. Outside of her room, everything else was completely neutral. As I pointed out the face, the B and the Brookie blue to others, they pointed out a few other things to me. The face of the woman had the exact shape as Brooke's, with a jawline so close to hers that it could have been traced. In addition, there is a perfectly clear halo over the woman's face and a few angels looking down from above. Most shocking, is the perfect replica of Paige's Elf on the Shelf—clearly as obvious as can be—but we didn't notice for several months, Paige's "Elfie," as she calls him, played a significant role in helping her through her first Christmas without Brookie. Pretty incredible, considering I had nothing to do with selecting this picture!

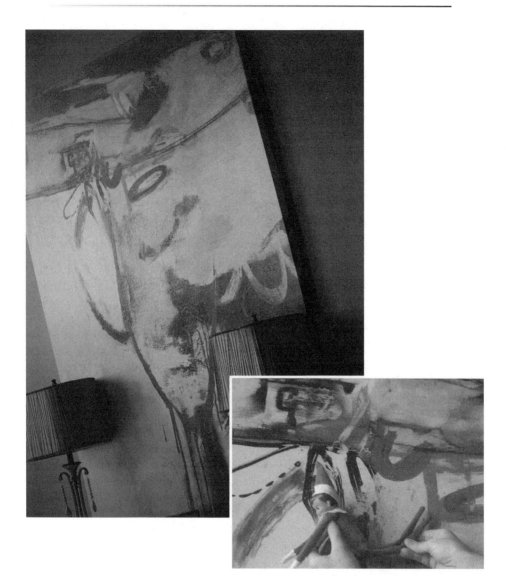

"There are only two ways to live your life.
One is as though nothing is a miracle.
The other is as though everything is a miracle."
~ Albert Einstein

The Light of a New Beginning

As time goes by, we can lock our self's away.
Close our heart and souls,
build big walls to keep us safe.
Not happiness, just the life as we know it.
Then one day, a wind blows softly.
Opening a window that was nailed shut.
A streak of light comes shining through.
Not wanting to change,
but tired of the way it is.
Stepping gingerly into the light.
Testing the waters.
Over powering surge of faith,
replacing hopelessness.
Not sure which way to turn,
lost in the mixture of feelings.
A soft hand takes yours,
a gentle voice with encouraging words.
This is your moment to choose.
You go into the light,
and a new hope is born.
Gathering strength from a source unknown.
Letting the wall crumble around you.
Seeing yourself for the first time,
as the person you were meant to be.
Overwhelmed by the weight taken off of you.
Tears falling on your cheek,
saying good-bye to the chains that held you back.
As new strength surges through you.
Happiness filling your heart.
I watch this transition take place in you.
And say, "Here is the person I have always seen
This is the beginning of your journey.
Never forget the past,
it has brought you to where you are now."
When you feel a gentle breeze blowing,
and a soft hand leading.
Open your eyes and follow your angel
into the light.

~ Chapter Twenty Seven ~

"We turn to God for help when our foundations are shaking,
only to learn that it is God who is shaking them."
~ Unknown

The month of April was extremely busy and equally emotional. Within a few weeks after I returned from Colorado, George and I had started talking more and seeing each other some. On top of moving and trying to get himself and Little George settled, he was faced with the death of his uncle, and then his grandmother only a few days later. His grandma passed away on Monday, March 29 at Progress West Hospital, the hospital that the phone call came from at exactly midnight on Brooke's birthday.

Attending the wake and funeral for his grandma was difficult, since it was the first I had been to since Brooke's. I had a lot of anxiety about being at the mortuary and seeing the casket, but I wanted to be there for George, so I did the best I could.

George's father, "Big Big George," as I am sure Paige would have called him, passed away at the young age of thirty-two, when George was only six. Unexpectedly, his grandfather passed away within a few months of that.

As I sat in the church and listened to the priest during the funeral, I thought to myself how ready she must have been to be reunited with her son on the other side. After all these years, I imagined she was at peace in a way very few could understand. For a mother it is so hard to want to be in two places, and I am sure that she had felt that way for many years during her life. Although she had other children and grandchildren here and loved them very much, I imagine she felt tremendous peace when she crossed over and joined George, Sr. and her husband for eternal life.

George and I started spending more and more time together, and I felt better when I was with him. It was obvious we both missed each other. George and I share our desire for a deep, passionate relationship in which we both are willing to work hard to keep the romance alive and never let our relationship grow stale. After Brooke passed, I doubted my ability to do this; I didn't think I had the strength to put forth the effort required for the type of relationship we had both wanted. After our separation, I also knew I didn't have the courage to be alone, either, and I didn't want to lose George. I missed our relationship and all the fun things we did together as a couple and as a family. I was happy to be back together and finally committed to getting professional help to deal with our issues and focus on what needed to be done to save our relationship.

George had been attending regular sessions with psychologists for about a month. It was a big commitment, but he really felt it was helping him. He saw one doctor for his regular therapy and then he also saw another doctor in the group, Dr. Thomas Lipsitz, who is highly respected for his work with psychological trauma, using individual therapy, EMDR, hypnosis, and other techniques.

George had been seeing Dr. Lipsitz for EMDR (Eye Movement Desensitization and Reprocessing), a type of therapy developed to resolve symptoms resulting from traumatic life experiences. For him, the process utilized stimulation that activated opposite sides of the brain to help unlock the negative memories associated with the accident, and what George witnessed when he reached Brooke at the base of the cliff. Distressing memories such as this get trapped in the nervous system and make it hard for those involved to move past these memories and for the brain to successfully process the experience and find a place of peace.

George informed his primary therapist that I had reconsidered and was willing to try couples' therapy to help our relationship. She explained that she would continue to see George as his primary therapist and I would see Dr. Lipsitz as mine. We would each have several sessions on our own, and then, eventually, all four of us would meet to address our issues and set goals to improve the relationship. Both George and I agreed this sounded like a good plan, and we both liked the idea of having advocates who understood us individually.

I had my first meeting with Dr. Lipsitz on Saturday, April 3, the day before Easter. The timing couldn't have been better, as I felt a lot of anxiety about the holiday, knowing it had been the last major holiday we were able to celebrate with Brooke. I knew that, from that point forward, there would be no new holiday memories with Brooke. Most of the session was me explaining all that had transpired in my life, and as much as I have always been anti-therapy, it really did help to have a neutral party to just let everything out to. It is a good thing that I talk fast, because that was a lot of material to cover in an hour. I really felt like I connected with Dr. Lipsitz and that was important to me. I knew I liked him the moment he asked to see a picture of Brooke. I could tell that he is more than a psychologist. He is also a husband, and a compassionate father to three daughters; he cares and it shows. Unfortunately, his schedule was so full that it would be weeks before I could see him again.

On Saturday evening, the kids went to church with Sean. I wandered into Brooke's closet as usual; all of her Easter candy and trinkets from the Fantastic Four from the year before still sat in her closet, most of it unopened. Brooke was quite thrifty and made sure anything of value lasted her a long time. As I put together Easter baskets for Blake, Paige and Little George, I just held Brooke's soccer Easter basket with bunnies she had collected over the years, reminiscing about the memories related to each one. I took several of the smaller Easter trinkets—carrot pens, bunny pins—and put them in Paige's basket, knowing Brooke would want her to have them. We celebrated Easter morning with Blake and Paige and then, while the kids went to see Sean and his family, George and I went to church.

We got LG shortly after church and then, later that afternoon, my family came to my house for dinner. I had the bigger kids hide Easter eggs full of candy and money throughout the yard. I guess I was a little distracted with everything on my mind, and Brooke wasn't there to be in charge of things as in years past, so I forgot to tell the little ones not to hunt the eggs until we were ready.

Before I knew it, Paige informed me that they had already collected all the eggs and dumped them out. They weren't really interested in doing it again, so we missed the Easter Egg hunt. The kids assured me it was fun. I imagine Brooke watched and got a good laugh out of that.

During dinner, my Aunt Nancy told us about a woman she had just met a few days before. The woman, Michelle Struttman, had gone to Nancy's work to buy a gift certificate for an organization she runs named Harrison's Hope. Nancy explained to me that Michelle had been involved in a tragic situation several years ago when two young children, left unattended in a car at a park, accidentally drove the van into Michelle and her two-year-old son, Harrison, as they sat on a bench nearby. Michelle's injuries were extensive, but she survived. Unfortunately, Harrison did not.

Nancy told her about the foundation we had started in Brooke's honor and Michelle offered to assist us in any way possible. As Nancy explained this to me and gave me Michelle's card, I kept trying to think how I knew this story. Then the connection hit me, another unbelievable coincidence. Brooke actually hosts the Spirit Colossal Section of *C3 Magazine*, a section dedicated to sharing positive resolutions of grief following the death of a child. Her picture and story are in every issue, next to similar stories each month. Just a few days before Easter, Harrison's story had been published in *C3 Magazine, Volume 2, 2010*. A picture of Michelle with her son Harrison was directly below Brooke's in the Spirit Colossal Section. It is crazy how everything in life connects.

My anxiety continued past Easter as I started to worry about another tough day, April 6, my fortieth birthday. I wasn't upset because

I was getting older. I was upset because, in the past, I always knew Brooke would plan my party and I always imagined how much fun it would be. I didn't really feel up to a huge celebration. Considering that George and I had separated, it really wasn't something I looked forward to. In addition, the timing was just bad with the holiday, so my friends and family and I agreed to all get together a few weeks later, towards the end of the month.

George knew I was apprehensive about my birthday. The day before, he realized he had an appointment scheduled with Dr. Lipsitz for EMDR and he asked me if I would like to go in his place, knowing it would help me if I could see Dr. Lipsitz sooner. I thought that would definitely help me get in a better frame of mind for my birthday, so I met with Dr. Lipsitz first thing that day.

I was glad I did; I felt better and we had a very productive meeting. Dr. Lipsitz and I spent a lot of time talking about Brooke and the foundation. He eventually asked me about my spiritual beliefs, since he noticed that I had used the word faith far more than religion. I explained to him that it was our goal to help people from all religions and my wishes were simply to increase faith in others. We had an interesting discussion on the soul and we learned we share very similar spiritual beliefs. At that point, I told him about the reading with the medium Laurie Campbell and how certain I was that she had indeed been communicating with Brooke.

During the session, Dr. Lipsitz explained to me how he had evolved, professionally, to where he is today. He spoke of Brian Weiss, the leading psychiatrist involved in past life regression therapy, who had traveled for years with James Van Praaugh. I shared with him how James Van Praaugh's books had really helped me more than any others. He said he had initially questioned James Van Praagh's legitimacy, but then Brian Weiss had reassured him by saying that, as hard as it was to believe, he knew without a doubt that James VanPraagh talked with "dead" people. Weiss is a Yale Medical School graduate and a well respected psychiatrist. I was once again stunned by the connection.

Dr. Lipsitz went on to explain to me that he specialized in hypnosis and something called past-life regressions, and that he believed I would benefit from this. He explained I would learn about my soul and the relationship of Brooke's soul and my soul in past lives. He said he really thought this therapy would help me deal with my grief. He explained I would need to schedule a two-hour session for the appointment.

Randomly being able to meet with Dr. Lipsitz first thing on my birthday, in addition to the fact that regression therapy came up at all, made me feel like it was a sign I was supposed to do this—I considered it a birthday gift from Brooke. I had never before heard of past-life regression and didn't quite fully understand it, but I trusted my therapist. If he felt it would help me, what did I have to lose? Additionally, in a way that was starting to feel familiar, the entire sequence of timing and events felt more than coincidental, another indication that I should proceed.

When I left his office that day I felt so much better. I scheduled my two-hour appointment for Monday, May 3 at 11:30, the soonest I could get in. I knew I would be hard-pressed to fit it in that day, since I had an 11:00 conference call to host with my team, and then another at 1:30 with my boss and his team. It would be tight, but I figured I could do it and I didn't want to delay this session. Other than sharing the details with George and a few members of my family and friends, I really didn't give the upcoming session much more thought, nor did I research past-life regression.

The rest of the day was uneventful. I met George for breakfast after my session and then returned to my office to work a typical day. I didn't really feel up to going out and celebrating; I just wanted a quiet evening at the house with George and the kids. It was important to me to feel close to Brooke, and for that, there is no place like home.

That weekend, George and I attended his cousin Krista's wedding in downtown St. Louis. It was a beautiful night; George and I had a wonderful evening as we strolled hand in hand from our hotel to the historical Old Cathedral, a symbol of the expansion of faith through the West.

An emotional person, I cry at happy events as much as sad ones; a wedding usually does make me cry. But this wedding was different. As the bridesmaids made their way down the aisle, I was consumed by the realization that Brooke would never be a bridesmaid in her best friends' weddings. I would never shed happy tears for my daughter Brooke and witness her as the beautiful bride. I couldn't stop the tears, though George tried to console me.

A Christian band played live music, which reminded me of our church. I had never seen this done before in a Catholic wedding. Everyone stood as the beautiful young bride started down the aisle, and I literally felt dizzy as the words to Brooke's favorite Christian song, *I Can Only Imagine*, resonated through the church. I had never heard that before at a wedding, and I thought to myself how odd it was that this song would be played at both a funeral and a wedding. The band sang *How Great is Our God*, another of Brooke's favorites, and I couldn't help feeling sad that I would never share this beautiful occasion with Brooke. I cried nonstop.

As soon as the wedding ended, George and I left to walk back to our room at the Hilton so I could freshen up before heading down to the ballroom for the reception. I quickly pulled myself together— something I was accustomed to doing. I wanted to make the most of this special occasion, to join in the celebration for this beautiful young couple who had just partaken in such a meaningful ceremony.

We enjoyed a nice dinner at a table with George's closest cousins. As the band began playing, my love for music and dancing took over. I spent the entire night on the dance floor having the time of my life. It felt so good; I was so happy. My joyous mood showed so clearly that even Krista, the bride, commented that she was glad to see I was having so much fun.

As the month progressed, I continued to see Dr. Lipsitz. On one occasion, I even took Paige with me. She had been asking me a lot of questions that concerned me. For instance, we were driving in the car once and she asked me, "Momma, you know that thing that cuts down the trees?" I wasn't sure what she was talking about. She kept explaining until I finally realized she meant a hedger. After I confirmed that I knew what she was talking about, she asked if I thought a hedger would open the thing that Brookie was in. I told her that we couldn't open it because it was sealed shut, and that we didn't want to open it. Then she asked me what Brookie looked like in there. As I explained that Brookie was ashes, like what is left after we make a fire. She started laughing and talking about how Brookie loved to put ashes on her cheeks and be silly. Then, in her most concerned, sad voice, she said, "Momma, I sure hope one of my kids don't die." My heart ached and tears streaked down my cheeks.

A few days later Paige and I were talking about something completely different and out of nowhere she made the comment, "I sure hope that doesn't happen to me." I hugged her and told her not to worry, that we would be careful and always keep her safe. She looked at me and said, "No! I sure hope one of my kids don't die." It is interesting even young girls have maternal feelings already; Paige worries so much about her kids and fears the loss of one of her own children, whereas Blake doesn't give thought to that at all. And, while he is a victim of my paranoia, he constantly reminds me that I can't make him live in a bubble and that I have to let him live life, no matter how terrified I am. I know he is right.

As a parent, after all that we have been through, I struggle with how to love and protect my children, but not smother them. It is a tough thing to do successfully, as we are all emotionally scarred and confused, living from one day to the next, facing that day's fears. It is hard to understand what the kids are feeling, and their feelings vary so often. One moment, Paige will ask me to hold her tight as we sleep and make me promise to not let her die. Then, a few days later, when I grab her hand as we walk across a parking lot and tell her we need to be careful or she could be hit by a car, she looks at me and tells me that it's okay because she wants to go to Heaven because she misses Brookie and she wants to be with her. I tell her Momma could never survive that, and that she can't do that because I need her here with me. But, deep down, I know exactly how she feels.

One day, Paige had a low-grade fever at school and then did not feel well later in the evening, so I kept her home with me the next day. She watched movies most of the day, and didn't seem sick at all, but I couldn't send her to school until she had been without a fever for 24 hours. So, that afternoon, when I had my appointment with Dr. Lipsitz, I decided to go ahead and bring her. After some of our recent conversations, I felt the timing was good.

When we first went into his office, she jumped up on his big couch, holding her American Girl doll—her favorite because it resembles Brookie. I was surprised how comfortable she was with Dr. Lipsitz, right from the start. She felt comfortable enough that she told him she was cold and asked for a blanket and snuggled in. She proceeded to brush her doll's hair as we talked, leaving her mark with tons of blond doll hairs strewn all over the blanket. I asked her to stop, but Dr. Lipsitz looked at her with complete admiration and told her it was okay. He asked her some questions about how she was feeling and she didn't hold back at all.

I hadn't realized some of the things that were on her mind—memories that haunted her from the accident. She spoke of her fears as she tried to look over the side of the road, and her recollection of a foreign man who was holding her, and how she couldn't understand him when he talked. She needed to know the details of how Brooke's body had been positioned and what she looked like and how many boo boos she had. She wanted to visualize the base of the cliff, something she couldn't picture at all because, from up where she was, even if she went to the edge, she could only see the ocean below.

I felt better when I left; I was glad to hear that the doctor thought Paige was dealing with the tragedy very well and was grieving in a very healthy way. Paige does her best to keep Brooke's memory alive; her sister is a part of her everyday life. We all have to do what works for us. Paige has a blanket with a life-sized picture of Brooke. Each night before bed, Paige looks for Brookie—her blanket—and spreads it out on the bed next to her. Brooke's head rests on the pillow and Paige often rolls on top of the blanket and hugs it and kisses Brooke. It helps her to feel close to Brooke and know she is always beside her. She even tucks her Brooke blanket under the covers sometimes, just as Brooke would be.

On April 30, George and I had our first joint therapy session, which became a little tense at times. I did not yet relate to his therapist, since this was the first time I had met her. So I became defensive when she expressed her view that I was emotionally unavailable. Both therapists could clearly see the passion between us, but seemed to recognize that we had very different wants and needs. Unfortunately, unlike our regular sessions, I think this session left us both feeling worse. I didn't let this bother me; my appointment for regression therapy was only a few days away so I focused on my excitement about it.

"It is simple. We are where we should be,
doing what we should be doing.
Otherwise we would be somewhere else,
doing something else."
~ Richard Stine

~ Chapter Twenty Eight ~

"We are not human beings having a spiritual experience.
We are spiritual beings having a human experience."
~ Pierre Teilhard de Chardin (1881-1955)

as quoted on www.brianweiss.com

*E*verything seemed to be lining up to make it obvious to me that this regression therapy was part of the plan. Events not only reassured me that I should go ahead, they also helped me understand the concept better. That, in turn, enabled me to relax enough to be successfully hypnotized.

I have to give some background so this will all make sense. In January, Robyn had called me and told me she wanted me to meet her stepmother, Lynn, who was a writer. Robyn wanted to get Lynn to help write a children's book series aimed at inspiring younger kids, eight to ten years of age, with short stories that incorporated the many values that Brooke practiced regularly in her daily life.

Lynn, Robyn and Kelli Blue all came out to the house one evening so we could brainstorm on topics, and so Lynn could get a better feel for who Brooke is. We talked for hours. I shared stories of Brooke's life, and they left with a ton of topics to write on. A few days later, Robyn called me and apologized. She told me Lynn had decided not to do the series, that she wasn't sure she could do it justice. She told me that I would receive a strange letter from Lynn, but the bottom line was that, because the topic was so important, Lynn was concerned. I never gave it much more thought than that. We had so many ideas that I figured that, maybe someday down the road, I would pursue it.

On Friday, April 30, months after it had been mailed, I finally received the letter from Lynn. In a large envelope, marked "personal and confidential" and postmarked January 28, I found a five-page letter and a book. In the letter, Lynn explained that she had left the meeting feeling all kinds of emotions. She was touched by my courage and willingness to use my energy to make sense of the loss and to try to help others, but she just couldn't see how she fit in or what her role needed to be. She told me that when she got in her car, she spoke out loud to Brooke and asked her if she was to write the books or if she was there for some other purpose. She asked for a sign so that she would know what she should do.

Lynn said she not only received a sign, but that it was very clear to her. She didn't explain it to me, she said that it was personal and wouldn't necessarily make as much sense to me. Based on all I have been through, I didn't need any other evidence; I knew it was true. She said she waited a bit before communicating her decision, because she wanted to be sure. She explained in the letter that although she was unsure why, she knew I would understand and it would make sense to me.

Lynn said she thought maybe her purpose had been to share her spiritual path with me. She explained her beliefs: we are soul, soul is eternal, soul exists because God loves us, reincarnation, karma, and the importance of learning how to give and receive love. She also spoke of her belief of the significance of dreams and the need for me to seek input from Brooke on what she wanted. If I kept my awareness open, she believed I would get the answers I needed. She went on to say that maybe Brooke would want her closest friends (the Fantastic Four) to write the stories for the children's book series. She thought I should explore the possibilities and to take my time, that it would come to me and there was no rush.

Lynn said, "God works in mysterious ways and if we let things work on His time versus ours, it all works out so much better, at least that's how I feel." She told me that she felt the need to step aside, but she appreciated the opportunity to get to know Brooke through me. She was sorry she didn't know her when she was alive.

Lynn enclosed a book, *The Call of Soul* by Harold Klemp. When I opened the book, I reviewed the table of contents and thought about how the package had spent three months in the mail in order to arrive on that exact day. I smiled, knowing I had received my sign that regression therapy was the right direction for me. I didn't have the kids that weekend, so it was the perfect opportunity to read the book before my appointment on Monday. The book addressed how we are Soul, a divine Spark of God on a journey homeward, and that the destiny of Soul is to be a coworker with God.

I was shocked to find a section of the book entitled "Let It Be" that actually went through the words of the beginning of the song. We had played *Let It Be* at the church service for Brooke, and I had had the odd experience of hearing it at the restaurant in California. The book reviewed different spiritual exercises that allow practitioners to access different planes, including the past lives that influence their lives today. The book offered some techniques to help calm the mind when attempting these exercises, or meditation. I was finding all of this quite "coincidental" as usual.

A few other concepts from the book spoke to me. Spiritual freedom is growing into a state of more godliness. By becoming aware of the lessons behind our everyday experiences, we grow into a loving awareness of the presence of God. A person who realizes God's hand is in everything that occurs in that person's life is someone who has a degree of spiritual freedom. All the lives you have ever lived were for the polishing of the Soul. You are now at a higher and more spiritual level than in any prior incarnation.

After finishing the book, I felt confident I was following the path that had been set for me.

Over the weekend, I joked with my mom and sister, who both knew that I was doing this therapy on Monday, that I was sure I was a man in a past life. We all laughed and concluded maybe even a military leader. I tend to be quite type A and excellent at issuing orders, so that weekend they both teased me and called me "Patton." We were really curious to see what the outcome would be. We weren't quite sure what to expect, since none of us had ever heard of past-life regression or known anyone who had done it. I didn't understand the experience that lay ahead of me, and I certainly didn't anticipate the impact it would have on my healing process.

On Monday morning, the day of the appointment, I had a few other signs that continued to reassure me. First, my girlfriend Angela called me from Texas to tell me about an unbelievable coincidence. She had recently gotten very involved in the youth group at her church, and I knew she had grown extremely close to a few young women there, all of whom knew about our story. She told me she couldn't believe it, one of these young ladies, Lauren Margerber, had just taken an internship back at her hometown church. Shockingly, the church was Calvary—our church. Talk about a small world—Lauren had heard Brooke's story from Angela, but never knew the connection to Calvary.

Then just an hour later, my girlfriend Rhonda emailed me to share her disbelief about how connected everything is. She had just found out that two different employees on the team that worked for her were actually in some way connected to me. One of her employees, Lindsey, is actually the cousin of one of my closest friends at work, Kraig. The other, Jenny, is the wife of the Chuck, who I have known for years as the owner of the company that takes care of our yard. In addition, my sister is actually good friends with both Chuck and Jenny. I took it all in stride; it was pretty much a typical occurence for me by then.

Because the appointment was scheduled for two hours, I had to multitask to make it work. I sent my boss a quick email before I left the office to let him know there was a chance I would be a few minutes late for his weekly staff call at 1:30. I hosted an 11:00 conference call with my team from my cell phone, so I could lead the call on my way to my appointment. I walked into Dr. Lipsitz's office promptly at 11:30, leaving someone else in charge of wrapping up the final few topics on my call. Thankfully, I was pretty rushed all morning, so I didn't have time to be nervous, or to even think about the appointment.

Dr. Lipsitz explained to me how the hypnosis would work, and suddenly I felt a little anxious. I became aware of all kinds of little things that kept me from relaxing. I have trouble falling asleep and pretty much consider myself an insomniac, so how in the heck was I going to relax enough to be hypnotized? Of course, then I started worrying what would happen if I had to go the bathroom. I quickly excused myself so I could put my fears to rest. I hurried back and settled into a comfy leather recliner. Dr. Lipsitz dimmed the lights and put on a relaxing CD. I asked for a blanket and took my heels off.

He asked me to visualize myself in a peaceful setting at the base of gorgeous, snowcapped mountains, taking in all of the natural beauty. I had no problem putting myself there and started to relax. He told me to visualize myself facing the doors of an elevator on the tenth floor. He told me to step in the elevator and that, as I descended to each floor, I would go deeper and deeper into a state of relaxation. At the tenth floor, I was to imagine a beam of light that entered my skull and slowly worked itself down the base of my neck. And then, at the ninth floor, the light worked its way through my neck and shoulders, relaxing them. My brain started questioning if this was real or my imagination, but I swear I felt the tingling from this imaginary light as it worked its way through my body. As I went down the floors, I was to go deeper and deeper. Dr. Lipsitz said that I would not be able to move those body parts. Tingles ran through my arms down to my fingertips and I felt the strangest sensation work its way down my back.

Suddenly my anxiety took over. My brain kept saying that there was no way this would work; I struggled to calm my mind. I thought back to the techniques in the book, *The Call of Soul*, that Lynn had sent me. I focused through my spiritual eye as the book had described (the center of the forehead, about an inch deep), and then also utilized some of the other techniques to get myself to a more relaxed state. It worked. I believe that if I hadn't read that book just the day before my appointment, there was a good chance the hypnosis wouldn't have been successful. For me, this was further proof that the book arrived when it did for a reason.

Dr. Lipsitz asked me to describe what I was seeing, and during the session, he jotted notes as quickly as he could. As I lay there unable to move, unable to open my eyes, I struggled to get the words to come from my mouth. Finally they came out, quietly and slowly.

I describe a young girl, maybe seven, with long, blond hair in long braids. She wears an old-fashioned flowered dress. She stands in a beautiful field with yellow and purple wildflowers, and she gestures for me follow her.

I was skeptical, thinking I was willing this thought. Dr. Lipsitz told me to go with her, so I did.

Next I see a horse, and then a man. Something about this man was bad, but not in a criminal way. I am not supposed to be with him. Eventually I realize it is George and I am worried about him. He is a bit of a rebel in his own way and gets in a fight.

Next I see wooden saloon doors, and a lot of people.

Dr. Lipsitz asked me to find myself.

I see myself. I am in a beautiful, bright yellow, shiny dress with large hoops. My dark hair is pulled up, with curls flowing out the back of the bun. I am younger, maybe in my upper twenties. I am from an affluent family and, for some reason, forbidden to be with George, who is named John.

I see a large mansion with white pillars out front and a tiled entry. There are many women there, all dressed up, and I can sense I am unhappy in this social setting. I don't like how formal my life is.

Dr. Lipsitz asked me if I was pretty, and I told him, yes, I am very pretty in this lifetime.

Dr. Lipsitz prodded me along by telling me he wanted me to go forward into my future and explain what I saw.

I smile and feel an amazing sensation of joy. I am so happy; I am having a baby. The joyous sensation taking over me is so wonderful. I move from the vision of me giving birth to seeing the baby and feeling tremendous love. The child is Brooke. Even though she looks different, it is obvious to me. An image of Brooke as a baby in my current life flashed into my mind, making it clear to me it is her.

Dr. Lipsitz asked me to look for the father.

In my mind, I look for Sean and then George, searching for the answer. I see George holding the baby. He spins her around in circles as she changes from a baby to young girl. While it is so obvious to me that she is definitely Brooke, we name her Samantha. George and Brooke are laughing and so happy. I know he isn't her father; he raises her, but he isn't her father, he came into her life later. Then it becomes clear to me. I am shocked, but, then again, not really. The father is a friend in my current life.

I had met this friend for lunch after Brooke passed—my friend who had little faith. In the current time, I had explained to him that he had to trust me, have faith, and understand eternal life is real. As I had told him that—in the midst of our conversation—the fire alarm had gone off in the restaurant, as proof of what I was saying.

It all came together. When we first met, this friend and I experienced a strange connection that neither of us really understood. We had joked within a few hours of first meeting one another that we were soul mates. We were both so drawn to each other that we spent four or five hours together that first day and then the entire next day together. I always felt some strange pull towards this friend, and even though we never had an opportunity to be more than friends, there was always something there. I couldn't quite rationalize why I felt the way I did. Now it made complete sense to me and I understood the connection I felt.

I suppose, at that point, it would be easy to question. Was my subconscious mind creating what, for some reason, I wanted to be true?

Brooke's father is in his early thirties and I am in my early twenties. Then an upsetting image comes into my mind. This friend,

Brooke's father, is on a horse and he is shot in his chest, below the left collarbone. I see it in a quick image, not like a movie. I see him on the horse and then on the ground with the bloody wound in his chest, above his heart, and he is gone.

I can see it all, but I know I did not witness it and I don't know the circumstances of how he had been shot. I comment that I think George was in my life before this happened, and then he comes back into my life after my husband (assuming we were married) passed.

Again, I see the image of George holding Brooke and I sense great happiness. We are very happy and my life is much simpler. We live in a shack and I see myself cooking outside on an open log fire in a large cast iron pot. My mom stands nearby and I sweep the dirt porch of our dilapidated wooden shack. Only my mom isn't my mom in my current life; she is the mother of one of my best friends from grade school, Kim Fronabarger's mom, Kathy.

Of all my closest friends growing up, Kim is the only best friend I do not stay in touch with. Kim was my neighbor and lived two doors down from me. I haven't talked to or seen Kim in years, and I haven't talked to or seen her mom since I was thirteen. After reflecting on this regression, I recalled that both Kathy and Kim had been in the long line of people who waited to visit with the families at the church. Kathy had hugged me and told me how, even though she never knew Brooke, Brooke had greatly impacted her life. I had completely forgotten that not only had Kathy been there to show her support almost 26 years after she had last seen me, she also sent an email to the foundation telling how she really wanted to volunteer and help in any way possible. In my dazed state of mind I had forgotten about it entirely until the therapy jarred the memory free.

My mom, Kathy, worked hard to help me, and was there by my side.

Dr. Lipsitz asked, "Do you have any other children?"

> *I do, a little boy, but not Blake or Little George. I see him as he gets older. He looks familiar, but I can't place him.*

Dr. Lipsitz asks me to move forward through that life; I do and I tell him I think I die young. He tells me to go to the moment of death.

> *I know it is some kind of sickness; it is not an accident. I am in my upper thirties and I can see a doctor with me; I am bedridden. Brooke is by my side, so upset, and is crying. George is there to comfort her, reassuring her that I will always be there for her, no matter what. I see my son and, this time, I recognize him. It is my uncle, Mark.*

I have felt the need to mother Mark my entire life. I have helped him out emotionally and financially any time he has needed me. I constantly worry about him and have always stressed over his actions. I try to help him in any way possible, and I know that, if he had to name the one person in his life who has done the most for him, it would without a doubt be me. When I shared this therapy and "discovery" with him, he was not at all surprised. Now when he asks me for something, he just tags "Come on, Mom" on at the end!

The lesson from this lifetime, I believe, was that I had given up all my worldly goods after the death of my significant other. The mansion, the money, and the social status did not make me happy. It was people that mattered. A life with riches, without the people you love most, isn't a rich life at all. I knew initially there was a bad vibe around George, but he wasn't a "bad" person. He was poor and considered not worthy from the perspective of social status. My mother and I were able to find happiness, but it had nothing to do with money, only love. Surprisingly, I was a very docile woman, very feminine and happy in my life as a mother and wife. I did not work. I was completely fulfilled with life's greatest assets, the two things in life worth more than anything—people and time. Relationships with the people I loved and time with the people I loved made me the richest woman ever.

As I focus on the moment of death, I feel myself going up. I am able to look back on the scene of my family around me as I pass. They are consumed with grief. Someone is there for me and at first I am not sure who. Then I realize that it is my mom now.

It isn't really sad at all. It is more like a peace that overtakes me. As I look back, I tell Dr. Lipsitz that the best way to describe it is like turning a page in a book. I now understood what the medium meant when she explained Brooke's passing: Brooke saw it as a "matter of fact." There is no panic or intense emotion for the soul as we cross over from the physical world to the spiritual world. I am never scared or afraid as I die, I just feel tremendous peace. I can't see what Brooke goes on to do after my death, but somehow I know she had made me very proud.

Another image comes and at first I am not sure if it is that first life or another. But I see Brooke as a grown woman, around forty, standing at the front of a one-room classroom. She is the teacher and my grandchildren, Brooke's children, are in the class. I see myself and I am much older, so I know it is a different life. Then I am very surprised; I know that my husband is my father-in-law, Ron, in my current life.

I said to Dr. Lipsitz that this was so weird, and it was hard for me to understand, because I was thinking of it in context of this lifetime. Dr. Lipsitz asked me why I thought it was weird and explained that it wasn't unusual or strange at all.

We are there in the classroom and Brooke's children, four girls, are all there. There is an intense energy that moves through the room as Brooke looks at her oldest daughter and smiles. I can see the great love and friendship they share. Then Brooke looks at me, and as our eyes connect, I feel the most intense energy fill the core of my body. I know that we are closer than ever and have an amazing relationship.

The energy Brooke feels with her oldest daughter runs parallel to what she feels with me; I experience the intense love she, too, experiences as a mother. (Here Dr. Lipsitz notes in his file how peaceful I looked.) *Suddenly it becomes clear to me who her daughter is and I smile. I feel so excited—her daughter, Kelly, is her best friend Lauren in my current life. I immediately sense how close they are. I am filled with a great sense of pride and a really warm feeling as I watch Brooke teach and I observe the chemistry between her and Lauren. They are like me and my mom, who is my actual mom in this life. They all make me laugh and feel so happy. Brooke's love for her children is so evident, and the joy I feel seeing this comforts me. In this lifetime, Brooke is my only child.*

Dr. Lipsitz asked me how I died and I shared that I died peacefully and old. It was much different than in my previous life.

When Dr. Lipsitz asked me what I think the lessons were from this life, I told him that I think it had to do with the grandkids and how amazing they made me feel. I felt confident that, in my current life, my soul would continue to be blessed with more and more love.

I see the image of the young girl in the field again. She runs and laughs as I follow her. She looks back at me, and as her eyes sparkle and she smiles at me, I know who she is. (Dr. Lipsitz noted in his file that at that point I smiled.) My spirit guide is my sister Meghan. I comment that we are very openly showing our love for one another, though in our physical life we don't always show it as explicitly. I am witnessing the greatest love ever, and she is pulling me along, excited to guide me.

Dr. Lipsitz asked me to locate Brooke.

Suddenly, the most awful feeling I have ever experienced overtakes me. I clench my teeth as I struggle to deal with the image I see and the sensations I feel. Brooke is in a fire and it is not good. She is panicking; she is screaming. Tears stream down my face.

The doctor asked me who Brooke was with, and I explained that she is by herself. He noted that I grimaced as I told him nobody can help her and that I am seeing her from Heaven. My soul is waiting for her to cross over. I am not physically with her. I feel her pain; I am consumed with tension and panic. I want to help her but I can't; it is terrible.

I can tell it isn't an accident. (The doctor noted how upset I was.) I know she has been in a fight or a struggle. I keep seeing an image of Dale (my dad, who committed suicide). *I know that he had set her house on fire. Then it comes to me; he had raped her and then murdered her so he wouldn't get caught. She is in her late teens and he is somewhere close to forty. I see all of this from afar; I don't witness him raping her, but somehow I know it happened.*

Suddenly, all the turmoil inside me quiets and I feel an inner peace when I see her take her last breath. I feel inside me that she has just died. She floats up towards me, both of our bodies prone, at a 45-degree angle. As her body approaches mine, our fingertips touch. I feel the most intense sensation, a current that fills my entire being as our souls reunite.

No one else knows what happened to Brooke; that she had been raped and murdered. Everyone thinks the fire was just an accident; no one knew the truth. Sean is her dad again in this lifetime; he is devastated by the loss and clearly struggling to survive it.

Despite the tragic circumstance, the doctor noted that I smiled and I told him it was okay, that Brooke still went on and found happiness; we were definitely reunited.

We are in Heaven together. All I see is white, blank space; it is the three of us—Brooke, Dale and myself. We can all look back at the incident with forgiveness. I am so happy and I feel such amazing love and peace during a time of great tragedy.

I commented that it is not the same as in our human life; there is no anger, no hatred, no judgment. It just happened. It was like watching a play. Dale was simply playing his part, as was Brooke, and I was in the audience watching.

I continue to feel this most wonderful sensation, a love and peace greater than I have ever imagined. No words can adequately describe this euphoric sensation.

Dr. Lipsitz told me that he wanted me to go back to the safe place where my journey started.

I see Brooke, my sister Meghan and myself running in the beautiful meadow with the yellow and purple flowers. It is as if the three of us are one. We don't let go, we just hold on to each other tight, hand in hand.

After he brought me out of the hypnotic state, Dr. Lipsitz thanked me for sharing such an incredible experience with him. He told me how much it all made sense, and how so much of it connected, though he was surprised that Brooke and I shared several lives in the same roles as mother and daughter. I told him that I was surprised as well. I thought that Brooke would have been the mother at some point. The fact that Brooke had lived three other lives before her life that ended so tragically in Costa Rica did not surprise me, though. Those who knew Brooke best often spoke of her as a wise old soul. And, of course, I had joked with my mom and sister about being a dominant male leader, which could not have been further from the docile, demure woman I saw myself being.

He commented about Dale's actions in the past, and how it would make sense that his soul needed to continue to develop through additional life lessons. So he came back to the physical world with an abusive father, suffered through Vietnam, was always tormented by the memories of what he had to do to children there, and then his struggles with alcohol brought out his violent side. It seems clear that his soul tried hard to overcome his weaknesses, but in the end, when he knew he could not, he took his own life so he would stop hurting others. His soul had grown enough to recognize and end the violence, even if he still struggled.

Pretty intense stuff! I wasn't sure what I thought, but I didn't have time to analyze. I grabbed my phone as I walked out, planning to dial in for my conference call. I noticed an email from my boss; the subject line just said, "Running seven minutes late." I figured he must not have gotten my email and was wondering where I was—and commenting that I was making the call late. I quickly dialed in. I apologized for my tardiness and asked if he had gotten my email. Scott didn't sound like he knew what I was talking about, so I figured he must not have gotten it. We proceeded with the meeting. When I returned to my office, I noticed my email about running late had, for some reason, not gone through.

Later, Becky came over and I described the entire session. She felt exactly the same as I did—shocked, but not really. It all seemed logical, and nothing surprised us anymore.

George and I went to dinner that night. We dined at a restaurant nearby, sitting outside on the beautiful patio with a cascading waterfall and relaxing tranquil setting—a perfect place to attempt to convey the magnitude of the emotions surrounding the day's events. George was not surprised in the least; he never once seemed to question or doubt it.

For some reason, later that night I ended up opening the email Scott had sent earlier in the day. Again, the email said nothing other than "running seven minutes late." I noticed the email was sent at 1:30, and I was not the only person it was sent to. Initially I had thought Scott sent it to me because I was holding the call up and I was seven minutes late. But, since it was sent at 1:30 and it was to all of us, the email really meant that Scott was running seven minutes late himself.

In all the years that I have worked for Scott, he has never been so precise as to say he would be seven minutes late, he would simply say five or ten. How odd that he said exactly seven minutes, precisely, to the minute, when I walked out of my appointment. As usual, strange things happen to me and everything just falls in place. I took this as a reassuring sign that I had done the right thing and this regression therapy was supposed to happen. As if that weren't "coincidence" enough, I received an email that night with a recommended book selection from Amazon. The book was written by James Von Praagh, the very author and medium Dr. Lipsitz and I had discussed on my birthday, which opened the door to his suggestion that I try past-life regression. The book's title is *Unfinished Business: What the Dead Can Teach Us About Life*.

I emailed my sister Meghan that I guessed I was supposed to order this book. She joked and told me that, as my spirit guide, she would suggest it. Of course I ordered the book.

That night, as I finally settled in for bed, I found myself completely wired and worked up, but not in a bad way at all, more like excitement. I felt at peace, I felt a love greater than I had ever before imagined. I was so amazed and touched. I got to feel Brooke's joy at being a mother, and to experience our love as our relationship evolved; we were even closer friends when she was an adult. The love, admiration, and respect warmed me and sent a feeling through the core of my body that I can still take myself to and feel through and through. The sensation is so intense that I cannot do it justice in words; it is a feeling that, until my past-life regression therapy, I would not have even been capable of comprehending.

I can't explain it, but for whatever reason, this therapy was part of the plan. I received signs before, reassuring me this was the direction I was to go. I can't say I had ever given much thought to reincarnation before, and I certainly hadn't thought of hypnotic regression. I didn't feel compelled to research it one bit prior to my session, which is extremely unusual for me, as I am the epitome of "paralysis by analysis." I typically overanalyze everything to death. I haven't reviewed studies on it since, and I don't feel the need to do so.

I haven't concluded for certain if I am convinced this background is real, or if it was in my imagination. It doesn't matter. One way or another, it is in my mind and this therapy has helped me heal. Maybe I just needed this "dream" to be able to relate to the peace Brooke is experiencing in Heaven, so I could pull myself from the darkness and evangelize. I now clearly understand that life here on Earth is temporary; there is certainly a much bigger, brighter place ahead. I think I needed to heal so I could be strong enough to help and inspire others. Now that I have this new inner peace, I don't really feel a compelling need to know more. I am confident my soul will be reunited with Brooke's, and beyond that, I'll wait to go to Heaven to find out the rest.

Although it is controversial, I have no regrets whatsoever about my decision to do this. Immediately following the therapy, I found that I had significantly greater patience. I am able to better understand the time dimension and how fast life here goes by. I can now visualize and sense the enchantment of Heaven because of past-life regression therapy. During the hypnosis, I sensed the immediate peace that spreads through your being at the very second the soul sheds the physical body, a sensation that began centered in the core of my being but then seeped through me like rays of sunshine working their way through the clouds. Regardless of the severity of the pain and the horror in the moment leading up to death, I know the incredible feeling that takes over—no matter what pain was present, even something as traumatic as burning to death in a fire. The peace is so strong and so defining that nothing else matters. All of that existed prior to that moment, and now ceases to exist.

The most compelling part of the experience was the unconditional love and the ability not to judge, even as I found myself side by side with my daughter's killer in Heaven. I viewed the rape and murder of my daughter without any anger or blame and it did not even come into my mind that I should pass judgment. Instead, I felt the greatest joy and happiness, so deep and intense I cannot even explain it. More than anything, this feeling convinced me that there is more to regression than just a dream or experience in my imagination. No matter what, I am certain I was supposed to experience these feelings, feelings that I never viewed as humanly possible. I know for a fact that prior to this therapy, I was not capable of these feelings. I didn't understand love to this degree.

I have a vivid memory of reading John Grisham's book, *A Time To Kill*, when Brooke was a baby. In the book, a young African American girl is badly beaten and raped by Caucasian racists. Like it was yesterday, I remember looking at my beautiful baby as she slept and thinking that if anyone ever hurt one of my children like this, I would without a doubt seek revenge, regardless of the consequences. Like the father in the book, I would not rest until I killed the assailant myself. I found this book so disturbing that I opted never to see the movie; I knew I couldn't handle it. So imagine my astonishment when, in my hypnotic state, I knew this happened to my daughter, and within moments, I found myself in the happiest place ever with the very person who committed the crime. I am confident that I experienced this feeling for a reason.

Although some may question why, as a Christian, I would agree with this therapy, I know I made the right decision. Signs, both before and after, reassured me. Since then I have healed tremendously. I consented to this therapy out of my compelling need for assurance; some may interpret it as a sin committed by going against the words of the Bible. I have asked God for forgiveness for my weakness, but I honestly believe that both God and Brooke led me to the events that took place, knowing it was essential to my survival. If I am certain of anything, it is that Brooke's story, along with all we have been through, has inspired and helped many. If I had not been able to pull myself from the darkness, I would not be able to use this terrible tragedy to help make a difference in other's lives. Until someone has walked in my shoes, they cannot know for sure how they would react or what they would do—judging me would not be fair. I am not suggesting that this is the right thing for others, or telling all grieving parents to rush out and do past-life regression. I am simply telling the story of my journey—my life and how I searched for the answers I needed.

I first started putting my thoughts together for this book within a few months after Brooke passed. I have come a long way from where I was then to where I am today. My inner struggles with the death of my child have changed. I accept this as a part of life and spiritual growth. I never understood for certain what my beliefs were before; now they are clearer than ever. My path to spiritual discovery enlightened me, and I have a newfound peace, along with a new sense of purpose to my life. I am proud of my daughter and the amazing ability she has to inspire others. I have learned so much from Brooke and her faith.

"Each person comes into this world with a specific destiny—
he has something to fulfill, some message has to be delivered,
some work has to be completed.
You are not here accidentally—you are here meaningfully.
There is a purpose behind you.
The whole intends to do something through you."
~ Osho

IN MEMORY OF
BROOKE SCALISE
2009

Blake and my Mom

Dad's final tattoo:
"We may go parted...
your light still shines."

Brooke Scalise Foundation braclet

Costa Rica Memorial Service
at site August 4, 2009
(Brooke's 13th Birthday)

~ Chapter Twenty Nine ~

"We make a living by what we get,
but we make a life by what we give."
~ Winston Churchill

*Y*ou really have two choices in your life when it comes to dealing with tragedy: you let the grief consume you and ruin your life altogether or you learn to survive and become a stronger, better person because of what you have been through. Although I am not certain why I had to encounter so much hardship and tragedy, I am confident it is all part of my life's lesson; part of the plan that God has for me. Clearly, some of us are faced with more challenges than most. Possibly God knows we can survive and will, in some way, help or inspire others through hardship.

Regardless, I can't help wondering why the plan was for me to face two of the most difficult challenges in life, the suicide of a father when I was only ten and then the tragic loss of my twelve-year-old daughter. Losing a parent when you are a child is extremely challenging. However, I worked hard to recover from the challenges of my childhood and did so successfully. I actually always thought that what I had been through had shaped me into the strong, successful person I later became.

The loss of a child is beyond comprehension for those who have not experienced it. No words can describe the pain and agony that tear through your body. And, although this tragic death has taken an unimaginable toll on me and my family, I know Brooke would want us to find a way to help others because of this.

There are so many possible consequences of grief; it affects those who suffer loss in tremendously varied ways. Even within our family, many of us grieve differently, though we all agree that we want to keep Brooke's spirit alive and with us always. Her presence will forever be with those she was close to. No one can walk into our house with-

out feeling Brooke's spirit. Pictures are everywhere and we constantly reminisce about our many wonderful memories. We all wear Brooke Scalise Foundation apparel, most of us drive with her name and cross decaled on our cars, some family members are tattooed, and we all wear our foundation bracelets and other jewelry to constantly remind us of her. While she is not with us physically, we want to always remember her and feel her presence in our life.

As I fought hard to make it through the year of challenging "firsts," I found strength and courage to go on because of the many signs Brooke sent—reassurances that she will forever be by my side. I know God has a hand in so much more than I ever imagined; my faith could

not be stronger. I never expected to become the person I am today. Brooke's faith has changed me, along with many others.

The Brooke Scalise Foundation, a 501(c)(3) government-approved nonprofit organization, has given us the opportunity to respect Brooke by helping other children. We have several dedicated volunteers leading in every aspect. The foundation's primary purpose is to increase the faith of kids in junior high school, during the years they are most vulnerable to peer pressure. We strive to help these children make better decisions in their lives and be accountable for their actions because of their relationship with God. Hopefully, by instilling the values that Brooke demonstrated daily, we can prepare the children of today to be the leaders of tomorrow.

Sending other youth to church camp in Brooke's name has been a tremendous honor; we feel proud to see Brooke's legacy live on through these children; the heartwarming stories they share on how they have grown closer to Christ or first accepted Christ into their life because of the experience helps give purpose to Brooke's death. The scholarships benefit a diverse segment of area youth, including: children in foster homes, inner city schools, and the family next door struggling through today's tough economic times.

The numerous fundraisers we do for the foundation give us an opportunity to get together often with the people who were closest with Brooke. We can raise money for an excellent cause while having fun together, exactly as Brooke would want us to. I highly encourage others dealing with grief to get involved in a cause important to your loved one and do something positive in remembrance—this is a big step towards finding peace.

I have learned many lessons through this tragedy; I am sure there will be many more as my journey continues. I try to share what I have learned with others, hoping I can in some way help them enrich their lives and help them understand and focus on what matters most. It is so easy to get caught up in the hustle and bustle of life and forget what it's all about.

For me, I would sum it up quite simply: faith, family and friends matter most. If I could choose one piece of advice that relates to every aspect of your life, it would be to spend time on these. Maybe we need to coin a phrase like "FFFF"—faith, family and friends first, so we all keep our focus where it needs to be. A constant reminder would help us all make the most of our lives. I am blessed to have four girls who are the Fantastic Four in my life, but faith, family and friends first can be the Fantastic Four in everyone's lives.

So many people who have not suffered a loss such as this fail to recognize that the people in our lives, our relationships, the time we have with these people and the memories we share make our lives rich. So often we let money or material items distract us from what matters most. I would gladly give up everything I own for just another day with Brooke. We need to treasure people and time, to treat them as life's most limited resource and the true source of our wealth. We take time

with our loved ones for granted, and seldom live our lives as we would if we knew our time together would be cut short.

At least fifteen years ago, I had an associate who lost her husband to a brain aneurism. They were both young and his death was completely unexpected. Sadly, they had fought that morning. He left for work angry and they were not speaking. His wife told everyone she knew to never leave the ones you love when you are mad; no matter what, always kiss them good-bye. Life is far more fragile than we assume; at any minute we could lose someone we love. So hug the people you love often; tell them how special they are to you. Remember that you can have a plan for your life, but there are things outside of your control, yet still part of God's master plan. You never know when it will be your last moment, or your loved one's. I learned the hard way how drastically life can change in mere seconds. Fortunately, I hugged Brooke often and she passed knowing I loved her more than anything. I cannot imagine had the circumstances been different.

Since my loss, one of the hardest things for me to deal with is seeing other parents so glaringly oblivious to how blessed they are to have their children. This has been extremely tough on me. When I witness a parent treating a child poorly, my heart breaks. I am filled with a feeling I cannot explain—hurt, sadness and anger all bottled up together. Wrong or right, on more than one occasion I have spoken up and told the parents they need to recognize how blessed they are to have their child in their life.

> *"The real voyage of discovery*
> *consists not in seeking new landscapes,*
> *but in having new eyes."*
> *~ Marcel Proust*

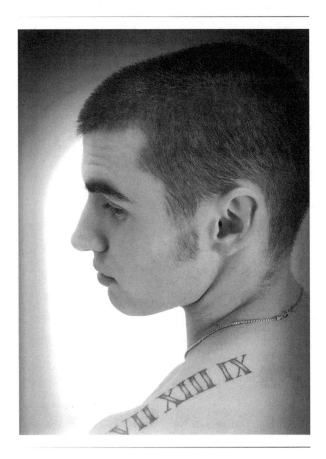

~ *Chapter Thirty* ~

"We are not here on earth to change our destiny, but to fulfill it."
~ Guy Finley

The day of Brooke's death changed many lives. Brooke's eighteen-year-old cousin, my godchild Brandon, took the loss especially hard. Being a popular high school senior and football star—All State Wide Receiver—didn't keep Brandon from showing how much Brooke touched his life. The day of the service at our house, Brandon proudly wore a new cross necklace with Brooke's name engraved on it. He keeps the memory of Brooke near him always, and even has a decal of a large blue cross with her name and years of birth and death on the back window of his Trailblazer. Then, to my surprise, one day I received a text with a picture of a tattoo, VII XIII IX, Roman numerals representing the day of Brooke's passing, a day that forever changed his life and now a permanent marking on his left shoulder.

All of Brooke's cousins and relatives struggle with this horrid calamity and the loss of someone they loved so much. The hearts of all were broken, and they all sought out ways to honor her. We have bunnies named after Brooke, dogs, tattoos, and even a wedding dedicated to her memory. When my Aunt Nancy was married, her wedding party consisted of the six children that made up their new blended family wearing Brookie blue, and of course, their matching foundation bracelets. At the reception, Nancy asked that the DJ play *Let It Be* and then Brooke's cousins Hayley, Sydney and Kali dedicated the song *I*

Can't Wait To See You Again to Brooke. We weren't suprised to find orbs in the photos as we danced and had fun on this special day. The entire family needed this time of love, a celebration that had intentonally been

scheduled in July to give us a happy, joyous day during the month that served as the one-year mark from the acccident.

Many caring friends sent notes to Brooke and posted comments on her Facebook page about how much they missed her and how she had inspired them. As a family, we continue to grow stronger from the outpouring of love for Brooke from people everywhere. Young kids share that Brooke has made them believe in God and start wanting to go to church; adult men email to tell me that they were "spiritually challenged" before and Brooke has now inspired

them. Parents with a new sense of appreciation commit to spending more time with their children.

Brooke's soccer team, Glavin U-13, both parents and players, have all helped so much by keeping Brooke's spirit alive. The players all wear armbands proudly displaying the number six—Brooke's number—as a permanent part of their uniforms. The parents have buttons with Brooke's picture and green soccer ribbon. Before every game the team cheer is "We do not walk alone." They know their teammate Brooke is always beside them. For practice, the girls wear a shirt designed by one of the player's older sisters. The team trophy from the first tournament proudly sits amongst the other trophies on display with Brooke's button looped on it by its ribbon.

Brooke touched the lives of everyone on the team. She had played with half of the girls for years, but the other half are players and families she had only known for a few weeks before her death. However, they all feel like Brooke has been in their life forever.

I try to stay connected with the team and, on occasion, attend their games. I attended the game where we awarded our first camp scholarship, a touching experience for us all. Coach Rocky emailed us all after the game, pointing out how special the night had been. When he got in his car and was pulling off his number six armband, the score of the game came to mind. He was sure that it was no coincidence that

the final score of the game was 6 – 0. The other coach replied that he, too, had a strange experience that night. As he drove home, his cruise control stuck on 60—a sign from Brooke. Then another father emailed, pointing out that the date was also the sixth, and then finally another, saying how he had never experienced anything like this and how Brooke's presence was so obvious that he could absolutely feel her there with the team during the games. It made me feel great to see the reach of her inspiration.

My dear friend and associate Briana, who loves to bake, created Brookie Cookies, a cupcake with brownie on the bottom and chocolate chip cookie on top, beautifully packaged with a label identifying them as Brookie Cookies, made in loving memory of Brooke L. Scalise. They have become a staple at any special event we have. I cannot guess at this point how many hundreds of these she has made. Briana honors Brooke in a way that has great meaning to her personally. This is what healing is about. In dealing with grief and trying to manage it, we all have to do what helps us personally. There is no right or wrong way, and the healing process is unique to each individual. Understanding this is key to survival.

"Nothing can bring you peace but yourself."
~ Ralph Waldo Emerson

~ Chapter Thirty One ~

"When we choose not to focus on what is missing from our lives
but are grateful for the abundance that's present…
we experience Heaven on Earth."
~ Sarah Ban Breathnach

May 19, 2010

I spend the evening with Blake and Paige. Blake is excited about his new room that has just been finished. He and I struggle with it, but together we get his furniture in. We haven't finished setting it up when Blake and Paige decide to play Paige's version of volleyball in what used to be not only Blake's, but also Brooke and her friends' favorite room. Blake happily makes plans for the weekend, conning me into letting him invite nine friends over to spend the night on Saturday. They want to BBQ, swim and sit by the bonfire all night. He explains that they are determined to stay up until the morning light fills the sky.

I agree, but on my terms. I immediately lay out the safety rules I will cover with them all and make them promise to adhere to. I am trying to let him out of the bubble that I want to keep him in. We search for compromise and find peace somewhere for us both.

Paige and I play outside. She rides her favorite "bike." Watching her on it makes me laugh. It is an old-fashioned, red, Radio Flyer tricycle that most almost-seven-year-olds wouldn't fit on. It starts to mist lightly and she decides we should go for a golf cart ride instead, since it has a roof and we can stay dry. As we head out on the golf cart she tells me where she wants to go. We take in the scenic views on the golf course, enjoying sitting close. The mist is light, so she asks me to stop at Number 11 South. She wants to race me. She takes off her shoes and tells me to do the same; I do. We run through the fringe surrounding the green. At first I let her run ahead of me, but then, after seeing how fast she is, I run harder. It takes all my effort to keep up with her as she beats me. She is fast like her sister. We race around the green several more times, enjoying the feel of the wet grass and soggy ground beneath our feet.

Next, Paige directs me to Number 14 South. She hops off, joyously running up and down the moguls—the small, beautifully manicured rolling hills that go along the back of the green. She hollers for me to join her and I do. We laugh together, having fun at the very spot where Blake and Brooke used to love to do the exact same thing when they were her age.

We head back on the course to Number 10 South, a long par four with a very uphill fairway. She wants to race me again, up the entire fairway to the green. We do; I am amazed by her energy and her speed.

We head back to the house and go out to the swing set together. We get on the swings and both start pumping our legs as hard as we can until we are swinging high into the air. She challenges me to see who can jump furthest and I tell her no, it is too dangerous—we could get hurt. Our swings move in rhythm together, exactly the same. She looks at me and puts up her hand to me and says, "High five—we are married!" I give her a high five as she explains that is what they call it when they swing in unison. We laugh and have fun and eventually get off to go in. She grabs my hand as she says to me, "What a fun girls' day. But it would have been more fun if Brookie had been here, too, right, Momma?"

I think to myself how blessed I am to have my family. I find peace and comfort in knowing that someday, sooner than I can comprehend, we will all be reunited together again for eternity. In the meantime, my life here continues.

"The longest journey of any person is the journey inward."
~ Dag Hammarskjöld

~ *Epilogue* ~

October 2011

*I*t is difficult to believe over two years have flashed by since that tragic afternoon on July 13, 2009. Oddly, it feels like yesterday that Brooke and I laughed as we shared those special last moments together, while at the same time, the traumatic experience of the accident itself is so surreal that it feels like a distant dream from long ago.

I feared that as time progressed, my memories of Brooke would fade. Thankfully, that is not so. In fact, I can imagine her in my mind as vividly now as when she stood physically before me, two years ago. I treasure the wonderful memories of all the special things we did together and I reflect on them often. Each day, I stop and take time to connect with Brooke—this may be looking at photos, watching home videos, reading her journal, or simply closing my eyes and reliving a moment in time when we were together. Feeling close to her brings a smile to my face and a sense of peace in knowing she will forever live on in my heart.

The reassurances that Brooke is still with us are now typical every-day occurrences that many others have also been blessed enough to experience firsthand. Most find it captivating and inspiring, but on occasion, someone will consider it unnatural and eerie. Recently, Blake had an experience that I told him he should tell his teacher about; his response was hilarious. Adamantly, he said, "You can't tell people that. They will think we are crazy. We will for sure be labeled as 'special' people." I just smiled and laughed, as the thought came to mind: *Yes indeed, we are special.*

A little over a year after the accident at the start of his sophomore year, Blake's suppressed emotions erupted and he was diagnosed with Post Traumatic Stress Disorder. Little things, insignificant to those around him, such as a map of Costa Rica hanging on the wall in a classroom, the assignment of creating a timeline of the major events in his life, or a discussion on the Theory of Evolution, would send him into such a panic that he would have to excuse himself as he broke down. I know exactly how isolated from the rest of the world you can feel at that moment, with so few able to relate, let alone understand why you are upset.

According to the doctor, this was normal; Blake needed time to properly grieve. His concern about Sean and me kept him from addressing his own pain after Brooke passed. He became deeply depressed for a full year. He did not go to school, and mostly lay in bed every day. Thankfully, our school district offers a program for students who are absent for an extended length of time based on a doctor's recommendation. Blake maintained an exceptional GPA while remaining enrolled in his honors classes.

Blake learned to seek help when needed. He formed a close relationship with the counselors at school and took advantage of their guidance as necessary. Blake is doing much better this year and has learned how to deal with situations that may upset him. He prefers to spend his time with a smaller, intimate group of close friends or family members as opposed to crowded social settings. I can relate; there is something uncomfortable about being around people that in no way understand what you have been through.

Paige still constantly talks about her sister and comments often about Brooke being with us. She pretends Brooke is beside her when she swings, eats breakfast, etc. I feel she is grieving and dealing with the loss in a very healthy way. I am sure, though, for her teachers and classmates it can be uncomfortable at times, not knowing what to say in response to some of her comments. Her life is so different from many. A few months ago Paige was drawing on a dry erase board. She held up the drawing and I just laughed; it was hysterical. Photos of orbs

are so common to us that when Paige drew a self portrait, there beside her was a big circle—the orb representing Brooke that we see so often.

Paige and I discussed her day at school recently; she explained to me that one of her classmates wasn't sure what to write about for a class assignment. Paige proposed that she write about God. That night, she worried that maybe she shouldn't have suggested this to her friend because of the possibility that God wants those who write about Him to join Him in Heaven sooner. I hugged her and told her not to worry.

Paige and her friends are always looking for ways to feel close to Brooke. Recently, Paige and her friend, Lexie, set up a lemonade stand on the driveway. Paige proudly made a sign that indicated they were selling the lemonade for her sister that had "past away." Not quite sure how to explain the foundation, she noted "the money was for people with no money." They were quite successful and raised $68 in two hours!

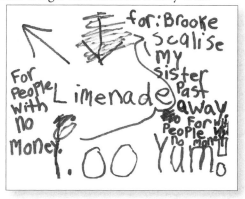

At present, my pain has lessened and the anxiety and panic attacks triggered from the constant flashbacks of the accident are getting to the point of being rare. My faith in God; however, continues to grow. The pain will always be there and I am sure I will continue to struggle with my emotions for the rest of my life. Anger or sadness can creep up on me at the most inopportune times. My grief has caused me to flee from a store in tears, excuse myself in the middle of a business dinner unable to gain the composure to return, cry openly while seated next to complete strangers on an airplane, and inappropriately lose my temper with someone undeserving. It is going to happen, and it is all part of the process of grief and dealing with the pain.

Grief does not necessarily have to be associated with death; it can be caused by any sort of separation or loss. Based on what I have learned in therapy and from what I have read, the stages of grief include denial, anger, bargaining, depression, and acceptance. As I look back and review my actions and emotions over the past two years, I can now see them clearly as the stages of grief.

Shock and denial took over for several weeks after Brooke passed. I simply got by in a fog and felt like there was no way this could be my life; it was just a bad dream that I would soon awake from. I took Xanax to numb myself but regardless, I slipped into an even deeper depression. I bargained with myself. *What if I had been in front of her? What if she hadn't ridden on an ATV? What if we hadn't gone to Costa Rica? What can I do to make this not be real?*

Initially, I demanded accountability for the negligence that resulted in Brooke's death. My anger consumed me. If necessary, I was prepared to take on a foreign country! I couldn't believe that this could happen to my daughter and there was no way I was going to let them just sweep her death under the rug as if it had never happened. I had raging anger that I directed at the tour guides from the moment of the accident. Later, my outrage was aimed at the tour company owner and eventually, I implicated the Costa Rican Government for their lack of enforcement of policy and the corruption that prevents justice by ensuring accountability. Over time, my hostility has subsided, and although I would like to have seen some accountability or have at least received an apology or some sign of compassion from the tour operator, I have stopped obsessing over it. The information exposed by WikiLeaks through U.S. Embassy Cables pertaining to Costa Rica made it clear my efforts would be futile and in the end, it wouldn't bring my daughter back.

As I continued to grieve, I did everything I could to occupy my every moment in my "save the world quest" which meant taking on all things possible and impossible, focusing on everything but my own life in an effort to distance my mind from the real turmoil that encompassed me.

George and I struggled to make our strained relationship work. We had long ago reached the point of no return in our heartache, yet we continued to turn back, feeling a pull to one another. The cycle continued and the emotional drain was exhausting and unhealthy. Because of our souls' connection, we both struggled to let go. I am confident, no matter how painful the lessons are that we endured through this process, in Heaven together there will be love and peace. As for our future together here on Earth, although I am not certain where life will take us, I know that George was meant to be in my life when he was for a reason.

I do my best to stay focused on the path Brooke is leading me down. I consider myself much wiser and my soul significantly more evolved than before this tragedy. My most profound lesson through all of this; however, is one that others may not be able to relate to, as they have yet to reach this place in their own lives. I have found a place of peace that I can escape to and put my mind at ease, no matter how bad the storms are around me. I have learned how to reach inside of myself and connect with my soul.

Each day, I look at the events as they transpire in my life and allow these experiences to enlighten me. On occasion, I still find myself off track, left feeling worn out and exhausted, but when this happens, I now stop and dig deeper. I think about the lesson God has put before me and I try to take the right steps that will lead me back to the place where I am supposed to be. I objectively review my actions, the consequences, and most importantly, the lessons I need to learn for my soul to grow. What I find is that when I go against my gut instinct and make a decision that "intuitively" I know I shouldn't, it almost always leads me down the wrong road. God guides us all, but in the end, it is up to us to recognize His guidance and step into the light.

Each of us is unique and therefore, the path that leads us will vary. It isn't that I didn't want to have a relationship with God before; it was that I didn't know how to. I would go to church and listen through the service, and while I would absorb some of it, there was a lot that was difficult for me to truly relate to. I still have not read the entire Bible, and I still don't attend church, except for on occasion. But I will venture to say that my faith could not be stronger and I have learned how to feel God in my life—always.

Brooke is forever with me and I constantly feel her guidance. Through our souls' connection, she has led me to places I have never been or imagined. She has allowed me to experience some of *her* journey—to a place I never before knew existed—a place that when I close my eyes and focus, I can sense for a brief moment. I have tremendous peace knowing this purely euphoric sensation is what Brooke feels constantly, now that her soul has returned Home.

Although it is difficult to explain, I believe I know what Heaven feels like and I stress it is the "feels" that is most important. I used to try to visualize Heaven, but Brooke has taught me it is not what we see that matters, rather, it is what we feel. The concept of Heaven was always difficult for me to grasp; I wanted to see it in my mind but couldn't. Finally, I understand why. It is impossible to see a feeling of pure bliss, therefore, trying to picture Heaven does not suffice. We are limited by our experiences in this lifetime, hence, we cannot imagine a feeling of contentment and peace like we will feel in Heaven. Now, I cannot only feel Heaven, but can picture it in my mind. Heaven is the place you find yourself freely at peace with no outside noise or distractions. That might be me as a child running through a field of purple and yellow wildflowers, laughing and playing as I hold hands with Meghan and Brooke. Blake may find in his Heaven that he and Brooke are joyfully together at our friend's 200-acre farm. They play next to the lake, in the shade under the huge 100-foot Pin Oak. They feel tremendous happiness as they take turns on the tire swing, smiling at one another in understanding that their souls are forever joined.

Imagine, the scene from the movie *Titanic,* where Jack and Rose are at the bow of the boat together with their arms spread wide, hands entwined, and the magic so wonderful Rose opens her eyes and says, "I am flying." Take yourself to that place where the feelings of pleasure are simply at their peak and you, too, can start to imagine what Heaven feels like.

As I write the final few pages of my book, my life is honestly chaotic, both personally and professionally. I have been overloaded with working on the book, my career and the foundation to the extent that I have had to sacrifice the very thing that is most important to me—time with the people I love. I will continue to remain focused on the path I must follow, and refuse to let outside disturbances keep me from the inner peace I have now found. I am in a different position now that I can sit back and reflect on the bigger picture and recognize the need for our individual souls to grow and the lessons we must learn.

Regardless of the noise around me, I am in a good place; at peace, with calmness in my heart. I continue to let God's plan unfold. In doing so, I was again led somewhere completely unexpected when a situation came up regarding a seventeen-year-old girl, Rachel, who came into my life. Her mother died when she was young and she doesn't have much family. The kids and I considered it to be a perfect fit. We wanted to help and offered for her to come live with us. Initially, it didn't look as though it was going to work out, but I received a call on the afternoon of August 1, 2011, asking me to appear in court the following morning. Shockingly, I was awarded custody, effective August 4, 2011, Brooke's 15th birthday. We accepted this as a clear sign that Brooke wanted us to help Rachel. It is just like Brooke to bless us with a gift on her birthday. It was reassuring to Rachel, as well, to know that Brooke had welcomed her into our family.

Shortly after moving in, Rachel, too, grew accustomed to Brooke's presence. We have a digital picture frame in the kitchen that Brooke picked out for me for Mother's Day the year before she passed on.

Brooke loaded the photo frame for me herself and I haven't changed it since. I love to watch it as the hundred or so pictures flash by, often taking me to that memory and moment in time. There is one picture in particular that seems to always come up as I walk into the room or when I need a sign from Brooke; it is the black and white photo included at the end of the Intro section of this book. This is the same photo that came up during the reading with Laurie Campbell. I feel certain Brooke communicates through the digital version of this picture. Each time I walk into the room, she is there to greet me and her eyes gaze into mine as the photo freezes for the longest time. I often pick up the frame and kiss Brooke as I say, "Good morning," or "I love you, princess." Silly, I know, but it makes me smile and feel good, and that is what truly matters.

Several others have noticed how often this picture is displayed and how it always seems to be the one that comes up as you walk into the room. We know she is still here with us; the many photos of orbs reassure us. It seems like on holidays and special occassions we always end up with orbs in our photos. On Blake's sixteenth birthday, a quick snapshot of Blake, Paige and me had an orb exactly where Brooke would have been if she were here with us physically.

Strange things also happen with others that I am close with. Rhonda and Robyn, who did not know one another at the time, both e-mailed me the same night describing a vividly realistic dream they'd each had about Brooke the night prior. Their dreams were unusually similar, right down to the details, including the denim shorts and white shirt that Brooke wore and the hairstyle that made her appear so angelic. Robyn commented that it was odd because in the dream, Brooke was an inch or so taller than her. I smiled and explained to Robyn that Brooke was taller than her, by about "an inch or so." Robyn had never met Brooke when she was alive, so she imagined her being shorter since she was only 12-years-old. Robyn also shared with me that in her dream, Brooke stood by her and pointed to the lake where Robyn used to go as a child. They watched together as Robyn's grandmother, who appeared much younger, was riding a boogie board with her brother, "Uncle Red," whom Robyn believed was still alive. Brooke's exact words to Robyn were, "Everything is going to be okay." The next day, Robyn's grandmother passed away, and upon describing the dream to her mother on the phone, she was told that "Uncle Red" had died years ago. While it was certainly a strange dream, for Robyn, it was incredibly comforting.

Recently, I was having a weird experience at night where I would smell a candle burning. It had a unique, fruity smell to it, but it was definitely a candle. The first time I smelled it, I thought maybe Rachel had lit a candle in her room, but she was asleep already. I smelled this same candle night after night for several days. One evening that week, Rhonda, Robyn and her daughter, Logan, were at my home. Logan was downstairs playing with Paige and Rhonda, Robyn and I were upstairs in the kitchen talking. I explained to them how I had been having this strange experience with a fruity-smelling candle. Robyn started laughing and hollered for Logan. Robyn asked her what she had smelled the night before and Logan's replied, "A fruity candle, like an orange, or a melon or something." She described exactly what I had been smelling.

All these random events give me tremendous peace and comfort. Nothing is coincidental; God puts the right people in your life at the right time for a reason. I see this time and time again, and it has now become "the norm" in my life. I did an interview with "ABC New York" on ATV safety the summer of 2010. The producers flew into St. Louis from New York, but they hired a local cameraman—Phil Lapkin—as opposed to flying in all the equipment from the east coast. When Phil came in the house, he immediately expressed how sorry he was for my loss. He explained that he did not know the details of what he was filming until just a few minutes prior. He told me how shocked he was because he was already very familiar with the story. Phil lives in Columbia, Missouri, a small town outside of St. Louis where the friends we traveled to Costa Rica with also reside. He told me he knew the family that owned the condo we stayed at and when I said it didn't surprise me, he proceeded to explain that that wasn't the half of it. It turns out that Phil owns a house in Costa Rica in Flamingo Beach, of all areas, and to top it off, he was actually in Flamingo the day that Brooke died. Many residents in the small community of Flamingo were upset by Brooke's needless death and when several of them pulled together to share their concerns, Phil, too, was there. He actually took an active stance against the government and even signed the petition following the accident that pushed for change.

The loss of my daughter has changed my life forever, but our souls will always remain united. Brooke has inspired me to dig deeper, to look inside of myself, and to discover who I really am. I have found my true being, my soul. Through my sorrow, I have grown stronger. I accept that I am not in control and I must let go of the reigns with complete confidence and trust in God, letting the light shine from within me as I feel His peace. I have allowed myself to live more openly, and I have gained the insight of knowing Brooke will always be by my side. I have learned to not let my trust falter when the road becomes rocky and steep. I perceive adversity as a means to grow, and I feel certain I am on the right path. I have found peace in my life—a beaming calmness radiantly shining inside me.

Appendix

Brooke and I
By Paige scalise

Brooke is Paige,s sister. Brooke is the best sister ever. I love my sister so much. I never get to see Brooke. I miss my sister so much. Brooke played with me and sleept with me. I love Brooke so much but now I sleep with my mom and dad because Brooke past away. Brooke was 12 when she past away but I still see Brooke and I still love her and I still miss Brooke. The end of Brooke and I. Love Paige scalise and love Brooke to.

Brooke's science project—Randy the Raindrop—is full of symbolism ranging from a teardrop to the very words that describe the circumstances of Brooke's death.

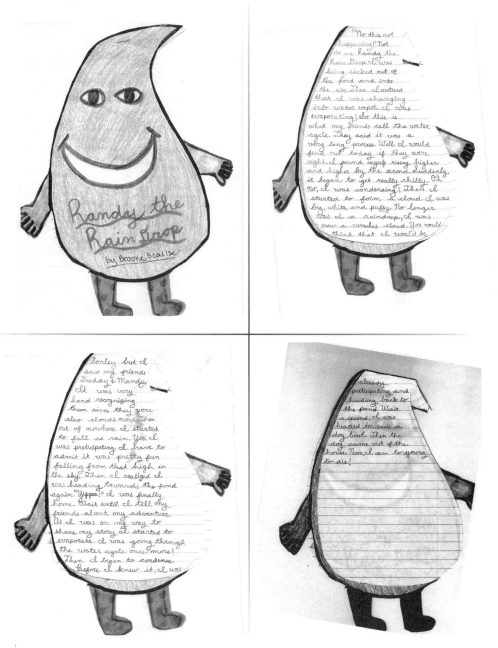

Randy along with "Hello Grandpa" make up part 2 of my Dad's tattoo.

"No, this is not happening!"

Not to me, Randy the Rain Drop.

I was being sucked out of the pond and into the air. Then I noticed that I was changing into water vapor. I was evaporating!

So this is what my friends call the water cycle. They said it was a very long process. Well, I would find out today if they were right.

I found myself rising higher and higher by the second. Suddenly it began to get really chilly. Oh no, I was condensing!

Then I started to form a cloud. I was big, white, and puffy. No longer was I a raindrop, I was now a cumulus cloud. You would think that I would be lonely but I saw my friends, Freddy & Mandy. It was very hard recognizing them since they were also clouds now.

Then out of nowhere I started to fall as rain. Yes, I was precipitating. I have to admit it was pretty fun falling from that high in the sky. Then I realized I was heading towards the pond again.

"Yippee!" I was finally home. Wait until I tell my friends about my adventure. As I was on my way to share my story, I started to evaporate.

I was going through the water cycle once more! Then I began to condense. Before I knew it, I was already precipitating and heading back to the pond. Wait a second, I was headed towards a dog bowl. Then the dog came out of the house.

"Nooo, I am too young to die!"

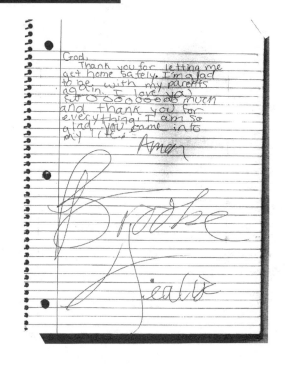

⑤
11-19-08

When I see the American flag I think about all of the wars our country has been in. The soldiers in the army are fighting for all of the citizens in the United States and that makes them heros. They are fighting to keep us safe and sound. While we sit in our homes and watch television the soldiers in Iraq are fighting a bloody war and are in danger of being killed. So, every time I see the American Flag I think about how great the people fighting are, and I silently pray to God and ask him to keep them safe.

God,
Thank you for letting me get home safely. I'm a glad to be with my parents again. I love you soooooooo much and thank you for everything. I am so glad you came into my life.
Amen

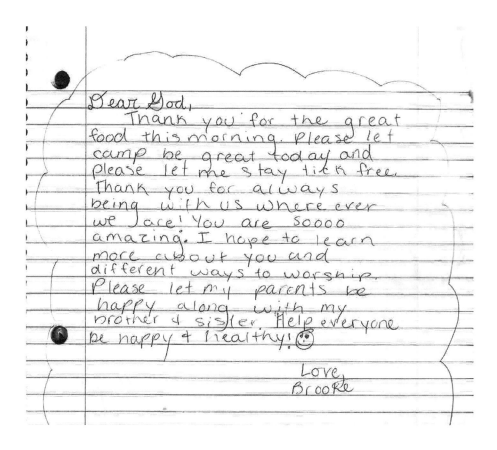

Dear God,
Thank you for the great food this morning. Please let camp be great today and please let me stay tick free. Thank you for always being with us where ever we are! You are sooooo amazing. I hope to learn more about you and different ways to worship. Please let my parents be happy along with my brother & sister. Help everyone be happy & healthy! ☺

Love,
Brooke

If I could have three wishes for my future, I would wish for…

Bleas my granpa
1

Bleas my grandma

bleas my hole
family

Mom,

You are such a
good mother.
You treat us kids
so well! You mean
the world to me
and thank you
for caring about
my feelings. You
have raised 3
wonderful kids
that all love you
to death. ♡ -Brooke

Dear Mom,

I know we have been going through a tough year and I just wanted to let you know that you mean everything to me. I could not live without you. I know how much you care about me and that makes me very happy. You are always there for me, like the time I broke my chin and the time I needed help pulling out my tooth. You know me better then anyone. I love spending time with you, I cherish every second of it. You are not only a great mother but you are also my best friend. I love you so much mommy!!

Your Thankful Daughter,
Brooke

Brooke Scalise

In a million words or less, tell us about your child.

I am sure all parents say it, but without a doubt Brooke truly is a wonderful child. From the day she was born and slept ten hours straight through the night and each day on I knew she was special!! In my opinion, one's greatest accomplishment in life is raising a good hearted, caring, successful child and I can say with Brooke I have succeeded this goal. Last year her 5th grade teacher literally had me in tears telling me what a wonderful child Brooke was and how proud I should be as a parent and telling what a great job I had done in raising her and what a positive reflection she was on her parents. She continually stressed what a positive influence Brooke has on other children and encouraged me to keep her active in school programs, etc. where she could be a role model for other children because of her many great attributes.

Brooke is the middle child, she has a 13 year old brother and five year old sister. She is very family oriented and very close with her siblings, her father, her grandparents, her aunt, and me. But I have to say honestly Brooke and I share a very special bond. We love to spend time together and any time I can make for one on one with her she will put before anything else — even fun with her friends. I am a very career oriented mom that travels every week so from a young age Brooke has learned to really value our time together.

She is very driven and determined to be successful in anything she does. I believe in holding children responsible from a young age, I have never ever told Brooke she had to do her homework or study and she has always been a straight A student. Brooke works very hard to ensure her success. Sometimes she strives too hard for perfection and there was actually a point in time I had to tell her to relax a little and not work so hard or worry about getting A+'s in every class that A's would suffice!

She can at times be very serious and this coupled with her maturity makes you doubt she is really only 12 years old! She is extremely responsible and sometimes I have to remind her I am the mom and can handle things and for her not to worry — but often her responsibility helps me out at challenging times.

She is a very loyal person and very much cares about people's feelings. I have always stressed the

importance of living your life by the golden rule and Brooke certainly does this. A perfect example would be when we got back from a week vacation this summer three different friends called and asked her to do something the first day back. She declined to all of them because she didn't want to hurt any of their feelings by just picking one as more important. A very mature, responsible, caring decision that few children would have concluded as the right thing to do.

She has a big heart and loves with all her
might. She likes to laugh and have fun
and be silly with friends and I am often
glad she can let her hair down and have
that side too!

My greatest challenge with Brake is giving her
as much love and attention as I wish I
could due to being a single career oriented
mother of three! She is so incredibly special
and every day grows into a more and more
beautiful loving person that I know will
achieve great things in her life.

She plays soccer, is very competitive. She likes to
be called on in class and is without a doubt a leader.
she is outgoing, confident, and extremely conscientious.

I am proud to be her Mother!

----- Forwarded Message -----
From: "jenniferscalise
To: brookescalise
Sent: Wednesday, January 7, 2009 8:17 PM
Subject: Re: please read

Brooke, you are the most amazing gift, I love you more than you could ever imagine. Thank you so much for sending this, I will read it often! I am going to do a better job trying to give eveyone some quality one on one time. Love you, sweet dreams.

-----Original Message-----
From: Brooke Scalise

Date: Wed, 7 Jan 2009 19:09:33
To: <jenniferscalise
Subject: please read

January 7,2009

Mom,
   Thank you for everything. I know you think that no one appreciates what you do but inside we really do appreciate every single thing you do. I can't even begin to tell you how sorry I am that I lost the present I gave you. It's just that I didn't like coming home to see my artwork laying on the ground. I honesty have no clue where it is at the moment but I will try my best to find it. I know that it has been a while since the divorce but I am still getting use to everything. I think that you having a new person in your life is great but while growing up I had a lot of time with you and now the time I get with you has decreased. I know this is not your fault its just that you have to take care of two 5 year olds which obviously takes up most of your time. Also, not to mention the divorce playing a big part in this. The divorce was a good thing in my life because I could not stand watching you and dad fight. But, it also had some disadvantages.
 Like not being able to see one of my parents every day. I know this may sound dramatic but I love you so much and can't stand when I can't see or talk to you for a while. I guess you are just a person that is loved very much by your 3 kids. I know we can all be mean and cranky at times but kids are kids. I know I am not perfect and I am sorry for all of the times I have messed up and said something rude or hurtful to you. You buy us all the food we LIKE and you pay for all of the house bills. I promise that I will be more responsible about turing my television and lights off because it increases your electric bill. I know that you do make a decent amount of money but I know even though i have 3,000 dollars in the bank at the moment I try to spend the least I can. I can understand why you are the same way. Extra money is always good :) I know you work so hard at your job to be successful and thank you for that. I know I work hard at school to do a
 good job and it takes a lot of effort. By the end of the day I am worn out. I never really sit down and think that you probably feel the same way after a long day of work. I understand that I can be high maintenance at times and expect to much from you and I am sorry for that. I am coming to the age in my life where I am going to probably start my period soon and you probably already know this. When this time reaches I hope that my attitude will not ruin how close we are. I know that you should not be considered as anything but my mother but I still consider you my best friend. I love you so much and I hope that this letter wasn't too long. I just had so much to write!!!!

♥ Your daughter,
Brooke Lauren Scalise

6/22/09

Brooke, well you just left this morning and
I miss you already!! I hope you are
having fun and making some special
memories. You have a great group of
friends and I am happy you get to
do this with them. It is going to be
a busy week and week-end with tryouts
and all. I got an email today from
Eric that he is no longer going to be
soccer coach. Stue will still be working as
a trainer and there is a new coach - Rocky
Rodriquez. Sounds like they really have
big plans for the team. So I imagine it is
going to be tough and a lot of hard work!!

It is so hot here today, I am sure
it is hot there too. Wear lots of
sunscreen!!

Can you believe our vacation is only
a few weeks away. I am starting
to really get excited. We are going
to have so much fun!!

You will have to start packing for it

a few days after you get home! At least there you will mostly just need swimming suits!

Becky brought me by a big gift basket from Lauren for taking her to San Francisco! Tell Lauren I said thank you – guess she figures you guys must have drove me to drink (it has margaritas in it!)

Take lots of pictures. Tell all your friends "hi" for me. I imagine you are all being very silly and having a great time.

Be careful and have fun – I love you very much princess.

Big hug + lots of kisses!
Love you –
Mommy

July 13, 2010

Jennifer & Family:

Though we are neighbors, I would not know you if we passed walking on the
street. Yet, you and your family have become known in our household in the past
year. We were just in the throws of our move here when the presence of so many
cars and well dressed people on a sunny Tuesday afternoon 'announced'... God
had taken a child to be with him (too soon). The impact was strong and (I hope)
enduring and I hope you will not find it inappropriate to say that since that
moment, I've resisted a gravitational pull toward you.

My fears were soon confirmed by a neighbor as I waited at the bus stop with my
children. I quickly learned that your Brooke was a sweet and friendly middle
schooler. The details of the accident were only pertinent to me as they reinforced
the shock that you have endured. Still this day, there are no words to convey the
sorrow for your loss, but I am so very sorry.

As my family returned from a dinner to celebrate my own birthday, the draw to you
became even more obvious. I share Brooke's birthday ... albeit a 'few' years
prior! I have to admit this coincidence makes me smile, though I am not in
position to claim so.

There is not a day goes by that I don't drive by your home and think of you. It has
been a privilege to read descriptions of your precious daughter via the foundation
website we have only recently found. No being could be more FULL of LIFE.

At this juncture it would be polite to express that this note is not about me, my
family and our discovering of a tragic loss of a beautiful girl. But that wouldn't be
entirely true. In contemplating this note it occurred to me that, aside from wanting
to convey that you are in our thoughts and prayers often, I wanted to share
another example of Brooke's far reaching impact. Though you already know this...
Brooke's light shines in an ever reaching scope. Thank you for allowing me to
share that sentiment. As I anticipate the knot I'll feel attempting to deliver this note
to your home... I do hope that someday we will meet and perhaps share a chat.
Until then, you and yours will remain,

In prayer,
Bonnie McClanahan (& Family)   *Bonnie*

Jennifer-

There is no way to start a letter like this. I've tried everyday for the last two weeks and it hasn't gotten any easier. Mark and I are saddened by the loss of Brooke. Though we never met her, from knowing you we know what a wonderful young girl she was. We've thought of you and your family almost hourly as we have moved through our "routine" days knowing that your days are anything but routine now. We've asked ourselves how we would move forward if something happened to one of our children and honestly we don't have a good answer. But, what we do know is that Brooke is not who we are saddened for. Her life was full. It was complete. You can see it in her smile. She felt love and she felt joy. I'm amazed by the power that Brooke has to change lives she never physically touched! I know that words alone won't heal the large open wound that was left by this tragedy, but I wanted to share with you what Brooke taught me already…

- I am not in control. In all my feeble attempts to meticulously plan every aspect of my life I must ultimately hand the reigns over. My happiness and success are not tied to an outcome or the end result (because they are subject to change without notice) but more to the journey…

- Stop and listen. So many time in my life I give canned responses to my kids when they talk to me, or tell them "just a minute"…Brooke has taught me to take the minutes I've been given and not let them pass by…

- *"Death ends a life not a relationship"*- Robert Benchley. My mother died when I was eight and I've spent the majority of my life mourning the relationship that I never had with her. I just now figured out that I do still have a relationship with her. She is still here. She is all around me. Her life may have ended but our relationship never ended. I may call on her whenever I need…

- It is better to die alive than to live dead. When we are kids we live in the moment but somewhere along the way we loose that as we become adults and take on responsibilities. Seeing Brooke's beaming smile from eye to eye makes me ask the question everyday…Am I really living in the moment? Am I feeling joy? Am I allowing myself to feel love? And if not…am I really living at all?

As hard as it was to start this letter it is equally as hard to end it. There is nothing I can say to change anything. I just wanted you to know that my family's thoughts and prayers are with yours. Brooke's life may have ended but her light is shining bright for others to feel her warmth.

Sincerely,

Mark, Jill, and family - We are holding you near our hearts!

Let children walk with Nature, let them see the beautiful blendings and communions of death and life, their joyous inseparable unity, as taught in woods and meadows, plains and mountains and streams of our blessed star, and they will learn that death is stingless indeed, and as beautiful as life. – John Muir

When the sky is darkest, we can see the stars - Unknown

Young U.S. visitor dies
in quadracycle crash

By the A.M. Costa Rica staff January 4, 2005

A young tourist died while on a quadra bike tour in Jacó. The victim, Bryan James Avery, 13, was on the tour Dec. 28 with his father and two brothers, said an employee of the Cruz Roja.

Avery is believed to have lost control of the four-wheeled motorized bike he was on, veering off the road and plumeted down a 20-meter (65-foot) ravine that ran alongside the road.

As this accident occured during the Christmas holidays, information about the incident was not made immediately available to reporters.

Avery's was one of 42 deaths in Costa Rica during the holiday period. Nine lives were claimed on the roads of Costa Rica. Ten people were murdered between Dec. 24 and Jan. 2 with two separate incidents with knives in Pérez Zeledón causing the deaths of Alberto Zarate Meza, 39 and Alvaro Rodriguez Harra, 55.

Of the fatalities eight were caused by drowning, the youngest victim being Cristian Morales Chaves, 9, from Valle La Estrella. On Jan, 2 alone, four persons died from drowning. Andres Alvarado Fonseca, 16, drowned in Puntarenas. Orlando Torrentes Jimenez, 38, drowned in Liberia. Diego Alvarado Sandoval, 23, drowned in Nicoya, and Jose Francisco Gonzalez Vargas, 59, drowned in Sarapiqui.

Included in the toll are the deaths of three of the four women and a man murdered in the Nicoya Peninsula Sunday night and early Monday morning.

A.M. Costa Rica: Published Wednesday, July 29, 2009, in Vol. 9, No. 148

<u>Our reader's opinion</u>

He'll pay for lawyer to press claim for girl's fatal mishap

Dear A.M. Costa Rica:

Failure to accept responsibility:

Is a national pastime in Costa Rica and this case is no exception. The waiver of risk the parents or <u>Ms. Scalise</u> signed is a clear example of this. G. McKinnon has obviously never travelled to any tourist destinations outside of Costa Rica.

Parents have a reasonable expectation to have the risks explained to them on any tour regardless if a child is involved or not. While 4-wheelers are not inherently dangerous. Lack of planning, explanation, and failure to reduce risk on the part of the tour operator is.

I'm 100% sure the parents of fallen Brooke were not told about the sharp mountain drop offs. Additionally, the tour operator failed to maintain a safe speed in which all riders were able to keep pace. Ask any motorcyclist or quadracyclist who ride in groups in the mountains, and you'll find that one leads to make/decide the trail, and one follows the group. Additionally people in between stop at intersections etc, so that those who are behind know where to turn.

Taking a zip line tour, there is a reasonable expectation that you might fall. There is also a reasonable expectation that the zip lines aren't completely rusted, and can support a person's normal weight. There is ZERO regulation in Costa Rica with regards to safety. Tourists are not told that. Most tours in other countries are rated: beginner/easy, moderate, advanced, expert.

A 4-Wheeler tour could be beginner/easy if on flat terrain, moderate if on hills, advanced if on mountains. etc. Furthermore, when taking a zipline tour you aren't expected to be able to harness yourself. The tour operator should have known the skill level of the riders and acted accordingly.

The tour operator needs to take responsibility for the death of the girl, It could have and should have been prevented. The tour operator knows there are ZERO repercussions to his actions. It is too bad we will never know the condition of the brakes and mechanics of the quadracycle.

Should the family of Ms. Scalise wish to pursue legal action against the tour operator. I will provide an attorney and pay the legal fees for them.

Craig Salmond
San José

Reports...

Updates on happenings in the Flamingo community with details on bite reports, dive reports, guest experiences, restaurant reviews and special events!

TUESDAY, JULY 14, 2009

Open Letter To Ministra De Transporte (Costa Rican Minister of Tranportation)

OPEN LETTER TO MINISTRA DE TRANSPORTE:

Dear Mrs. Gonzalez,

Yesterday was a sad afternoon for the entire community in Flamingo and Reserva Conchal. A 12 yr old girl rode her rented Quadra cycle (4 wheeler) off a cliff to her death! Today the community continues to feel saddened and ask why and how could this happen? Some of us ask how it was that she was even allowed to ride on one in the first place! She came down from the U.S.A. with her friends and family to enjoy a holiday! Mrs. Gonzalez, I urge you to consider a few things from the perspective of a hotel manager living in Guanacaste.

Last night after hearing of the tragedy I ran into a language student (Andrew Bama) who told me of his weekend trip back from Limon. His rental car was stopped six times, two times of which they were asked to get out of the car and were physically searched, including his wallet! He said that there was not one police checkpoint along the way back that did not stop them. He is a university student over here for a couple of weeks and vows never to drive in Costa Rica again! What were the traffic police really looking for? Again, he was stopped six times! WHY?

On my way back from Tamarindo last night I passed two young girls on another Quadra cycle without helmets and then I passed another two young girls on a scooter without helmets! I also passed several bicycles without lights or even reflectors. Last night I tossed and turned trying to sleep as I recalled you on channel 7 several months ago introducing two gentlemen on TV. One was from England and the other was from France and you were so proud to introduce them as witnesses to the stricter traffic laws similar to the ones in Europe and the ones that have recently passed here! In Europe cyclists without reflectors would be fined (given a "Multa"), besides that they would have wider roads along with proper lighting and maybe even side walks! Wake up Mrs. Gonzalez, we are not in Europe! As in much of the legislation that passes here it is "over-kill" on one end and complete negligence on the other!

I feel that the new traffic laws here verges on the absurd and now with the new points system, we will open a Pandora's box! Yet again, a 12 year old can ride a deadly vehicle to her death! No one should have to receive a call like that from a friend regarding a fatality regarding the death of a child on holiday!

And finally what really gets me stirred up is everyone in the tourism industry keeps talks about "Turismo Sostenible" (Sustainable Tourism). How about a crack down on the real problems mentioned above and the ones we all witness daily out here...lets just call it "Tourismo Responsable!" (Responsible Tourism!)

I implore you to reconsider your new laws and work on laws that focus on realistic regulations on all vehicles especially after the sad and unnecessary loss of life of an innocent 12 years old tourist.

Ulrik N. Oldenburg

Followers

Blog Archive

▼ 2009 (9)
  ▼ July (3)
    Open Letter To Ministra De Transporte (Costa Rican...
    Flamingo Coast Guard Commander Makes A Young Mans ...
    Flamingo Bite (Fishing) Report!
  ► June (1)
  ► May (3)
  ► March (1)
  ► February (1)

About Me

Ulrik Niels Oldenburg

View my complete profile

Trademarks & Permissions

These Trademarks are mentioned by name in the book:

COMPANIES:

American Airlines® is a registered trademark of American Airlines, Inc. All rights reserved.

©2011 Delta Air Lines, Inc.

Discovery Channel™ is a trademark of Discovery Communications, LLC.

Facebook® is a registered trademark of Facebook, Inc.

© 2011 Fidelity National Information Services, Inc. and its subsidiaries.

History Channel™ © 1996-2011, A&E Television Networks, LLC. All Rights Reserved.

Honda® is a registered trademark of Honda Motor Company, LTD.

Lowe's and the gable mansard are registered trademarks of LF, LLC.

McDonald's® is a registereed trademark. All Rights Reserved.

MySpace® is a registered trademark used for Audio Recordings featuring Music and owned by MySpace, Inc.

NASCAR® is a registered trademark of the National Association for Stock Car Auto Racing, Inc.

PETSMART® is a registered trademark of PETsMart, Inc.

Pizza Hut® is a registered trademark of Pizza Hut, Inc. All rights reserved. An affiliate of YUM! Services Group.

Sephora® is a registered trademark of Sephora USA.

Target®. The Bullseye Design and Target are registered trademarks of Target Brands, Inc.

PLACES:

Reserva Conchal Golf Club – Guancaste, Costa Rica. © 2008 Robert Trent Jones II, LLC. All Rights Reserved.

Walt Disney World® Resort in Florida. ©Disney. All rights reserved.

The Twilight Zone Tower of Terror™ attraction: The Twilight Zone® is a registered trademark of CBS, Inc.

PRODUCTS:

Ambien® is a registered trademark used for Pharmaceutical Preparations For the Treatment of Sleep Disorders and owned by Sanofi-Aventis, Synthelabo.

American Girl® is a registered trademark of American Girl, LLC

Apples to Apples® trademarks and trade dress are owned by Mattel, Inc. © 2010 Mattel, Inc. All Rights Reserved.

Corona® is a registered trademark of Grupo Modelo S.A.B. de C.V.

Elf on the Shelf® is a registered trademark of CCA and B, LLC.

Hilton® is a registered trademark of Hilton Worldwide.

PRODUCTS (Continued):

Hollister is a trademark of Abercrombie & Fitch Trading Co.

iPhone® a registered trademark of Apple Inc.

The Jim Henson Company, Inc.®

Kleenex® Registered Trademark of Kimberly-Clark Worldwide, Inc. © 2011

KONAMI® is a registered trademark of KONAMI Corporation.

Merry Christmas From Heaven Ornament © 1990 John W. Mooney Jr.

Pokemon™ is a registered trademark of Nintendo/Pokemon.

PowerPoint ® is a trademark of the Microsoft group of companies.

Radio Flyer® is a registered trademark of Radio Flyer.

Segway® is a registered trademark of Segway Inc.

Trailblazer® is a registered trademark of General Motors.

Xanax® is a registered trademark of Pfizer Inc.

YouTube™ is a trademark of Google, Inc.

Ziplock ® S.C. Johnson & Son, Incorporated.

MOVIES, MUSIC AND TELEVISION:

Flicka (2006) Written by Mark Rosenthal and Lawrence Konner and Mary O'Hara, Directed by Michael Mayer, a Fox 2000, Twentieth Century Fox Film Corporation and Zucker-Netter Productions Production.

Ghost (1990) Written by Bruce Joel Rubin, Directed by Jerry Zucker, a Paramount Pictures Production.

Home Alone (1990) Written by John Hughes, Directed by Chris Columbus, a Hughes Entertainment and Twentieth Century Fox Film Corporation Production.

How Great is Our God ©2004 by sixsteps records/Sparrow Records, written by Chris Tomlin, Jesse Reeves, Ed Cash, performed by Chris Tomlin.

I Can Only Imagine ©2001 by INO/Curb, written by Bart Millard, performed by MercyMe.

Let it Be ©1970 by Apple Records, written by John Lennon and Paul McCartney, performed by The Beatles.

The Medium (2005-2011) Created by Glenn Gordon Caron, Produced by Paramount Network Television, Picturemaker Productions and Grammnet Productions.

See You Again © 2008 Downtown Music Publishing LLC, written by Antonina Armato, Miley Cyrus, Tim James, performed by Miley Cyrus.

WORK OF ART:

Van Rijn, Rembrandt. "The Return of the Prodigal Son." c. 1661–1669. Oil on canvas. Hermitage Museum, Saint Petersburg , Russia.

PHOTOGRAPHY:

Most photos in the book are from the author's personal collection of family photos and used with permission. Additional photos are courtesy of :

Rachel Ballard Photography – page 112, 113, 114. Second color insert page 7 (top photo).

Blonde Tulip Photography, Lisa Neighbors – page 201, Bridget's wedding.

Drift Agency Group, LLC. – 214, 215, 240, 272, 273, 274, 275, 284, 285. First color insert pages 2, 3; second color insert, pages 12, 13; third color insert, pages 2, 3, 4, 7 (bracelet), 8 (painting).

PUBLISHED MATERIAL:

A Time to Kill by John Grisham. ©1989 by John Grisham. Published in New York by Bantam Dell, A Division of Random House, Inc.

Death of US Citizens Abroad . U.S. Department of State Website, May 2010 http://travel.state.gov/law/family_issues/death/death_600.html

Don't Kiss them Goodbye by Allison DuBois. ©2004 by Allison DuBois. Published by arrangement with Smarter Than They Think, Inc. Published in New York by Fireside. Fireside is a registered Trademark of Simon & Schuster, Inc.

Healing Grief: Reclaiming Life After Any Loss by James Van Praagh. ©2000 Spiritual Horizons, Inc. Published in New York by New American Library, a division of Penguin Group (USA).

Holding Fast: The Untold Story of the Mount Hood Tragedy by Karen James. © 2008 by Karen Oddy James. Published in Nashville, Tennessee, by Thomas Nelson. A registered trademark of Thomas Nelson, Inc.

I Love You Forever by Robert Munsch ©1986 by Robert Munsch. Published in Buffalo, NY, by Firefly Books. Ltd.

Talking to Heaven: A Medium's Message of Life After Death by James Van Praagh ©1997 by James Van Praagh. Published in New York by Signet, an imprint of Dutton NAL, a member of Penguin Putnam, Inc.

The Call of the Soul by Harold Klemp. ©2010 by Eckankar. Published by Eckankar.

The Shining by Stephen King. ©1977 by Stephen King. Published in New York by Pocket Books, A Division of Simon & Schuster, Inc.

Unfinished Business: What the Dead Can Teach Us About Life by James Van Praagh. ©2009 by James Van Praagh. Published in USA by HarperCollins Publishers.

What to Expect When You're Expecting by Heidi Murkoff, Sharon Mazel Copyright © 1984, 1988, 1991, 1996, 2002, 2008 by What To Expect LLC.

We Are Their Heaven: Why the Dead Never Leave Us by Allison DuBois. ©2006 by Smarter Than They Think, Inc. Published in New York by Fireside. Fireside is a registered Trademark of Simon & Schuster, Inc.

PERMISSIONS:

A.M. Costa Rica – Articles copyrighted by Consultantes Río Colorado 2011.

Jesus Calling, Sarah Young, © 2005, Thomas Nelson Inc. Nashville, Tennessee. All rights reserved. Reprinted by permission.

"Letter from Heaven" by Ruth Ann Mahaffey. Copyright © 1998-2009 by Ruth Ann Mahaffey.

"The Light of a New Beginning" by Tammy McK. Copyright © 2001 Tammy McK.

Scripture taken from the *Good News Translation in Today's English Version* - Second Edition. Copyright © 1992 by American Bible Society. Used by permission.

THERE YOU'LL BE (FROM *"PEARL HARBOR"*). Words and Music by DIANE WARREN. Copyright © 2001 REALSONGS (ASCAP) All Rights Reserved. Used by Permission.

For More Information:

For more information on the Brooke Scalise Foundation
please visit www.BrookeScaliseFoundation.org

For more information on author Jennifer Scalise
please visit www.JenniferScaliseAuthor.com

A portion of the proceeds from
A Mother's Journey of Love, Loss, and Life Beyond
will be donated to the Brooke Scalise Foundation.